DATE DUE

AUG 1 0 1983	MAY 7 1987
AUG - 8 1983	NOV 4 1997
AUG - 8 1983	
NOV 1 6 1983	
NOV 2 1983	
FEB 2 2 1984	
FEB 2 2 1984 ER	
FEB 2 2 1984	
FEB 2 2 1984	
OCT 3 1 1984	
DEC 1 1 1984	
DEC 1 2 1984	
JUN 1 2 1985	
MAY 3 0 1985	
MAR 1 4 1986	
JUN - 6 1986	

DEMCO 38-297

Controlling

Production and Inventory

Costs

Albert Ramond and Associates

Prentice-Hall, Inc.
Englewood Cliffs, New Jersey

Prentice-Hall International, Inc., *London*
Prentice-Hall of Australia, Pty. Ltd., *Sydney*
Prentice-Hall of Canada, Ltd., *Toronto*
Prentice-Hall of India Private Ltd., *New Delhi*
Prentice-Hall of Japan, Inc., *Tokyo*
Prentice-Hall of Southeast Asia Pte. Ltd., *Singapore*
Whitehall Books, Ltd., *Wellington, New Zealand*

© 1978 by

Prentice-Hall, Inc.
Englewood Cliffs, N.J.

Library of Congress Cataloging in Publication Data

Albert Ramond and Associates.
   Controlling production and inventory costs.

   Includes index.
   1. Cost control.   2. Inventory control.
I. Title.
HD47.5.A35 1977   658.1'552   77-1434
ISBN 0-13-17186-2

Printed in the United States of America

ABOUT THE FIRM...

Albert Ramond and Associates, founded in 1916, is headquartered in Chicago and maintains field offices in New York, Washington and Toronto. The firm became a member of the Association of Consulting Management Engineers (ACME), an organization of professional management consulting firms, in 1948.

Albert Ramond has been engaged by many Fortune 500 companies and governmental agencies as well as by small family firms who wished to secure profit improvement through operating cost reductions in both private and public sectors.

This book represents the distillation of proven systems and techniques applied in a variety of client-industrial situations. The action program in the book was structured by key members of the staff.

Also by the Firm:

Effective Maintenance Management:
  Organization, Motivation, & Control in Industrial Management.
(McGraw-Hill, 1967)

HOW TO GET FULL VALUE FROM THIS BOOK

The purpose of this book is to provide production control managers, inventory control managers, industrial engineers and other members of manufacturing management with an up-to-date, practical tool to be used in controlling both production costs and inventory costs. The emphasis is on proven, practical methods. Case histories are used in the chapters to substantiate the information and the methodology that is described. There are over 100 forms and tables that illustrate the proven systems and techniques presented in the book. Many of the forms can be used in your situation without modification; the remainder can be easily converted by you to fit your needs.

This book is more than a look at the in-plant situation. It covers material management in terms of purchasing, warehousing, and selection of warehouse sites. It describes for both job shop and continuous line processing operations the flow of information, material and people from order receipt to order shipment.

This book will help you control production and inventory costs by showing you how to:
— Establish/analyze the right organizational structure for your company.
— Select the right people for your team.
— Select the data basis for control.
— Measure the characteristics of your system.
— Present forecasts in a usable form.
— Improve customer service.
— Establish effective communications with other departments.
— Control the quantity and quality of information in the communication system.
— Develop an effective production plan.
— Develop an inventory of production capabilities.
— Prepare an effective production schedule.
— Monitor schedule compliance.
— Simplify paper work, thereby creating working paper.
— Differentiate between "controllable" and "uncontrollable" costs.
— Construct a cost profile.
— Establish cost targets.
— Develop performance indices.
— Effectively eliminate bottlenecks.
— Understand and use the differences between theoretical, rated and deployed capacity.

5

- Increase the effective utilization of equipment.
- Establish equations and graphs for equi-value points to aid in increasing utilization.
- Optimize crew sizes.
- Evaluate economic alternatives between adding equipment, personnel and working overtime.
- Determine the proper ratios of machines to operators.
- Derive average interference curves.
- Schedule multi-man, multi-machine operations.
- Eliminate excess inventory and stabilize production even when sales are seasonal.
- Develop a production plan using horizon planning techniques.
- Select the right scheduling system for your plant.
- Involve purchasing in the cost control effort.
- Evaluate the cost factors that are determinants for sub-contracting.
- Minimize your inventory costs by utilizing EOQ and MRP.
- Establish ABC classes of inventory.
- Simplify inventory requirements forecasting.
- Simplify the control of work-in-process by "telescoping."
- Use value analysis to reduce work-in-process.
- Minimize warehousing costs by better utilizing the storage cube.
- Control the cost of off-site warehousing.
- Explore the advantages of off-site warehousing.
- Determine when to convert manual systems to EDP applications.

This book will help solve everyday problems encountered in many types of industries. The practical applications of the theories of scheduling and controlling systems are, in fact, fundamental in basis and universal in application.

The book is subdivided into three primary sections covering:

- Establishing the Basis for Control
- Controlling Production Costs
- Controlling Inventory Costs

Establishing the Basis for Control

Any good structure requires a solid foundation. Since each organization has its own personality, no set of specific rules can be developed that has universal applicability. Guidelines do exist, however, that can help any organization scope out its production and inventory control function. These guidelines are presented here in a five step approach. Several examples of different reporting relationships are presented along with a general discussion of their merits.

After the functional organization is established, inputs and outputs need to be streamlined to ensure a smooth operation. The characteristics, sources and nature of sales forecasts, along with customer service requirements are presented as primary input control. Communications within and between departments are addressed as the system linkage. Output control is presented in a practical mode and describes production plans, schedules, deviation reports and exception reports as the working paper required for control.

Controlling Production Costs

There are several factors that influence the production costs of products. The intensity of the contribution of each factor varies by company and, in some cases, certain factors are not cost considerations. In summary, the second section of this book addresses controlling production costs by the following:

Cost Profiles

To be most effective, cost control efforts should be directed toward the largest cost contributors. The first phase of any production cost control program is the construction of a cost profile that clearly identifies the cost elements of greatest significance. For example, if the direct material costs represent 60 percent of the manufacturing costs and labor represents 10 percent, it becomes apparent that the emphasis should be placed on material tracking rather than on labor control. Several alternative structures are presented that highlight the five major categories of cost: direct and indirect labor, direct and indirect materials, and burden.

Cost Standards

Targets for all five categories of the cost profile can be developed and are useful tracking tools. The accuracy of the standards can vary depending upon their derivation method. Obviously, variances from highly reliable standards deserve better scrutinization than variances from estimates. Some of the development techniques for standard costs are:

— Engineered standards for labor.
— Specific recipes, formulations for materials, or bills of material.
— Estimates for both labor and material.
— History for both labor and material.

The analysis and response to variances from standard costs focus management action on the specific areas that require concentrated attention.

Capacity Analysis

Production costs savings can be generated by improving equipment utilization and eliminating bottlenecks. The first step is to define equipment capability and capacity. After this definition, throughput requirements can be calculated and bottleneck operations can be highlighted. Specific operations analyses can be conducted and the causes of the bottlenecks can be corrected.

Equipment utilization considers downtime, set-up and changeovers, maintenance requirements and scheduling. A method known as "equi-value point" analysis assists in quantifying the various breakeven points of production runs. Alternative methods for increasing output are presented so that decisions can be made that optimize constrained situations.

Labor Cost Implications

Labor costs of production offer many avenues of control. The total cost implications of all aspects of labor need to be defined and analyzed. In addition to operating costs the following factors are considered controllable costs:

— The hiring and firing costs associated with changing manning levels.
— The man/machine loading systems.
— Overtime costs versus additional personnel total costs.
— Multi-man/multi-machine loading situations.

— Scheduling implications in batch, continuous and job shop environments.
— Training costs as an investment for flexibility.

Controlling Inventory Costs

An often neglected area of cost reduction potential is controlling inventory levels. As with production costs, all inventory cost savings are not available to all industries. This book presents specific approaches to controlling the following cost factors:

Carrying Cost

A significant cost factor associated with inventory control is the carrying cost of inventory. Carrying cost percentages vary by industry because of several conditions. The common considerations involved in calculating carrying costs are:
— Interest on money
— Space
— Deterioration
— Obsolescence
— Pilferage
— Insurance and taxes

The interest on money does not fluctuate by industry but is time sensitive and can vary by 3 percent within a year. The cost of space varies by the physical characteristics of the product, the utilization of the storage cube and the age and condition of the storage facility; excess inventory may require satellite warehousing at an additional premium charge. The cost associated with deterioration varies with the product life— the food and pharmaceutical industries are more susceptible to product deterioration than the structural steel industry. In some cases, like the manufacturer of radioactive isotopes with various half-life cycles, deterioration is expected and planned. Obsolescence is a factor whenever the product undergoes model changes—the toy, automotive and apparel industries are examples of industries where obsolescence can be a cost factor. Pilferage is almost a universal problem—there are inventory losses due to pilferage in maintenance supplies, raw materials and in-process materials as well as in finished goods. Insurance and taxes vary by product line and geographic location—some municipalities as well as states have inventory taxes. Because of the wide variations that can occur in tax structures and insurance rates, each situation has to be evaluated individually.

Since each factor in the carrying cost calculation is variable by product line, geography and time, average carrying costs become meaningless indices. The range of calculated carrying costs has been found to be as low as 12 percent to a high of 54 percent.

Market Fluctuations

The economic picture does not remain constant and therefore demand is either decreasing or increasing. This changing scene, if not properly monitored, can result in shortages or overages in finished goods inventory.

Cost control over the impact of market fluctuations is dependent on response time, forecast accuracy and tracking techniques. The key factor is timeliness of accurate information flows. In some industries, forecasting techniques are well-advanced and the accompanying tracking techniques provide sufficient information to offset market fluctuations. The food industry is an example of this type of business environment. Generally, most industries are subject to inventory fluctuations caused by activity in the general marketplace over which they have little control. In order to keep the inventory fluctuations at a manageable level, most companies preplan total inventory levels and establish ranges that are acceptable. Weekly or monthly reviews of actual versus estimated inventory levels are conducted. This information indicates if a change in the production plan is necessary.

Pricing Structure

Occasionally an industry can alter its selling price in order to reduce inventory. This only applies to products that are price sensitive such as clothing, furniture and appliances. The price reduction is generally less than the carrying cost, thereby economically justifying the price adjustment. This method of inventory control is utilized whenever production adjustments are not feasible or whenever obsolescence or deterioration would cause a total loss of inventory.

Physical Distribution

The number of warehouses in the distribution network has an impact on inventory levels. The total inventory increases as the number of warehouses increase. This is primarily due to a duplication of safety stocks and pipeline (in transit) inventories. A careful review of satellite warehousing and transportation, based on customer service configurations, could lead to overall inventory reductions. In one instance, a candy manufacturer was able to reduce finished goods inventory by 20 percent by consolidating warehouses without affecting customer service.

Cash Flow Implications of Inventory Management

Total inventory management should focus on minimizing the monetary commitment to corporate material resources. This implies control over the amount of raw material stored, the size of the work-in-process inventory and the elapsed time from final production stage to customer shipment. Each phase of this material resource control requires a different discipline. The first phase, control over the amount of raw material stored, is a coordinated effort by purchasing and production control. Whenever the discrepancy between production plans and production runs is high, purchasing must cover this contingency and therefore raw material inventories rise. Purchasing can also increase raw material inventories by increasing lot size orders for price considerations. Occasionally, the carrying cost is greater than the price decrease, especially if the material is stored for a considerable length of time.

The work-in-process inventory control requires the combined effort of operations, engineering and production control. Manpower flexibility and equipment capacity are the prime determinants of how long the production cycle will be. Bottlenecks, caused by skill availability or equipment constraints, increase the wait time between operations. Poor scheduling can also add delay time to the process. The delay factors should be investigated by responsible members of each function serving as a task force. The operations group should have the responsibility for personnel development, the engineering group should have the responsibility for equipment capacity, and the production control group should be constantly aware of breakthroughs that can be incorporated into the scheduling system. Production control also has the responsibility for defining the bottleneck operations.

The elapsed time from final production stage to customer shipment requires the cooperation and communication between sales, operations, traffic, inventory and production control. The carrying costs, storage costs, transportation costs and needed product availability are the cost factors that can be controlled. Producing what is needed, when it is needed and having the product where it is needed in the right quantities should be the goal of these four departments. Accurate information flow between departments is the key to the cost control efforts.

In summary, this book presents a multitude of practical, tried, in-place methods for both production and inventory cost control. The knowledge of the prime inputs to manufacturing costs are explained in detail with exhibits and charts translating proven principles into practical applications. The scope of this book also includes warehousing, warehouse selection, purchasing techniques, and other facets of material management that are applicable to production and inventory control. The reader can save time and unnecessary work by following the practical guidelines for recordkeeping and decision-making relative to production control and inventory control. This book shows how to reduce inventory carrying costs and provides guidelines for controlling labor and material costs.

The intent of the book is to provide a practical method for any organization to effectively increase their performance by controlling production and inventory levels, communicating properly, and minimizing stressful situations in their department and in their corporate structure. The knowledge of men and machines coupled with a proper interpretation of the sales forecasts can alleviate a considerable amount of stress normally associated with a controlling function in an undefined environment.

Albert Ramond and Associates

Table of Contents

Chapter 3 *(cont.)*

Chapter 4

Chapter 5

Chapter 6

Chapter 7

Chapter 7 *(cont.)*

Chapter 1

Seeking, Gathering, Measuring and Evaluating Data for Profitable Production and Inventory Control

In almost every industrial organization there is data available concerning production and inventory activities. In some instances there is too much available.

CASE IN POINT

An eastern manufacturer of mechanical and process equipment was using work measurement as a basis for evaluating the performance of his direct labor employees, about 1,000 people. The percent of people covered by the work measurement was low, about 50%-60%. Because the situation was properly considered throughout the company to be unsatisfactory, eight different department heads, acting independently, initiated the preparation of monthly reports showing performance against set standards and the percent covered. Each individual intended that his report would provide motivation for corrective action. Unfortunately, not all of the reports showed the same performance level or same extent of coverage for individual departments. There were also differences among the reports in information about the trends of the two factors. Some of the reports were showing improvements and others were showing deteriorations from month to month. Because all of the reports used the same source data, the differences must have arisen from differences in treatment of the data. The net effect was a great deal of data but very little useful information.

Proper resolution of the situation would have been the assignment of the responsibility for preparation of the report to one department. The assignment should have included an instruction to develop a method for treating the data to the satisfaction of all concerned. Instead of that action, however, the company's management discontinued all of the reports. The reason given for that decision: "The real results show up in the Annual Profit and Loss Statement." That may well be true but, during the interim period between annual statements, there are no controls over labor costs.

To achieve proper control of production and inventory costs, it is necessary to examine routinely and regularly the costs and determine if they are higher or lower than they should be. The examination should determine if actual costs lie between upper and lower cost limits established from a data base that reflects the characteristics of the individual production and inventory system.

For any production and inventory system there are essentially two categories of characteristics. One category describes the environment outside of the production and inventory system, the marketplace. The other category describes the system itself. The characteristics describing the outside environment include: sales volume and customer service considerations. One purpose for measuring the outside characteristics is to provide guidance in determining if costs are being kept too low so that service to the market is being impeded.

The characteristics describing the system itself include: capacity of resources, lead times, inventories, and quality considerations. One purpose for measuring the inside characteristics is to provide guidance in determining if costs are going too high; whether unnecessary or unproductive effort is being exerted. After the components of the data base have been identified and the input sources established, the incoming data should be examined for its direct usability and for its reliability.

CASE IN POINT

The founder of a large business machine manufacturing firm spent a great deal of time in his plant observing the production operations. According to legend, after one of his tours, he went to his cost accounting department for information. He asked the head of the department the labor cost for a specific operation. The department head went to a file of 3 by 5 inch cards and retrieved the card for that operation. The card showed details of both material cost and labor cost. The department head gave the card to the president and began explaining, "You have to understand that this cost. . . ." The founder interrupted him and asked, "Is this the cost or isn't it?" The department head repeated, "You have to understand that this cost. . . ." Again, the founder stopped him and asked, "Is this the cost or isn't it?" The reply came, "Yes, it is the cost, but. . . ." The founder, the story goes, stopped the man again and said this time, "I want all of these cards destroyed by this afternoon. I then want you to replace them with information that has no "Yes . . . but's."

He wanted reliable information, information that could be used for decision-making without any side issues being raised about the quality of the information. He knew that if the information could be questioned, to any degree, the decision-making process would break down into a debate about the reliability of information, no matter how trivial the question might be.

With the reliability established, or the degree of unreliability clearly stated, work can be started on the form in which the output data is to be presented for use as controls. Any given set of data may have to be presented in several different forms, depending on how it is to be used. Although format is important and can influence how effectively the data is used, format design occurs late in the process. The first step in the process is selection of the data to be used.

BE DELIBERATE IN SELECTING THE DATA TO BE USED

To establish good control over any situation or any system, it is necessary to understand its nature, its characteristics. The difference between production and inventory control situations is a difference of characteristics. A characteristic that is important to one situation may be unimportant to a second situation. The selection of data to be used to control a specific situation should be governed by the important characteristics of that individual situation.

CASE IN POINT

There are many items such as canned goods, inexpensive toiletries, paper products and confections for which the brand name is less important to the retail shopper than the immediate availability. If the shopper finds that one brand is unavailable, he buys a substitute brand. If his brand is absent from the store shelf, the manufacturer loses the sale.

There are other products for which the brand name has special significance to the shopper. These items include some pharmaceuticals, some items of clothing, some items that have special technical properties. If the brand is absent, the shopper may go to another place to get the brand he wants. In that case, the first seller has lost a sale, the manufacturer has not.

There are yet other items that have special qualities or properties to the extent that the purchaser is forced to, or is willing to, wait until the item is made available. The manufacturer of such an item is assured of the sale.

The characteristics of the production and inventory control systems related to each of these three classes of products are different to some degree. In fact, differences will be found among the systems best suited to individual products within each of the three classes; different kinds of data may be used to control the production and inventory system of individual products, even if the products fall into the same category.

There is only one general rule that can be applied to the selection of data: *The optimum control condition exists when the least possible amount of data is used to provide the necessary control.* Not only will the cost of control be minimized, but the quality of control will be maximized through avoidance of confusion and conflict among the data.

IDENTIFY THE CHARACTERISTICS THAT ARE IMPORTANT TO YOUR SITUATION

The selection of data should be started by preparing and examining the list of what are thought to be important characteristics. At first, very little attention should be given to the degree of importance. Those characteristics with relatively little or no importance will be eliminated later. The objective in the beginning is to make certain that no important characteristics are omitted. The task may be approached systematically by establishing categories, dividing within the categories and then subdividing further. The two major categories of characteristics affecting a production/inventory system, those that operate outside of the system and those that operate inside, are shown in Figure 1-1.

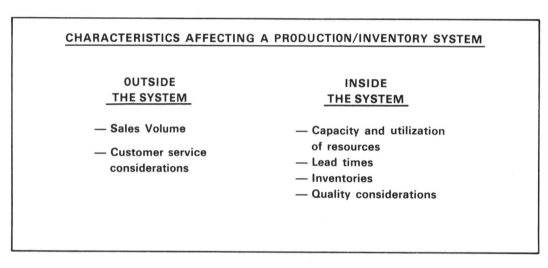

FIGURE 1-1

The characteristics that operate outside the system represent what the system is to accomplish for the customers. Those inside represent the capabilities needed by the system to meet the demands from the outside.

The task of data selection should be approached from the outside in by giving first consideration to:

— The number of units of each individual product expected to be sold.
— Customer purchasing patterns, whether periodic, seasonal or random.
— The acceptable time period between receipt of customer order and delivery.
— The acceptable degree of failure to satisfy customers' orders.

The measurements of these characteristics outline the magnitude of the job to be done by the production and inventory systems. The next step is to determine the measurements of the inside characteristics needed to do the job properly:

— Capacity and utilization of resources
  • Production
  • Facilities
  • Labor
  • Storage facilities
  • Material handling and transportation facilities
— Lead times
  • Customer order processing
  • Product processing
  • Labor procurement and training
  • Purchasing

—Inventories
  • Breakdown
  • Levels
—Quality
  • Production process capability
  • Product requirement

Care must be taken to maintain a flexible attitude about the relative importance of both inside and outside characteristics used for control. The reality is that conditions seldom remain constant, they always change to some degree because of external and internal influences.

CASE IN POINT

A midwestern firm manufacturing agricultural supplies was staffed by people who had been born and raised in agricultural environments. In their experience, agriculture is a seasonal activity. When they began their company, they designed their production and inventory system to operate on a seasonal basis. They operated with very little inventory, producing at a high peak of output for the short period of the growing season.

After several years of operation they sought to level out their activity. They had kept good records of sales, by individual products, and had been developing sales forecasting methods. They were preparing to build up an inventory of finished and semifinished stock. The main difficulty arose from the large amount of space required to store an inventory of meaningful quantities of products. They had tried outside storage, but their products were light and became damaged during wind storms that occurred in their area. They were able, after some effort, to obtain proper storage space at a reasonable price, and they started their inventory buildup.

They didn't stop there, however. While they had been working on their forecasting techniques, they had also been training their dealers to do forecasting. The final achievement was a buildup of a limited inventory at their dealers' locations so that the dealers could supply their customers very early in the season. There was also a backup inventory at the plant of a mix of products and accessories to help provide quick response to customer demands. The inventories of finished products provided a buffer, allowing the production activity to be leveled. The smoothing has resulted in better control and an important reduction of operating costs.

The characteristics of the above example went through changes of major significance. At first, inventory control was minimal, consisting primarily of ascertaining availability of raw materials. Production control emphasized keeping output current with actual sales demand. The controls now cover inventories in dealers' hands and an inventory at the plant composed of raw materials, semifinished products and finished products. The controls that are presently applied to production operations emphasize achieving the lowest possible costs. The change in conditions is reflected in the difference between the controls used at first and the controls used now; there has been a dramatic change in controls over a period of a few years. But the change in the data base has been confined to expansion of the source data, with particular attention given to avoidance of duplication of sources.

AVOID DIVERGENCE AMONG THE MEASUREMENTS

All data related to the measurement of all individual characteristics must be derived from a common source. This is true of data for forecasts and inventories, as well as for all other data.

CASE IN POINT

A manufacturer of pharmaceuticals in a mid-Atlantic state did not have a reliable forecasting procedure for sales. The manufacturing staff was aware that demands on production capacity had been increasing. The increase was not particularly rapid, but it had been steady over a period of years. From their observations they predicted that an increase in facilities was required. The forecast from the sales department did not support that point of view. The result was two different forecasts, with two different predictions. The company's management was conservative, and they decided to rely on the sales forecast. Had they been of a more aggressive nature, they might have accepted the production department's data, even though the sales department is properly responsible for forecasting sales. As time passed, conditions showed that the production people had been correct in their evaluation. Sales increased beyond the point of the plant's capabilities; the situation then became very emotional. It was finally resolved by a concerted effort within the total organization to establish one forecast that provided proper information, and the same information, to all who need it.

Whenever there is more than one source for any particular information, there is a good opportunity for misunderstanding and extra costs.

CASE IN POINT

In a food processing plant in New York state, three sets of inventory records were being maintained for the finished goods inventory. One set was maintained by the warehousing personnel. They were responsible for the merchandise and therefore were keeping a manual record to make certain they knew the status of the inventory. The order entry staff also worked with an inventory record; theirs was supplied as a computer printout. The order entry staff needed the inventory information for processing customer orders. They used the records as the basis for preparing shipping orders and customer billing, including notation of back orders. The comptroller's staff also maintained an inventory record, a manual card system. They were responsible for the financial reporting and therefore needed to be certain that the inventory records were correct. The three sets of records almost always provided different information.

The difference in information resulted from a difference in timing. The warehouse records were based on stocks physically on hand. The order entry information reflected the entries of customers' orders. The comptroller's records reflected billings mailed to customers. There were many conferences and discussions as a result of the differences shown on the different reports. As a matter of fact, each report was correct. The misunderstanding arose from expecting the three reports to show identical data. In this situation extra costs of record-keeping were incurred because of the maintenance of the three sets of information and because of the time spent on discussing the differences. The situation was simplified by confining the record-keeping to the computer, and by developing a standard procedure for reconciliation of differences between the computer data and the physical inventory itself.

When members of an organization use common sources for data they help themselves achieve common viewpoints and purposes. Opportunity for divergence of data exists when data that should be related is derived from different sources. When such opportunities are found to exist, steps should be taken to eliminate them for at least two reasons:

1. Multiple effort is being spent in dealing with the data, resulting in excessive costs.
2. More importantly, the divergence of data defeats the purpose of its collection. Data that is confusing provides poor guidance to the system.

EMPHASIZE THE FORECASTING OF SALES VOLUME

A major characteristic that should always be measured is the forecast of expected sales. This measurement provides primary guidance for all production and inventory systems. The best knowledge of anticipated sales should lie in the marketing or sales department. With the proper forecast coming from marketing or sales, there is the greatest probability that production and inventory system activities will be directed toward supporting marketing and sales activities. To strengthen the support, the forecasts should cover all expected and planned movement of product into the market.

CASE IN POINT

After a thorough analysis of costs, a pharmaceutical manufacturing company decided to stop preparing special packages of their products for use as samples sent to doctors. The smallest, regular size packages were to be used as samples, instead of special packages. Discontinuance of the special sample activity resulted in elimination of the design and purchase of the special packaging, as well as other related costs. Unfortunately, it also eliminated the planning of the production of the products to be used as samples; the forecast of products to be sold failed to recognize the need for some of these products to be used as samples.

The use of the standard product as samples was well-known; individual packaging production orders were written for the quantities of packages to be used for sample mailings. On the other hand, materials and production planning were being based on the sales forecasts, which were known to be extremely reliable. The planning people assumed that the forecasts covered the quantities needed for samples. The forecasting people were monitoring sales forecasts for projection of financial income for the company. This gap created a crisis because a stockout almost occurred. The approach of the stockout was clearly visible, but it was thought to be an error in reporting, since the planning was being matched so carefully to the sales forecast. When the near stockout was found to be factual, the matter was carefully examined and the real reason was revealed. Recurrence has been prevented by including quantities needed for samples in the forecast of *goods to be made*. The forecast of *goods to be made* differs from the forecast of *goods to be sold* by the amount of goods to be used for samples.

The change in the subject of the forecast from *goods to be sold* to *goods to be made* helps ensure that there need be no confusion as to whether the forecast can be used as published or whether it is open to further question.

PRESENT FORECASTS IN IMMEDIATELY USABLE FORM

Information contained in the forecast should be presented in the way it is most immediately usable. If interpretation or conversion of the data is required to make it usable for the production and inventory system, opportunity is provided for improper interpretation, with the possibility that the conversion may be incorrect. For example, a dollar volume sales forecast will have to be converted to unit volume for individual products to be of practical use to the production and inventory system. The product mix should be shown specifically in detail, even if it is expected to continue as in the past, to eliminate opportunity for misinterpretation.

CASE IN POINT

The toiletry industry has a tradition of using promotions and deals to motivate potential customers. The special packages often are composed of the standard products in various combinations, or in a unique package of intrinsic value, or with premium coupons in the packages. Some of the packages are related to holidays: Easter, Christmas, Mother's Day, Father's Day. Others are developed very quickly when sales fall below acceptable levels. At the time that annual sales forecasts are prepared, the exact nature of the package configurations of the promotions or deals is not known. Decisions as to the exact configurations are generally delayed as long as possible to make certain that they are current with the times. In some toiletry companies the uncertainty of the configurations does not interfere with sales forecasts. In some other companies the uncertainty has been found to have an adverse effect on the reliability of sales forecasts. Where the adverse effect has been found, it can generally be related to the inability to identify the package configurations. The condition has been expressed: "If we don't know what the package will contain, how can we make a detailed forecast stating expected sales in terms of quantities of packages?"

One approach that has given satisfactory results is based on ignoring the makeup of the promotions and deals. Instead, the forecast is made of quantities of standard products. This forecast is used to control an inventory of semifinished products: standard products in standard containers. The inventory of semifinished products is then used to fill orders for standard products, as such, or for orders for promotions and deals.

The promotions and deals generally require change only in the exterior packaging. The packaging coordination is handled separately from the standard product production.

DON'T IGNORE THE FORECAST OF DOLLAR VALUE

The dollar value of the sales forecast is also important to the production and inventory system. It is used as a basis for budgets, return-on-investment analyses, equipment justification analyses and other areas of mutual interest to production and inventory control and financial control.

CASE IN POINT

The importance of the dollar value of a forecast may be overlooked when the unit volume is high. A manufacturer of electronic components became interested in miniature circuit boards because of the potentially large unit volume. The company counted the number of products that could use such boards and the number of boards that might be used in each product, multiplied the two numbers and arrived at an astronomical figure. The potential market convinced the management of the company that they should make a strong effort to add the circuit boards to their product line.

To help make certain of the success of the new product, they undertook a research program for providing their circuit boards with a special feature. The research was successful, so a new division was created, staffed, housed, equipped and a sales effort was launched. After several years of strong effort but lack of profits, the division was closed down. The dollar volume of the market did not justify continuation of operations.

Based on examination of the planning memoranda, there is reason to believe that the large potential unit volume dominated the original evaluations to the point where the potential dollar volume was dealt with superficially. A return-on-investment analysis had been omitted.

Just as for other data, divergence in the dollar forecasts must be avoided. This can be ensured if the forecast is prepared simultaneously with the unit volume forecast, and in a related format.

DESIGN THE FORECAST FORMATS TO MATCH THE INFORMATION NEEDS

In designing the sales forecast format, it must be recognized that the forecast has to satisfy many information needs for the production and inventory systems. The information is needed for planning:

— Inventory levels
— Production schedules
— Personnel requirements
— Facilities requirements
  • Plant
  • Equipment

The specific needs within the production and inventory system for information from the forecast of sales vary by industry and even by company. An industry that is faced with long lead times for facilities' construction or preparation such as the petroleum industry, works with longer forecast periods than one that has short facilities lead times such as the needle trades industry. A company with highly seasonal sales, a greeting card company, requires more detailed time-related information than a company with low seasonal variation, one that prints lottery tickets.

The following details should be considered in designing the presentation of sales forecasts:

1. Period covered by the forecast
   — Long-term forecasts should more than cover the lead time for response to the forecast. Five and ten years are the periods most frequently used.
   — Short-term forecasts covering twelve future months normally provide sufficient information for good production and inventory system control.

2. Division of forecasts into periods
   — When there are periodic or seasonal sales patterns, the forecast should show as much detail of the timing as is practical. Quarterly calendar periods should not be used where their use would obscure possible monthly fluctuations of the sales patterns.

3. Product identification
   — The product identification details should be sufficiently fine to permit planning for procurement of purchased materials and planning for the production processing necessary to make each of the products.

4. Sales volume
   — The volume should be expressed in terms of units of sales for which there are clear specifications of units of production. For example, if the item to be sold is a sales package containing one dozen units, the sales forecast should state the number of packages to be sold with a designation that relates each package to twelve units.

5. Product coverage
   — All products to be produced by the production and inventory system should be shown in the forecast.

Preparation of a forecast isn't the end of an activity; it is really a continuing activity. To be of greatest usefulness to the control system, the forecast must be updated regularly to supply the production and inventory system with current information.

TRACK ACTUAL PERFORMANCE VERSUS FORECASTS TO STRENGTHEN CONTROLS

Production and inventory system plans are subject to change as the actual sales are found to differ from forecast sales. The magnitude of the difference between actual and forecast sales has an important influence on the ability of the production and inventory system to control costs. To measure that difference, it is necessary to track the actual versus the forecast sales. The tracking will guide marketing and sales in updating the forecast to provide the production and inventory system the best, most current information for planning. Good cost control requires planning that is directed toward meeting the most current objectives.

Forecast tracking can be accomplished in various ways and at various costs. It can be carried out easily through the use of a computer by making regular periodic comparisons between orders received and projected sales. The work also can be carried out manually, with more clerical effort.

The value of updating the forecast may be determined by examining the causes of schedule changes and interruptions and the extra costs incurred through:

— Reduced labor utilization
— Extra overtime
— Extra equipment setup labor
— Extra material handling labor

The costs of tracking and revising the forecasts should be compared with the extra manufacturing costs to determine which costs are lower. It has been found that identification of the lower cost alternative is not always obvious.

CASE IN POINT

In an example discussed earlier regarding promotions and deals in the toiletry industry, the lower cost alternative for one company was a simple change in forecasting procedure. Forecasts made on the basis of standard products (unit products packaged in standard containers), without getting involved with the complexities of the promotions and deals, have been found to be so reliable that the difference between actual and forecast sales is of minor significance.

CASE IN POINT

In the case of a problem division of a large chemical manufacturing company, the lower cost alternative also consisted of a simple change in procedure. The forecast for the problem division was done by marketing personnel and the company's computer was used merely as the vehicle for publishing the forecast for use by the planning people. Orders received were entered manually into notebooks by order entry personnel and were not used for forecast tracking.

The forecast for another division of that company was already being done by means of a computer program which utilized order entry information for tracking and updating the forecast. The computer program also has provision for input of specialized information from the marketing people to adjust the computer-prepared forecast. The situation was improved simply by using the computer for the problem division in exactly the same way that it is used for the other division. The extra cost is for additional computer time; there was insignificant programming cost.

Forecasting and forecast tracking give consideration to one external characteristic: sales volume. Measurements must also be made of the second external characteristic: customer service.

BE DEFINITE ABOUT CUSTOMER SERVICE CONSIDERATIONS

There are two major aspects to customer service, each consisting of two parts:

1. Customer order lead time for:
   — Products made to order
   — Products shipped from inventory

2. Back orders:
   — Frequency
   — Duration

The production and inventory system's influence on customer order lead time varies according to the way in which the order is received, processed and filled. Lack of clear understanding of the actual time required for that process may result in improperly short delivery promises being made to customers. Such promises cause the exertion of extra efforts with added costs and various other ill effects, including the possible loss of customers.

sembly, packaging, and shipping had never been made. The general manager had no real basis for his delivery promises.

The results of the short delivery promises were extremely sincere, though unsuccussful, attempts by the general manager's organization to deliver as promised. There was extensive expediting activity directed at vendors and at internal operations. Very little time was available for a systematic approach to permanent shortening of time requirements. Solving of the problem started when the general manager acknowledged to his people that the demands of the customers' purchasing agents were unrealistic. At that point, he and his people began dealing with the external conditions separately from the internal conditions. Dealing with internal conditions consisted of relieving the intense pressure to meet the improper delivery dates, identifying the activities with the longest lead time and systematically working on reducing the lead times. For example, purchasing lead times were improved, in some instances, by making commitments to vendors for the purchase of approximate weights or numbers of items in anticipation of design details. This practice allowed vendors to schedule production weights or quantities of items although lacking specific dimensions or configurations. Separating the external conditions from the internal ones provided sufficient relief to the plant staff. They were able to make time available to plan and work methodically on reducing and telescoping time elements.

Lack of clear understanding of actual time requirements may have other causes.

CASE IN POINT

The senior order entry clerk for a door manufacturing firm had been a salesman on the road for the same company before he was brought "inside." He was customer-oriented and was eager to do his best to please them. Each day he determined from the foreman of the production department, the types and quantities of door that had been clamped, the final regular production step. He then made delivery promises based on that information. In making his promises, he overlooked the fact that some of the doors leaving the clamps were put aside for patching. He did not take into account the fact that some doors went to a prime painting operation and that others required glazing. He did not consider the time required to move the doors through the plant to the warehouse. By omitting these considerations, he failed to account for as much as two weeks' time in some instances. The remedy was simple. He was instructed to promise delivery only of doors that were reported to be in the warehouse and that had not been earmarked for delivery to any other customer.

The adverse effects on cost of lead times can be minimized by:

1. Determining what the lead times actually are and promising deliveries accordingly.
2. Recognizing that different products may have different lead times, even if they are similar in nature.
3. Deliberately and systematically working at reducing the lead times when that is

found to be necessary, and promising shorter delivery times only after the reductions have been achieved.

Improper delivery promises result in back orders that may not only have external effects, but they may also have harmful internal effects.

CASE IN POINT

The materials manager of an eastern pharmaceutical company was being criticized over a long period of time because sales entry reports showed a chronic back order condition. The condition became so severe that the president of the company called for an investigation of the materials manager's performance. The investigation showed that, with an occasional minor exception, the back orders did not affect products that were in the normal finished goods inventory, but were all confined to promotions and deals for some over-the-counter products. Further investigation showed that forecasts of quantities for those special events were always understated by the sales people; they then found themselves promising deliveries for quantities in excess of initial plans. At one time in the past, the sales people had greatly overstated the quantity for such an event and had been severely criticized by the president. The sales people were determined not to put themselves again in the same uncomfortable position. When the true nature of the back orders was identified and it became apparent that the normally stocked items were not on back order, the president was satisfied. He preferred the risk of understatement of forecasts for promotions and deals to that of overstatement, so the matter was put to rest and criticism of the materials manager stopped.

A more general back order condition occurs when a product that is *normally* carried in inventory is in a stockout condition. Three questions are important for the establishment of controls to provide protection against those stockouts:

1. How many individual items are on back order?
2. What is the frequency of back order for each item?
3. How long do the back orders last?

The answer to the first question indicates if the situation is isolated or widespread. The best answer to that question will come from a detailed examination of a back order report. The other two questions can be treated more routinely.

The frequency of occurrence is generally measured in terms of percent stockouts. The percent stockout of an item is usually considered to be the percent of orders for an individual product that cannot be filled because of stockout out of the total number of orders received for that product. Because protection against such stockouts is provided by safety stocks, establishment of the acceptable percentage of stockouts should be a top management decision. The decision should be based on evaluating the cost of achieving the acceptable percentage against the gain to be derived from the achievement.

The duration of a stockout and its effect on customers is sometimes measured in terms of back order days. The measurement can be applied to individual products if that is important to the company or it can be applied to groups of products, product lines, or to total products.

A back order represents a customer order that cannot be filled for a specific item without regard to the quantity ordered. On a given day, the total number of back orders indicate the number of customer orders that are affected for that day by the stockout. By accumulating the daily totals for all of the days of the stockout, the effect of the length of time of the stockout is emphasized. This measurement is demonstrated in Table 1-1.

Day of Stockout	No. of New Back Orders	Total No. of Back Orders	No. of Back Order Days	
First	5	5	5	(5 x 1)
Second	10	15	20	(10 x 1)+ (5 x 2)
Third	12	27	47	(12 x 1) + (10 x 2) + (5 x 3)

TABLE 1-1

If the stockouts are not considered to be especially critical for a company, two simpler measurements can be applied to back order situations. Daily recording may be made of:

— Number of back orders for the day (27 in Table 1-1, on the third day).
— Number of days of back order (3 days in Table 1-1).

Daily observations and comparison of the records will provide information about changes in the number of back orders, and, of course, of the duration.

To summarize, control limits in the form of numerical values may be established for any of the measurements:

1. The number of items showing stockouts.
2. The percent stockouts.
3. The number of back order days.
4. The number of days of back orders.
5. The number of back orders for the day.

The selection of the measurement to be used depends on the nature of the product line, the nature of the company, personal preferences, convenience, costs of collecting and treating the data and benefits expected to be gained. The use of both upper and lower control limits should be given consideration. When customer service measurements are above the upper control limits, customer service requirements are not being met. When customer service measurements are below the lower control limits, an examination might be called for to determine if too much effort is being directed toward customer service. For example, it might be found that some safety stock levels are too high. The customer service considerations can be evaluated specifically by numerical measurements and targets.

ESTABLISH AND MAINTAIN MEASUREMENTS OF THE CAPACITY AND UTILIZATION OF YOUR RESOURCES

The two characteristics previously discussed provide measurements of the magnitude of the job to be done. It is now necessary to determine if the available resources are large enough to do the job, if they are of sufficient capacity, and if that capacity is being properly utilized.

It is common practice to express the capacity of a production and inventory system in terms of units of products. The automotive industry speaks of the number of cars per day, the steel industry in terms of the number of tons. Frequently, such simple broad measurements can be used very effectively by the production and inventory system for controlling itself.

CASE IN POINT

A midwest millwork company has made substantial improvements in manufacturing costs and meeting delivery promises using only the total number of doors, for that department, and the total number of sashes for that department, as the controls. The breakdown of total numbers into styles and sizes would create a very complex paper work situation that would be too costly to operate. The decision to avoid the breakdown was based on the judgment that the variation of the product mix would not have a significant effect. Experience has substantiated that judgment.

CASE IN POINT

A manufacturer of electric components is able to control his production operations by scheduling the number of coils to be wound daily. His production capacity is limited by his coil winding capacity, although he has great flexibility in all of his other operations. He has found that by simply planning the number of coils to be wound, he solves the major part of his scheduling problem. Scheduling the remainder of the operations takes very little effort. His labor utilization is excellent, as is his performance against schedule targets as a result of this simple control.

CASE IN POINT

The work flow through a company that produces railway car parts (ends, bulkheads, floors, roofs, etc.) followed the same distinctive pattern month after month. The pattern is shown in Figure 1-2. The curve in the figure shows that the production rate is markedly

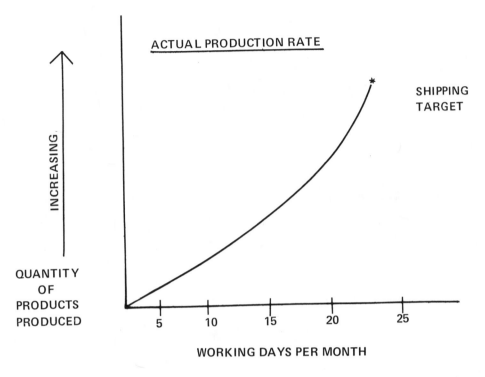

FIGURE 1-2

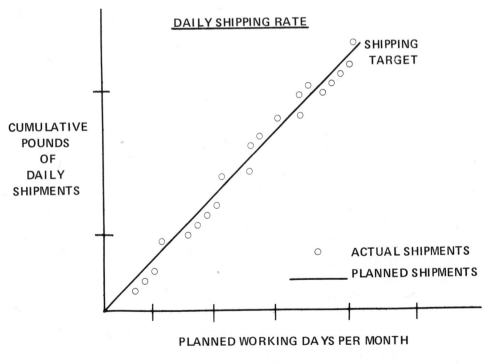

FIGURE 1-3

lower during the early part of the month than it is during the latter part. With the number of employees remaining constant during the month, the change in rate indicates that utilization of labor is lower at the beginning of the month than at the end. There was another undesirable condition at the end of the month. Because the level of activity was high at the end of the month, the equipment most suited for the work was in almost constant use so that some operations had to be carried out on equipment that was less suited, resulting in excessive processing costs.

An examination of the shipments of railway car parts showed that the sales dollar value of each pound of product (from shipping documents), regardless of the shape or identification of the product, was constant within about plus or minus 5%. This was true because the cost of the steel in the products averaged about 90% of the prime costs, and the overhead costs were fixed. The constant per-pound value was used to level out the flow of work through the shop. After the shipping target is planned each month, a graph is constructed as shown in Figure 1-3. The shipping target represents specific orders to be shipped, and is first expressed as sales dollars. The sales dollars are then converted to pounds.

A straight line is plotted, directed toward the total shipping weight of the shipping target, representing planned shipments. This is done before the beginning of each month. As shipments are made during the month, the cumulative weight shipped, taken directly from shipping documents, is also plotted as shown by the small circles. When the cumulative actual weight lags below the line for planned weight, this signals the need for corrective action. This graph is a simple device for tracking actual production versus planned production. The device pictures a daily rate of use of resources that can easily be compared with the capacity of the resources. Smoothing out the work flow helps ensure that the most suitable equipment is available as needed, reducing the use of less suitable equipment that adds extra costs. Leveling the work flow also helps ensure that the work force is of proper size and is well utilized. The good utilization now achieved is reflected by the level of bonus earned under a well-administered incentive plan in the plant.

The above examples demonstrate that measurement of the capacity of resources has two major purposes:

1. Determination of the ability of the plant to produce sufficient quantities of products to meet sales demands.
2. Control of utilization of the resources.

When the capacity of the resources can be stated simply, as for two of the above examples, the comparison between forecast sales and capacity can be easily and directly made. When the product mix is diverse and complex, other bases for comparison are needed.

The other bases most generally used are labor hours required per unit or equipment hours required per unit. The hours required per unit may be derived from industrial engineering work measurement analyses or they may be derived from historical data. Whatever the source of the derivation, the hours used for calculating expected capacity must represent the hours per unit expected to be required in the future. The expected hours are generally extrapolated from current utilization, modified according to planned changes. Multiplying the expected hours per unit by the number of units forecasted will yield the total number of hours expected to be needed to meet the forecast. For greatest convenience, forecasts are often broken down to cover weekly periods so that the multiplication will show the weekly hours required for labor and/or equipment. The weekly value is extremely important if the level of production is expected to vary during the year. The weekly value of labor and/or equipment hours needed to meet the forecast, when compared to the weekly capacity, will show the extent to which the build-up of inventory buffers will have to be planned to overcome capacity limitations.

A similar, systematic analysis can be used to examine:

— Cubic feet requirements for storage of various inventories.
— Volume of fluids or number of containers of materials to be handled.
— Number of truckloads or railway cars of materials or products to be handled.

This type of approach makes certain that the forecast of sales is converted into the language used for control of the resources by the production and inventory system. That, in turn, facilitates the job of making certain that the output capacity is capable of satisfying demand. With that taken care of, the production and inventory system can concentrate on controlling the utilization of resources between the two sets of limits: output and costs.

Capacity is the characteristic that applies to the production and inventory system's capability for responding to demand. The characteristics that apply to the system's sensitivity or rate of response to demand are the lead times.

USE FACTUAL VALUES FOR CLEARLY DEFINED LEAD TIMES

Because misunderstandings of meanings are so frequently found in reference to lead times, the definition of each lead time to be used should be the first step in the measurement process. After the item to be measured has been clearly defined, the measurement can be made with assurance that it will provide the proper information.

Basically, lead times should represent the length of time that elapses between initiation and completion of an activity. Typical definitions, related to production and inventory systems, are:

— Customer order processing: From the time an *order is received* from a customer until the time the *ordered material is shipped.*
— Product processing: From the time of *determination of need to begin processing* until the time the product has been satisfactorily produced and is *ready for use.*
— Purchasing: From the time of *determination of need to purchase* until the time the material is accepted and stored and is *ready for use.*

The values of time used for lead times must be factual, reflecting actual experience. They must represent the average times normally required for the activity. If excessive values are used for lead times, excessive costs may be incurred from carrying unneeded amounts of materials in inventory. If, on the other hand, the lead time values are insufficient, extra costs may be incurred because of the need to take emergency actions to recover from the lack of time. The use of factual lead times will result in the best possible costs, under the existing circumstances. If reduction of lead times is established as a company objective, the lead times must actually be reduced before the lower values are put to use. This point is being emphasized because experience shows that, at times, the numerical value of lead time used for planning is reduced without a reduction in the actual value of lead time. When that has been done, negative results have always been observed.

Examples of the use of unrealistic lead times have been observed in a wide variety of industries and companies. The general pattern is: delivery promises are made without thorough understanding of, or unwillingness to accept, the nature of the obstacles that will have to be overcome. Schedules are then established containing a series of unrealistic lead times. What follows is a series of failures to meet schedules, an initiation of expediting and other extra efforts, an accumulation of extra costs and, in spite of all that, unkept delivery promises.

On the other hand, examples have also been observed, again in a wide variety of industries and companies, where the needs for rapid response to customers' orders have been satisfied by a systematic analysis of possible alternatives and possible added costs. The result nearly always has been the development of a plan of action that has provided benefits to both the customers and the producing company.

Reduction in lead times on a real permanent basis has been achieved in many companies by the establishment of work-in-process inventories in the form of parts, subassemblies and semifinished products. This practice recognizes that inventories are more than just objects to be controlled; they are objects to be used.

PUT INVENTORIES TO WORK FOR YOUR SYSTEM

Physical inventories of materials are tools. They are tools to be used to maximize the utilization of resources. Their purposes are to help:

—Maintain the desired level of customer service.
— Optimize the flow of materials and products in order to obtain the maximum return on investment in:
  • Equipment
  • Materials
  • Labor

Discrete, or individually distinct, inventories should be established as necessary to support these purposes. Some examples of discrete inventory accumulations are:

— Area warehouses providing product to specific groups of customers
— Distribution centers, serving area warehouses
— Plants serving distribution centers
  • Finished goods

- Intermediate or semifinished products
- Work-in-process
- Purchased materials

The best breakdown of inventories for an individual company depends on the nature of the industry and company. Some of the reasons for breaking down the total inventory of a plant into discrete parts are:

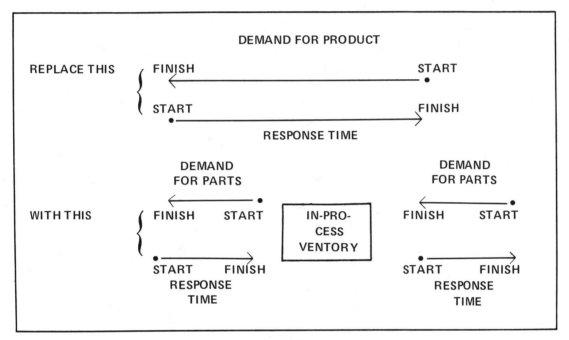

FIGURE 1-4

— To permit subdivision of its processing to accelerate response to demand for the final output of the plant, as shown in Figure 1-4.

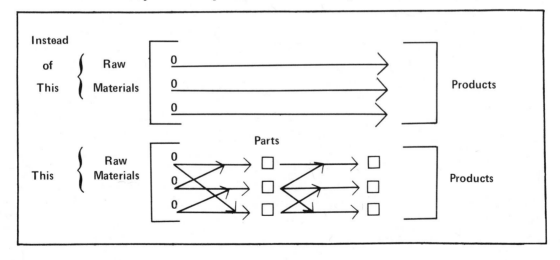

FIGURE 1-5

— To permit the use of common parts or components to reduce costs and to increase the flexibility of an operation, as shown in Figure 1-5.

— To provide protection against:
  • Uncertain or sporadic availability of materials
  • Short-lived materials, when the life can be increased through conversion or processing.
  • Uncertain or sensitive processing steps.

— In general, to optimize utilization of resources.

The establishment of additional, discrete physical inventories does not necessarily increase the total value of the materials in inventory. When protection against stockouts of finished products is provided, in part through inventories of unfinished product, the level of the inventory of finished product can be reduced. Because the value of unfinished products excludes the labor cost for finishing, the use of inventories of unfinished products sometimes results in a reduction of the total value of all inventories. The data needed for evaluation of alternative inventory arrangements are:

1. Cost of the items in inventory, including both labor and material.
2. Average levels of inventories under alternative arrangements.

Two simple measurements of inventory levels are minimum and maximum quantities. The minimum quantity frequently represents the reorder point. The maximum quantity frequently represents the largest investment that is desired. Because these two measurements do not define safety stocks, the average inventory can be assumed to be slightly higher than one-half of the maximum.

The two subjects, multiple inventories and levels of inventory, warrant a great deal of attention. These subjects will be covered in greater detail in subsequent chapters, because to give them that attention at this time raises the risk of distracting attention from the more general consideration of the overall data base. The discussion here will continue with more of the general aspects of the data base.

Broad consideration of inventory levels should include recognition of the turnover rate, a control device that is often used. The turnover rate is calculated by dividing the total annual value at cost, of materials entering and leaving an inventory by the average value of the inventory. Establishing target turnover rates should be given the same care as establishing other targets. It has been found, at times, that objectives to increase turnover rates place heavy emphasis on reduction of quantities of materials in inventory. It should be noted that turnover rates can be increased also by increasing the quantities of materials moving through the system. The numerator of the rate should be considered together with denominator.

It should be appreciated that values of inventories can be reduced by reducing the value, or cost, of individual items in the inventories. One cost factor is frequently found to be given insufficient consideration. That factor is quality control, not the operating expense of quality control but, rather, its influence on production costs.

BE CERTAIN TO EVALUATE QUALITY CONSIDERATIONS

Two major quality considerations that influence product costs are:

— The quality capability of the production process.
— The quality requirement for the product.

No production process will repeatedly make products of exactly identical quality. The quality of products coming from a process will lie within a range, with some products having higher quality than others. True, the range may be small but it is never exactly zero. Knowing that, producers and customers establish ranges of product acceptability defined by high and low limits. The limits will cover a variety of properties such as size, shape or color, or length of service. It is not always obvious that quality specifications are ranges with at least two limits. For example, it would appear that, in the case of length of useful service, there would be only a minimum acceptable limit.

CASE IN POINT

As a case opposed to that idea, compare the popularity of the disposable lighters with limited life, against the availability of inexpensive refillable lighters with longer life, and lower operating costs.

In some other cases such as the number of scratches on a car being considered for purchase, there would appear to be only a maximum acceptable limit (tempered, of course, by the degree of visibility of the scratches).

CASE IN POINT

As a case opposed to that idea, consider the effects on the quality requirements of the price of the replacement car together with trade-in offered for the old car. Consider also other evaluation factors such as: whether the car being considered for purchase is second-hand with a corresponding lowering of price, or whether the car is one with prestige price or a popular price.

Because quality always implies a range with upper and lower limits, the quality limits of a manufacturing process can be thought of as shown in Figure 1-6 and Figure 1-7. The range of capability does not coincide with the range of requirement in either figure.

In Figure 1-6, the range of capability is lower than the requirement. The result is extra cost, caused by scrap or rework. When the range of capability is lower than the requirement, the search for opportunities for improvement should start at the very

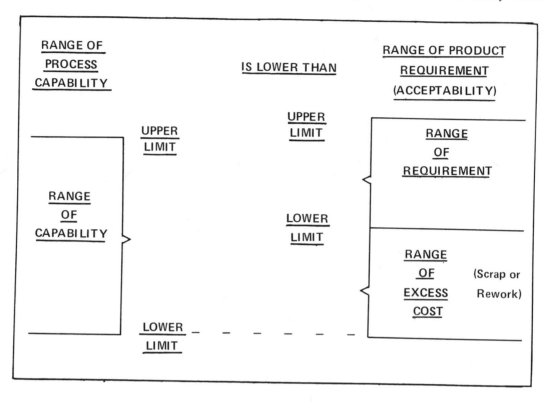

FIGURE 1-6

beginning of the process, with the raw materials. As a matter of fact, proper quality control includes consideration of raw materials.

CASE IN POINT

A manufacturer of galvanometers found that his poor quality came from an easily ignored source. His galvanometer consisted essentially of a mirror fastened to a coil of wire, with the coil and attached mirror being held between two small brass pulleys. After months of examining many other possible causes, he thought to examine his raw materials. He found that the brass rod, from which the pulleys were turned, contained scattered, small amounts of iron. The iron produced magnetic effects that interfered with those of the wire coil. The presence of iron in commercial brass is rare; it is generally assumed to be absent. In this case that assumption was costly.

CASE IN POINT

A manufacturer of miniature printed circuit boards was experiencing extremely high rework costs and loss of product because the locations of the circuits and terminals were found to be outside of the limits of acceptability. The magnitude of the problem can be

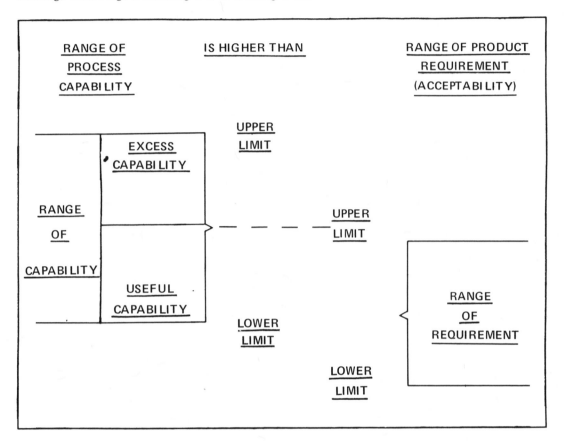

FIGURE 1-7

described very simply: Four boards were started through the process for each board that was shipped. As in the previous case, months were spent in examining many other possible causes before the raw material was considered. The raw material in this case was the photography of the circuit. For these miniature boards, engineering drawings of the circuits were reduced to size in the photographic equipment. A visit to the vendor of the photography revealed that his equipment did not contain any measuring devices for ensuring that the reduction was exactly that required. The vendor was relying on the coarse machine setting of his equipment to get the reduction. The specifications for the photography did not show dimensional tolerances.

These examples show the not infrequent lack of appreciation of the benefits of starting quality control at the beginning of the production process, even covering raw materials. It is sometimes judged, without investigation, that the establishment of specifications and testing facilities for raw materials represents an excess cost. In many cases, it can be demonstrated that the opposite is true; starting cost control through quality control at the beginning point often yields the lowest costs. Starting quality control at the beginning also often yields longer lasting beneficial results than the application of corrective action at a later point.

In examining a situation where the process capability is lower than the requirement, consideration of options should include such factors as:

— The effect of product price to the customer on the lower requirement (acceptability) limit.
— The effect on sales volume of a reduction of the lower requirement (acceptability) limit.
— Comparison of the value of the loss due to process limitations with the value of the two above effects (price and sales).
— The feasibility and cost of raising the lower capability limit.
— Comparison of the cost of raising the capability with the value of the two above effects (price and sales volume).

The identification of excess product or process capability has led to cost reductions in a variety of electronic and mechanical products and companies. This frequently occurs as competition for a given product increases the prospective purchaser's interest in price rather than in quality. This does not necessarily mean that the product is being cheapened; it might well mean that the original quality was higher than experience has shown is necessary.

Cost reduction opportunities based on excess capability may also arise as a result of experience gained in working with the process or equipment. Experience is often an important factor in getting the best use of equipment in that, as the user becomes more familiar with the equipment, he can:

1. Develop shortcut practices.
2. Predict its behavior more accurately.
3. Control its behavior more readily.

Experience shows that quality considerations are infrequently considered as being within the normal scope of routine cost controls. Most often, quality considerations are the subject of special projects such as those of value analysis. There is justification for dealing separately with quality considerations.

1. Evaluation of quality-cost alternatives many times requires a high degree of involvement of all major organizational elements, including:
   — Marketing and sales
   — Engineering and design
   — Purchasing
   — Production
   — Quality Control and assurance
   — Finance

2. There is usually a large amount of data involved in quality control, of which only a small portion is germane to cost control.

Enveloping quality considerations well within the production and inventory control system would tend to clog the production and inventory control channels.

KEEP THE DATA BASE SLIM AND NIMBLE

Data has importance only when it is put to use. The contents of the data base of any production and inventory control system should be limited to those items that will be put to good use by that system. Data that will be used only occasionally should not be constantly published but should be kept in the data base file, readily accessible for those times when it is needed. It should be kept in mind, however, that data base files frequently contain information that someone long ago decided "would be nice to know" and which is continually being collected but never used.

It can be argued that the absence of historical information is sometimes a disadvantage to an organization. On the other hand, it can also be argued that it is difficult to predict the identity of material that will be useful in the future. It might even be conjectured that the absence of historical information has forced the collection of current information, with greater benefit being derived than would have been provided by history. The fact remains that effort is wasted by collecting data that is never used.

A guide toward determining if data will be used is to establish, even roughly, how it will be used. Establishing how it will be used may begin with a description of who will use it and what the data will be expected to accomplish. The need for accomplishing that particular end can be examined, and, if the end is found to be of value, alternate means can be sought for accomplishing it. If there are no alternate means for accomplishing that end, only then should data be retained or new data be added to the data base. This point is being stressed for two reasons. The first reason is that the cost of handling unused data is an excessive expense. The second reason is that too much data in a control system can defeat the purpose of the control system. It is easier to pay close attention to a few bits of information than it is to handle many. Closer control can be provided from the intensive use of a few well-chosen control limits than from trying to cope with an extensive body of data. And the primary purpose of the data base is to establish control.

Chapter 2

Evaluating and Reviewing People and Procedures
in Production and Inventory Control:
A Five Step Program

ORGANIZATION RELATIONSHIPS

Every company is unique in terms of its need for organizational structuring. The best organization for company A can be the worst organization for their competitor, company B. This is true even though they both produce the same product and serve the same class of customers. The variance in organizational relationships reflects the difference in management philosophy, age of company, size of company and distribution network.

Decisions Create Organizations; Organizations Don't Create Decisions

Defining and structuring the proper organizational production and inventory control relationships for any company is not a herculean task. There are some guidelines that apply almost universally.

As an overview, a five-step approach involves these decision areas:

— Needs evaluation
— Program establishment
— Personnel selection
— Management mode
— Feedback systems

NEEDS EVALUATION

The purpose of evaluation is to identify the areas of involvement and the current and projected magnitude of the involvement of the production and inventory systems.

This review should entail a consideration of the five-year plan, current sales forecast and company growth objectives. This fundamental review of the business barometers will assist in the determination of the objectives of the production/inventory control program.

For example consider the impact that the following two items have on production and inventory system involvement.

Customer Service Levels—What percentage of customer orders will be filled within how many days? The first variable, *what percentage of customer orders*, will aid in determining inventory levels and reserves for forecast variance. The second variable, *within how many days*, will aid in determining the distribution and transportation configuration.

CASE IN POINT

A plant is located in the Midwest and its customer service policy is "95% of all customer orders will be delivered within three days." This translates into a requirement for finished goods not only at the plant but also in satellite warehouses located on each coast. The need for satellite warehouses would be eliminated if the policy was: "95% of all customer orders will be delivered within ten days." A ten-day lead time is sufficient for either rail or highway delivery from a Midwest location. Economically, it might be advantageous to have satellite warehouses but the purpose of this example is to isolate the impact of customer service policies.

Inventory Turns—How many times per year should the inventory be replaced or turned? This will vary by industry because of the different characteristics of the product. The food processing industry has to be concerned with product aging and deterioration. Obsolescence because of model changes is a consideration in the durable goods industry. A custom manufacturer or job shopper usually carries little or no finished goods inventory but may have a substantial investment in work-in-process inventories. A universal consideration is the carrying cost of money invested in providing the inventory. The tax structure in many states and municipalities also impacts on inventory levels. However, as a general rule, an overall average of four turns per year for industries with finished goods inventories can be used.

PROGRAM ESTABLISHMENT

Once the objectives are ascertained, the next step after evaluation is to develop the program that will be used to control production and inventory. Later chapters in this book will describe in detail some of the programs. The general outline of program content will be covered in this chapter.

The purpose of a program is to establish the criteria for the organization of a function. This organization is then accountable for the cost control information generation. The components of the program for a production control function and inventory control function will be addressed separately.

Production Control

There are three variables that significantly affect the production control program. They are:

— Job shop versus processing industry classification
— Product line configuration
— Size of company

Job Shop Versus Processing Industry Classification

The first variable, *job shop versus processing,* centers attention on material flow, process flow, and product flow. The size and complexity of the production control program is conditionally related to these parameters. Some typical inputs into program development are:

Material Flow

How many different materials are required to produce one product?
How many different materials are required to produce the total product line?
How many materials are interchangeable in how many products?
Do materials enter the production cycle at the same stage?

Process Flow

Who controls the process flow?
How many variations in production operations exist?
How many processing steps are there?
How many steps have to be monitored to know the throughput?

Product Flow

How many staging areas are required?
Is the flow continuous or interrupted?
Are there handling constraints?
Is there a quality control surveillance requirement?

The answers to the review of materials, process and product flow assist in determining the scope and magnitude of the production control function. They assist in determining the number and qualifications of the required personnel.

Product Line Configuration

The purpose of considering the product line configuration is to assist in quantifying the amount of data needed for control. The quantification of the data manipulation requirement will assist in determining the method of data handling, i.e., manual or automated and the scope of the system in terms of people and/or equipment.

Some of the factors involved in product line configuration are:

— Number of Line Items
  • How many individual finished products are sold?
  • How many different sets do the individual products represent?
  • Are there any line items that are seasonal and/or geographically isolated?
  • Are there price differences because of sales promotions?

— Restriction on Equipment
  • Can only a few machines produce specific products?
  • Are there different manpower skill requirements for different product runs?

— Plant Utilization
  • Are there many bottlenecks?
  • What percent of total capacity is utilized during peak production periods?
  • What percent of total capacity is utilized during the lowest demand period?

Size of Company

The larger the company the greater the risk and cost of poor management of the production/inventory control function. It is not always true that the size of the company dictates the manning requirements; but in most cases, if all other factors are equal, the larger company will require more personnel in PIC than the smaller company. Sales volume is not the only component of size; two other factors should also be considered—they are the coordination complexity and the number of plants.

The number of plants producing the same set of items initiates a coordination consideration into the system. If there is more than one plant in the system but each plant has its own set of items, the communication/coordination need does not include production control, except for raw material. This multi-plant configuration can impact on inventory control and especially the distribution function.

Inventory Control

There are three variables that significantly affect the inventory control program. They are:

— Distribution network
— Unit volume
— Product line configuration

Distribution Network

The size and number of warehouses is determined by the customer service policy and geographic dispersion of customers. If customers are statewide only, the required number of warehouses can be considerably fewer than if the customers were located in all the states. The time constraint imposed by the customer service policy impacts on the three factors that comprise time and service requirements. The three factors are: order processing time, material handling time and transportation. Each factor should be evaluated and quantified separately.

Order Processing

The order processing time can vary from one to five days. A one-day system usually involves dataphones and computers. A five-day system usually involves company mail, regular postal service and clerically maintained record systems. The interim time periods, two to four days, usually reflect a combination of systems. The three prime determinants of time are data volume, customer service policies and number of distribution sites. As the number of distribution sites increases and the volume of order processing data increases, the ability of any manual system becomes taxed and automation is required.

Material Handling

The material handling time can vary from one to three days depending upon the record-keeping, order picking and shipment systems. The record-keeping can vary from hand posted inventory cards to a real time automated locator/inventory system. Order picking system time requirements depend upon the amount of break pack picking and material handling equipment. Break pack picking refers to the small item picks that require breaking open a normal pack, usually a case. Mixed pallet loads of cases can also delay the order picking time.

The material handling mode can vary from shopping carts to automated retrieval systems using stacker cranes. Conveyors and in-floor tow lines are also used when the volume justifies the investment.

Transportation

The transportation mode and distance traveled are the prime determinants for the transportation time. The most popular transportation modes are trucks, rail, waterways and pipelines. Most companies use tractor trailer shipments most frequently. Truckload shipments over distances of 500 miles can make effective use of piggyback rail service. The size of the load affects the transportation time. Full truckloads (40,000 pounds) usually require one to three days to reach this destination while pool trucks or forwarded freight can require seven to ten days in transit. Figure 2-1 illustrates the many combinations that can exist for the three factors of order processing, material handling and transportation times.

Unit Volume

Typically, 15 percent of the items in the sales line represent 85 percent of the sales volume. The inventory control techniques need not be the same for all the items in the sales line. The ABC technique can be used successfully in a manual system.

THE RELATIONSHIP COMBINATIONS FOR SERVICE LEVELS

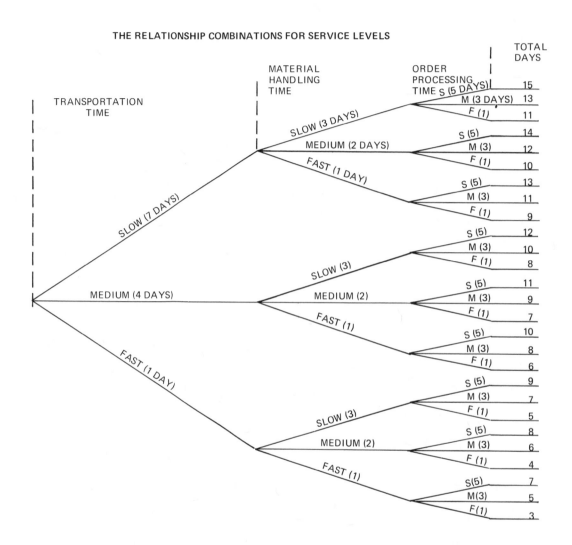

FIGURE 2-1

The unit volume for each line item is a function of total volume ordered and number of orders. Perpetual inventory records can becomes a massive clerical effort as the unit volume increases. When this effort starts to cause delays in order processing, it is time to seriously consider automating this function. Normally a Kardex system based on Economic Order Quantity principles can handle the inventory control information requirement.

The unit volume increases also affect the mode of transportation. As the unit volume increases, the material handling time and transportation time can decrease. This may become a factor in determining the number of days of inventory to carry.

Product Line Configuration

The product line configuration impact on inventory control is not as significant as its impact on production control. There are, however, some considerations that merit attention.

The item identification system should be structured logically. Most companies use a numerical code system that identifies three levels of detail. The number of digits used is based on the number of classifications required for each level. The three levels are:

—Generic family
—Size/color
—Pack/count

The generic family identifies broad classes of products such as paint, candy, hardware, canned food and pencils. The size/color designate identifies a specific physical characteristic of the product such as white paint, 20¢ candy bars, brass nails, can of tomatoes and #2 pencils. The last level of details refers to the quantity associated with the item such as 24 one-gallon cases of white paint, 8 boxes of 24-count candy bars, 100-pound bags of 4-inch brass nails, 16-24-ounce cans of tomatoes.

Automated Systems

Inventory control is one of the many areas of a company's involvement that lends itself to automated data manipulation. This is particularly true when the number of line items and frequency of transaction become so massive that delays in order processing are incurred. There are two things that need to be considered when contemplating a change from a manual inventory control system to an automated inventory control system.

— Would there be a time savings in order processing? If so, how many days and will there be a reduction in required inventory? Another time consideration centers around management's subjective judgment regarding customers lost due to longer order processing time in the manual mode.
— What are the costs that can be eliminated by converting? People, space and supplies are included in this consideration.

PERSONNEL SELECTION

After the program has been established the next activity is to select the personnel to operate the systems. The personnel selection step involves the following activities:

— Establish job qualifications and specifications.
— Recruit desired personnel.
— Orient and train personnel.
— Plan a development program.

Job Specifications

The job descriptions that are developed should reflect the needs of the system that the people will operate. If the initial system is manual, a heavy emphasis on computer understanding is misleading. Conversely, if the system is automated the job specifications should require exposure to automated data handling.

The job descriptions should follow the format employed within the entire organization. Each company has its own style. The specifications should reflect the different levels within the department. Table 2-1 illustrates one approach that can be used to indicate specifications and relationships.

REFERENCE JOB SPECIFICATIONS

JOB TITLE	EDUCATION	EXPERIENCE	SUPERVISION EXERCISED	JUDGMENT REQUIRED
Production Control Mgr.	3	3	3	3
Scheduler	2	2	2	3
Expediter	2	2	1	2
Inventory Clerk	1	2	1	1
Records Clerk	1	1	1	1

EDUCATION

1. 4 years High School
2. 2-3 years College
3. Degree College
4. Advanced Technical Knowledge

SUPERVISION EXERCISED

1. No responsibility
2. 1-2 people
3. 3-8 people
4. 9-17 people
5. 18 + people

EXPERIENCE REQUIRED

1. 12 months
2. 3 years
3. 6 years
4. 10 years
5. 10 or more years

JUDGMENT REQUIRED

1. Routine with considerable detail
2. Somewhat complex
3. Complex, requiring independent thinking
4. Highly involved, requiring analytical ability

TABLE 2-1

The job specifications contain the basic requirements for each position and are the foundation block for developing the position descriptions. The position description expands upon the specifications and defines the scope of the position in terms of relationships.

Recruiting Desired Personnel

Personality can be a key to performance especially in a production/inventory control department. The many different contacts across departmental lines require personnel who are excellent communicators and politically pleasing. In almost all companies, the production/inventory control function is a staff department that functions as a liaison between sales and operations. Ideally, the department head should be competent technically regarding operations yet possess a generalist's awareness of the total business cycle.

If the department is new, the recommended sourcing for a department head would be to recruit an experienced manager from outside the firm. His/her experience should be in a related type of industry, i.e., processing, heavy fabricating, electronic assembly or whatever best describes the manufacturing method. If the department is established, people within the organization can be considered first before recruiting from outside the company. Industrial engineers, plant engineers and production engineers are well-qualified candidates for this position.

The positions of scheduler and expeditor require a detailed understanding of the manufacturing process. For this reason, the best candidates are found in the production organization. Supervisors or assistant supervisors are frequently selected for these positions.

Orientation and Training

It is important that new members of the department fully understand the role of their department in the total organization. The orientation should include:

— Explanation of the production process, highlighting the key operations and bottlenecks. (Include a plant tour.)
— Review of marketing strategy, current and long-term.
— General background information regarding customers and how they use the product line.
— Personal introductions to key personnel in other departments.
— The department's role and contribution to the total effort.

Once the individual acclimates to the new environment, specific training can begin. The specific training should include:

— Administrative policies and procedures.
— Departmental policies and procedures.
— Functional systems.

— Information flows, sources and distribution.
— Departmental forms and records.
— Departmental goals and objectives, current and long-term.

Training and upgrading of skills should be a continuous process. The initial training phase is designed to equip the individual with the skill sets required to perform the job; the on-going program should prepare the individual for growth within the organization.

Planning a Development Program

Any organizational structure can be viewed as a temporary situation. Changing product structures, capital expansions and volume growths all contribute to the need for change. In conjunction with the five-year plan, there should also be a management development plan so that the production and inventory control function can keep abreast of progress. In some situations, the basic systems can change significantly; this is especially true when the systems are changed from manual to EDP. The development program can have the following components:

— Company-sponsored advanced education.
— Seminars.
— Supplier workshops.
— In-house training programs.

Management Mode

Where does the production/inventory control function belong within an organization? Ask five general managers of five different industries and you will probably receive at least five different answers. On the other hand, is there really a *best* place within the organization or should it be varied depending upon the specific organization or industry?

In many organizations the production and inventory control function is placed in a staff role to a major department i.e., sales, purchasing or production. Occasionally it is even the major department with production, purchasing or other functions in subordinate roles.

Staff to Production

A common location of the production and inventory control function in many companies is as a staff position to the production operation. As has already been described, the primary function is to plan and control production (Figure 2-2.)

In a staff role to the production operation it would be expected that the production and inventory control function would be responsive primarily to production and only secondarily to sales and other functions within the organization. In many instances, the function is relatively simple in scope and most logically fits into the

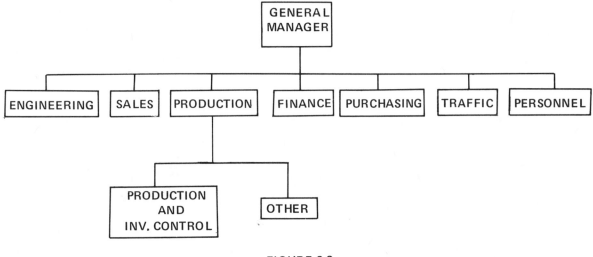

FIGURE 2-2

organization structure at this level. This also provides the opportunity for closer control of the production operation to be maintained and the development of a strong working relationship between the two functions.

On the negative side, if the goals and objectives of the entire organization are poorly identified, this organizational relationship can be detrimental since the objectives of the production department will come before those of the entire organization. Adequate and objective leadership within the production organization itself is a necessity under these conditions. If the particular product or process is of a complex nature requiring coordination with many other departments or functions within the organization, it is doubtful if this organizational relationship will be satisfactory. The production and inventory control function would simply lack sufficient status to be successful in discharging its duties.

For the most part, this kind of an organizational relationship is in existence in relatively small companies (under 500 total employees). Typically as companies originate, a function of this nature does not even exist. As they continue to develop and grow and the need for a planning and scheduling inventory function becomes apparent, the task will be assigned to someone in the production area on a part-time basis. This step may be followed by a division of responsibility and the assignment of personnel on a full-time basis.

Eventually it evolves into a separate department under the production function. More than likely a separate traffic function will not exist and will be the responsibility of purchasing on inbound material and production and inventory control on the outbound material. Occasionally an organizational relationship of this nature will be found in larger companies as well. In these instances the product or process is usually simple in nature and does not require a high degree of planning or control. These might include process or product type operations where the real control exists primarily at the sales level.

The specific functional organization structure that exists will usually be rather simple in nature and small in physical size. Because the nature of the task is not complex, it can be expected that it will be a relatively low-key job without a great deal of status.

Combined with Purchasing

Another frequent location of the production and inventory control function within the organization is in combination with purchasing. For the most part, in this concept, the function is termed materials management (i.e., the management of purchased and manufactured materials and parts—Figure 2-3). This structure is particularly common to those industries where material cost is very high relative to total product cost. It is also found in organizations that are pointed in a direction of functional consolidation and centralization.

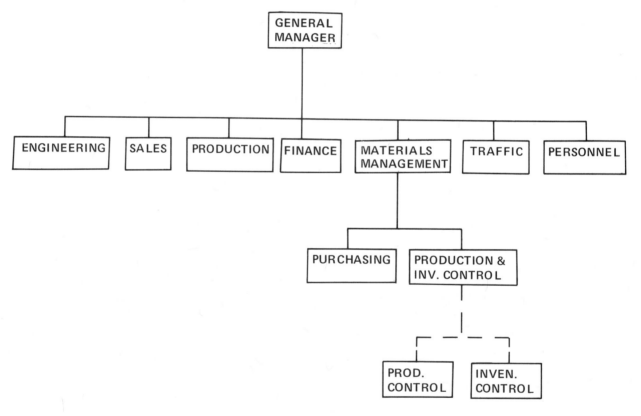

FIGURE 2-3

What are the advantages? How well does production and inventory control "fit" with purchasing? Both activities are concerned with material; both have a concern for on-time delivery; both have a responsibility for cost; both should have a direct interest concern for serving the needs of the customer. In addition, procedures and paper work can be streamlined with the combining of functions in this manner. In summary, the advantages are found in a singleness of purpose of these functions in combination.

Along with the advantages outlined above, there are some disadvantages. In combining these functions, the opportunity for a "check and balance" system of material procurement and usage is considerably reduced. There is always a concern with placing too large a responsibility within a single centralized function. In addition, there is often a basic difference in business philosophy between purchasing and production and inventory control. In the one instance, purchasing is primarily concerned with the acquisitions of material or parts on a least cost basis (consistent with quality requirements) for specific delivery schedule. In the other instance, production and inventory control is also interested in material acquisitions and in addition is concerned with planning, schedules and meeting delivery requirements.

In summary, it would be suggested that for many organizations this may well be the best organizational structure to employ. It is one that has gained substantially in popularity in recent years—and for good reason. It is the one structure that encompasses the entire material management function and directs its efforts toward a total program of control. Materials management may be considered a third generation organization and evolves out of a production and inventory control function under production and a purchasing function under top management. Although typically this structure of organization would be expected to exist in larger organizations, it should by no means be ignored as an excellent structure for even the smallest organization. The very real merits of consolidating control of material into a single center of responsibility should not be overlooked.

Staff to Sales or Marketing

To a lesser degree the production and inventory control function will be subordinate to sales (Figure 2-4). But why not? Is not the production control function merely an extension of the sales function? As indicated, the source data for the production plan is the sales forecast. It is only a matter of planning the material and parts requirements to support the sales forecast and the scheduling of production orders to achieve delivery dates. Again the commonality of purpose and a shortening of the chain of command tend to offer several advantages with this concept.

On the negative side is again the disharmony of basic philosophy that exists between sales and production and inventory control. By the very nature of its title "Production and Inventory Control," we are implying control of production and inventories. This is a "control" type function which suggests limitations or constraints and a regimentation of planning and performing tasks. This is considerably different from the normal sales attitude which appears unstructured with seemingly little control exhibited. In addition, sales and marketing personnel occasionally have only a modest interest in production activities and only a concern for inventory as to whether it is "on the shelf—available for sale." There is usually little interest as to what is required to get a product ready for sale. This organization relationship lacks a check and balance with the needs and desires of the sales function being of primary importance while those of the production and inventory control function become of secondary concern.

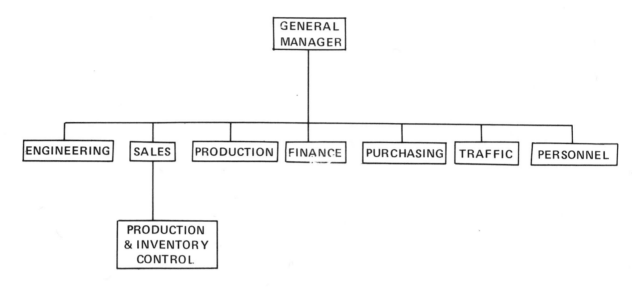

FIGURE 2-4

Staff to General Management

If the sales and production function are of sufficient significance to be responsible to top management, why is the function that translates a sales forecast into a production plan not equally important? It is and certainly in many organizations this is where it is located. There are many logical reasons for placing the production and inventory control function on a staff level to the general management function as shown in Figure 2-5. With the sales and production functions both at this level, it provides a leveling or balancing effect between the individual objectives and goals of each. Certainly, in larger more complex organizations that require complex planning and scheduling and resultant complicated inventory planning and control procedures, this may well be the only practical alternative short of the materials management concept. An additional advantage is that it provides an excellent means of communication and of maintaining credibility among sales, production and purchasing. When given equal status, it provides a check and balance among the various functions.

Even considering the exceptional reasons for placing the production and inventory control function at the general staff level there are also reasons why it should not be placed here. For example, is the production process so simple in nature that it does not require or deserve the status to be placed at this level in the organization? There are many organizations where the size and simplicity of the production function is of such a nature that it is much more practical to perform the planning, scheduling, control function as a direct support to production.

In general, this structure can be considered a second generation organizational structure. For larger more complex planning and control functions, it is virtually a necessity that the function be placed in this manner within the organization.

While it is one of the better locations within the organization, it should by no

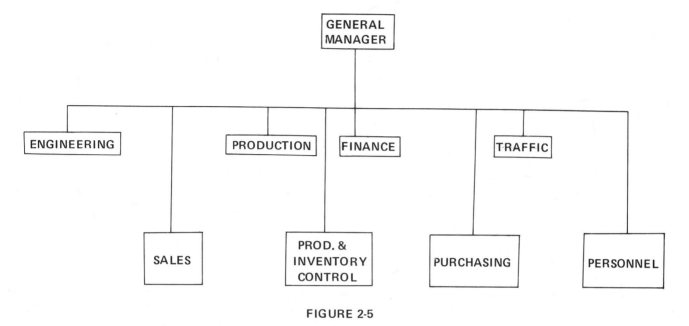

FIGURE 2-5

means be considered the optimum location. There are many factors that go into making a choice of location for the production and inventory control function that only after considering all factors can the best choice be made.

Other Locations Within the Organization

The discussion has centered on the more common locations and relationships that exist between the production and inventory control function and other functions of the organization. There are obviously other methods of organizational structure that can work and do work for various companies throughout the industrial and commercial community.

Summary

There is no one best location for the production and inventory control function within the organization. While there may be a best location and relationship for one company or industry, this location may not fit as well within other companies or industries. Another factor beyond the physical considerations discussed is the "people" factor. There are many examples and instances of organizational structure that have been based on the strength and/or weakness of the personnel within the organization. While it should not be construed that this be a strong consideration in the establishment of the organization structure, it is mentioned to recognize the fact that it does exist. In summation, the best location for the production and inventory control function is that which works best for you!

DEPARTMENTAL STRUCTURE AND MANNING

As there are a number of ways the production and inventory control function can be placed within the organization, so are there various methods to organize the function itself. Typically, the production and inventory control function will be structured in one of three ways:

1. Functional structure
2. Product structure
3. Process structure

Functional Structure

The most widely utilized structure for production and inventory control operations is the functional organization structure (Figure 2-6). This is not too surprising when one considers its versatility and capability of being adapted to a wide variety of industries. Typically, the functionally structured organization will be found in a variety of hard goods type manufacturing operations.

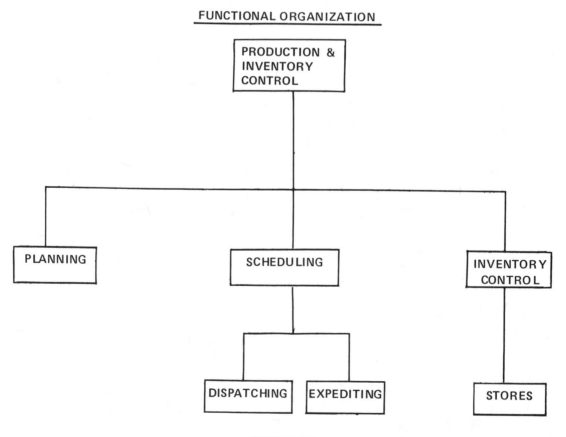

FIGURE 2-6

Key characteristics of this organization include:

1. Total function responsibility included in one responsibility area. This suggests, if information is required relative to a specific subject, it would only require directing the request to the specific function to obtain the information needed.
2. Flexibility—ability to adapt to a variety of industrial operations. It is effective for metalworking, printing, a variety of assembly-type manufacturing, packaging operations, electrical and electronics manufacturing, both heavy and light industries—a complete range.
3. Increased opportunity for control due to centralization of activity responsibility. For example, with one function responsible for all scheduling, we need only to look at one source for schedule status, shop load, and equipment availability.

Perhaps the greatest advantage to this organization structure is its adaptability to a variety of production situations. It is particularly well-suited to the more complex type organization where the planning-coordination effort is extensive.

The only disadvantage—if, in fact, it really is—is that for some organizations it may well be too complex, or more organization than is really required. For example, very small companies or those with a rather simple manufacturing process would not have the need for a structure of this nature.

Product Structure

The product structure organization (Figure 2-7) is frequently used where the particular products are of unique characteristics with minimal commonality of parts or processes. Often the entire organization from the top management to the production operation is aligned in this manner and all functions become subsidiary to sales and engineering. This type of organization is adapted only to specialized industries and

PRODUCT ORGANIZATION

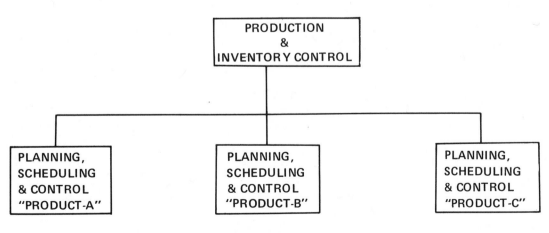

FIGURE 2-7

does not have the flexibility of the functionally structured organization. Although the product structure organization will consist of the functions encompassed in the functional structure, they will be product-oriented rather than plant-oriented. For specialized applications in a high volume, integrated manufacturing operation this type of structure is useful if the operation has these characteristics:

1. High volume
2. Specialized equipment
3. Minimum commonality of parts
4. Integrated manufacturing operations
5. Sales and/or engineering-oriented

Process Structure

The process structure organization (Figure 2-8) has many of the same characteristics as the product structure organization. This is a specialized type of organization that is primarily suited to process type industries (i.e., chemical, paper and basic metals). While this may result in a more simple organization from a structure standpoint, it may be more complex in actual execution. The characteristics of the operation are:

1. High volume
2. Specialized equipment
3. Process-type operation
4. Long-run infrequent changeover
5. Limited product line

PROCESS ORGANIZATION

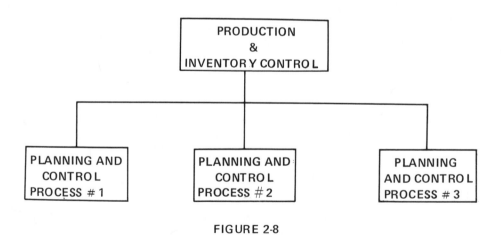

FIGURE 2-8

Relationships and Responsibilities

The primary objective of the production and inventory control function is to "provide control of the production/manufacturing operation and the inventory of material, parts, and finished product." Exactly what role does it play? What is its relationship to other departments—regardless of location in the organization? How are responsibilities assigned and established?

With Sales

Sales provides a sales forecast or market plan that would provide basic information as to quantity requirements of products or materials. In addition, an inventory plan that would indicate the level of inventory (finished product) may be specified. Sales would expect to be kept appraised of production lead times, inventory levels, and delivery status of orders from production and inventory control.

With Engineering

Engineering is the source for product and material specifications—including shape, size, type, form, fit, function and quantity required. Any changes, revisions, modifications or problems relative to the specifications are resolved by engineering. Along with sales data, the specifications provided by engineering form the development of the basic manufacturing plan. Production and inventory control has a responsibility to engineering to advise of requirements that may affect delivery or production capability.

With Purchasing

The relationship with purchasing is essentially one of being the representative source for obtaining purchased materials, parts, and supplies. In this regard, production and inventory control must work very closely with purchasing to develop adequate and reliable sources, be cognizant of lead times and delivery requirements. Purchasing should be appraised of revisions to normal requirements either in terms of increases or decreases. Production and inventory control is the source of requests for material requirements; purchasing is responsible for fulfilling material need requirements.

With Production

As has been stated previously, production and inventory control is responsible for controlling production, but exactly how is this accomplished? A production plan is developed from the sales forecast or marketing plan. From this a production schedule is developed and work orders written to perform the required work in the sequence scheduled and the time frame planned. It is incumbent upon production to maintain the schedule as nearly as possible and to keep production and inventory control advised of deviations or problems that may affect results.

With Personnel

What will be the level of employment required to support the production plan? This is information required by personnel to provide the groundwork for manpower planning. In the same manner, the availability of manpower in the market is information that is of interest to production. Will manpower be available to meet production objectives? Although the actual transactions relating to manpower will normally be carried out by others, knowledge of requirements and availability for planning purposes will be the major thrust of the relationship between production and inventory control and personnel.

With Traffic

The major relationship with traffic will normally be in the development of best methods and route of shipment of finished products. This may involve investigation of packaging techniques, methods of shipment, investigation of carriers and routing.

With Finance

A major relationship that exists between production and inventory control and finance is concerned with inventory of raw materials, parts, and finished products. Accurate inventory records are a vital necessity for the construction of accurate and meaningful financial statements and the determination of taxes.

Chapter 3

Establishing Effective Communications
Between Production/Inventory
and Other Departments

Communications is the instrument that unites all cost control efforts into an overall system. It is the means by which one effort reinforces another. Any ambiguity in the communications will impede this reinforcement and will thereby interfere with achieving desired results.

CASE IN POINT

The founder of a large southwestern foundry maintained a keen interest in the well-being of the operation that he had started and developed, even after he had relinquished all active management functions except acting as chairman of the board. He visited the plant at least once each week, touring the operations and speaking with the old-timers that he knew personally. At one point he decided that operations were out of control: deliveries were late too often, the output of the plant was out of proportion to the work force size even though incentive earnings were good. He made various attempts, over quite a period of time, to get improvement. He held meetings, conducted personal interviews, had studies made, all without any meaningful changes taking place. He could not understand why so little was being done about the condition that he saw so clearly needed correction.

The source of his perplexity was that he was not taking into account the existence of a formal supervisors' bonus plan that was paying the supervisors a monthly bonus in the range of 20% to 25%. The monthly bonus payments told the supervisors that they were doing a good job. They paid very little attention to any other evaluation of their performance. While they were receiving two separate communications that were at odds with each other, they heeded the one that was easier to accept, the bonus payment. The situation was changed by changing the basis of the bonus calculation to reflect more closely the contribution of each individual supervisor toward meeting the total objectives of the company. Under the revised plan, a clear message is given to each supervisor about the quality of his contribution.

65

The subject of "communications" is an extremely broad one, even when it is focused specifically toward cost control. This entire book contains many references to communications. This particular chapter provides some general rules regarding the use of communications. It also discusses specific examples of how good communications have helped organizations, how poor communications have hindered organizations, and how the poor communications have been improved. The discussion will contain the identification of some general principles that can be put to work to make certain that communications are operating in support of the cost control activity.

BE ALERT TO YOUR TOTAL COMMUNICATIONS

Communications is a system of processes that is composed of many elements. The communication system starts operating when someone *sends a signal*, furnishing information. Communication continues when someone else *receives a signal, responds to it and sends back another signal.* To stay in operation the communication process must continue with signal and response, signal and response, until the signalers begin to understand each other. When the process continues and when the signalers work at understanding each other, the signalers are in communication with each other.

There are many different kinds of communication signals. Any process that supplies information is giving a signal. Communication systems use all of the five senses: sound, sight, touch, smell, taste. That means there are many forms of communication. Formal reports, memoranda and discussions are only a few of the forms used in industry. Informal conversation, notes and even rumors are a real part of the communication system that operates in industry. The workings of a communication system are not always obvious.

CASE IN POINT

The technical management of an East Coast pharmaceutical manufacturer was implementing an intensive program for improving inventory planning and manufacturing operation activities. The implementation required many drastic changes in organization, procedures and practices. Quite expectedly the personnel involved were uncomfortable with the changes, even though they were participating completely in the evaluations, decisions and planning of the program. Their behavior was that normally demonstrated by others in similar circumstances. The question they asked repeatedly was: "If the company is genuinely interested in making improvements, why do they just focus on us? Why don't they also give attention to the sales group (in over-the-counter products) that plans poorly and is constantly changing requirements during intensive sales campaigns? Those sales people cause many disruptions to our packaging operations and add many extra costs, not to mention aggravations." Their main point was that they thought they were being treated unfairly, in that they were being called upon to make necessary changes, while other members of the company were allowed to continue practices that were in greater need of change. The inventory and production staff were quite sceptical about assurances that the sales people would also be required to change. Their scepticism slowed down implementation of the program.

During the implementation period, the sales group was to conduct one of its campaigns. They made their plans which were quite complex because the plans included the use of an outside vendor who was going to work with a new process. The new process condition called for an extra quality control effort, along with other special activities that imposed many complications on the packaging production planning. Soon after the campaign began, the sales group called for a change in plans that would have caused a major disruption to the packaging operations. The inventory and production people decided to take a firm stand, to respond to the change in plans with the least amount of disruption and extra costs. They made that decision with apprehension, because the sales people demanded that their new plans should be followed, just as they had always demanded in the past. Just as in the past, the head of the sales group threatened to go to top management if his changed plans weren't followed. The operating people decided to stay with their decision and waited for the call from top management. It never came.

The real question is whether the actions of the inventory and production people in previous years should have been to strive for the least amount of extra costs, instead of yielding to the demands of the sales group. Communications regarding the primary objective of top management had never really been properly established. The communication in operation for the past sales campaigns may well have resulted primarily from the strong personality of the sales manager. What is not known is whether his demands in previous years had been in support of top management's objectives or merely in support of his personal objectives. One thing is certain, the lack of clear understanding worked to the overall disadvantage of the company. The clarification that has now been made has benefited the company beyond the scope of the single sales campaign. The company, as a whole, has a better appreciation of the value of good communications.

In any organization, communication is good only when:

1. Each member of the organization has appropriate understanding of the organization's objectives.
2. Each member's efforts are being properly directed toward meeting those objectives.

Keeping the organization's members properly informed is part of having good communications. Analyzing their responses and providing guidance to help them reach the organization's objectives is the real purpose of communication. If an individual is given proper information, and he takes improper action, or improperly takes no action, the communication system is not being used to its full purpose.

The most difficult problem to solve may be getting the proper information to the individual who will put it to use.

CASE IN POINT

In some companies that have products composed of assemblies of formed sheet metal parts, there is poor communication between the people who design and lay out the assemblies and the people who establish the tooling and setups for making the piece parts. If there is a difference in concept between those two groups, there is good opportunity for an indiscriminate accumulation of tolerances to such a degree that the result is an interference among the piece parts that impedes the final assembly. The problem generally lies with establishment of datum lines and datum points. There are some inherent limitations in the establishment of datum lines or points for some specific equipment or types of tooling. There are also some logical limitations in the establishment of datum lines or points that exist for engineering design. Communications are not good when one set of limitations is not taken into account. Communications are good when both sets of limitations are taken into account in the design, construction and setup phases of piece part production. In those companies that understand that good communications in this area are important to cost control, devices are deliberately created to insure that the communications are good:

1. For each new product, a committee composed of design engineering, tooling, manufacturing engineering and production is formed to operate in concert to bring the product from the concept phase into the full production.
2. Project coordinators are trained to serve as communication catalysts among the design, tooling and production staffs.

Having needed information available within an organization is a good starting point, but it is just that: a starting point. One problem to be solved by a communications system is to help deliver that information to the individual who needs it to do his job properly. By the same token, another problem to be solved by a communications system is to help inform the individual that he does, in fact, need the information, that it is available, and that he has a means of getting it. In communications, the flow of signals always has at least two directions.

A communications system does not solve problems unless there are people putting effort into making the system operate. Each communications system is unique. For that reason, the people who operate it must understand the nature of their unique system.

UNDERSTAND HOW YOUR COMMUNICATIONS SYSTEM OPERATES

Any piece of information that can help an organization's members direct their efforts toward the organization's goals is potentially useful. However, the information realizes its potential only if it is put to work. That means that communications, the system that operates on information, must be established to include any source that can and does supply usable information and any destination that can and does put the information to work. The establishment of sources and destinations may be defined by an organization chart with its procedures or the communications system may be separate and apart from the chart and procedures.

The organization chart indicates the formal flow of communications. The formal communication structure is frequently described in company procedures, sometimes written. In addition to the formal structure, there is nearly always an informal structure. The formal structures are easy to identify; the informal structures are not easily identified. The informal structures generally operate because of individual personalities, special relationships and other such unpredictable conditions. That doesn't mean that informal systems are less important, or less desirable, or less useful than the formal ones. On the contrary, it is found that the informal systems often have more influence on the organization's activities than the formal ones. In many cases informal systems develop in reaction to inadequacies of formal systems.

CASE IN POINT

A very difficult communications problem exists in many jobbing foundries. The problem is in the cleaning room, and it is concerned with the quality specifications for individual customers and pattern numbers. Because it is a job shop condition, the product mix is highly variable and irregular.

When a customer's complaint about poor finishing quality is accepted by the foundry management, the castings are very often brought back to the foundry for rework. This seems to cause a reaction from the finishing operators so that all castings passing through the operation are finished to a higher level of quality than before the rework.

On the other hand, when more finishing work is being done than an individual customer requires, the customer may try to use that fact to negotiate for a lower price. He is sometimes successful in this negotiation, particularly when business is slow at the foundry. The problem is to communicate to the people doing the finishing work that a specific customer's quality requirements are lower than another customer's, or that a specific pattern number of a customer has lower quality requirements than other patterns for that customer.

There are at least two mechanistic, or formal approaches that have been tried in solving that problem. For one, work is sorted and segregated into two locations, one for high quality, the other for low quality work. An individual operator may be assigned to and supplied with one level of quality of work on a permanent, or temporary basis. It is possible to assign all operators to different levels of work for an entire shift or day. A second possible solution is to use different color containers for different levels of quality. When an operator receives castings, he is to work to the level of quality called for by the color of the container. The problem is confined to making certain that the individual who does the sorting is properly informed of the requirements.

Notwithstanding the possible use of the mechanistic, formal approaches, and the extra costs of excessive finishing, experience shows that most jobbing foundries use informal communications about quality. Evidently the informal communications are most convenient or more comfortable to use than the formal ones. Whatever the basis for that judgment and whoever made it, the important fact to recognize is that communications about quality of finishes in job shop foundries do operate, for the greater part, informally. Failure to recognize that fact can lead to unfortunate breakdowns in communications.

The fact that a formal communications instrument has been installed should not be allowed to lead to complacency. Failure to recognize how a formal instrument operates compared to how it is supposed to operate can also be unfortunate.

CASE IN POINT

In many companies blank sheets for engineering drawings bear printed title blocks. The title blocks show the company name and provide spaces for initials and dates for approval. Many also show a legend about tolerances, for example: "All dimensions must be held within plus or minus 0.005 inches unless otherwise specified."

It is not unusual to find drawings with dimensions that do not require such close tolerances, but where the broader tolerances are not noted. The result is that extra effort and cost is spent in working to close tolerances that are not needed. And the condition exists despite the formal checking and approval procedure. Correction often is called for via the informal structure by inputs from toolmakers or floor inspectors.

In a discussion of formal and informal systems, one informal system should be given the recognition it deserves. That system is the "rumor mill." Rumors have served and can continue to serve as strong signals to a company's management. They may cover many possible subjects: quality, employee relations, improper supervisory behavior, company plans, what the competition is doing and many other subjects too numerous to mention. It is not intended to imply that all rumors are true. In fact, many rumors are wholly or partially untrue. The point is that the existence of a rumor nearly always indicates the presence of a situation that must be investigated. Rumors are not necessarily to be believed, but they must never be ignored. Any kind of information that can be used to provide a benefit to an organization is essential to that organization. Too frequently, the response to a rumor is to take steps to try to stop the rumor by ignoring it, by trying to behave as if its existence isn't worthy of recognition, or by trying to prevent it from entering the communications system.

KEEP THE COMMUNICATIONS CHANNELS OPEN

All beneficial signals must be permitted to enter the communication system without restriction. This is true even if the information is of an unpleasant nature. Unpleasant information can be important to an organization, if it is used to create a benefit. It is not intended to suggest that any or all information should be permitted to flow through the system unrestricted. Information should be permitted to enter the system, so that it can be controlled by being given proper response. Employee complaints are many times considered to be information of an unpleasant nature and are given scant attention. In other words, the information contained in the complaints is not allowed to enter the communication system to be used to advantage.

CASE IN POINT

This condition has been the subject of many studies conducted by industrial psychologists in recent years. The studies have covered many industries and companies. In general, the findings of the studies show that employees' attitudes are not always understood by their supervisors and managements and this lack of understanding results in a great deal of labor unrest. The consequence is a loss of productivity and the expenditure of time and money trying to "patch on" remedies for the situations instead of getting to the basic cause.

The basic cause of the unrest is that the communication system is closed; supervision and management are not listening to what the employees are saying about the employees' wishes, about what is needed to motivate the employees. The forces that motivate individuals are not constant. They differ from individual to individual. For any individual, they change as external conditions change. When supervision and management attempt to apply motivating forces to an individual that are inappropriate at that time for that individual, there will be no positive results. To determine the appropriate motivational device, supervision and management must listen to the individual to learn his needs and desires, and thereby develop good communications with him. When good communications are in effect, when the appropriate motivational devices have been identified and are being applied, the results are beneficial to both the individual and the company. This doesn't mean that the company should always yield to each employee; it does mean that the company, working with the employee, should strive for mutual understanding. That in itself brings mutual benefits.

Keeping communication channels open doesn't mean that all available information should be allowed to flow without restriction. After information is allowed to enter the system its flow should be controlled.

CONTROL THE QUANTITY OF INFORMATION IN THE COMMUNICATION SYSTEM

Modern technology can produce almost limitless amounts of information. In any organization, therefore, it is not uncommon to find an individual flooded with detailed data, more than he can possibly assimilate and fathom. Consequently, the individual is forced to pay little attention to, or possibly ignore, some of the data that he receives.

Each individual should be furnished with only that data that he needs to discharge his responsibilities. If an individual uses some information only occasionally, he should not be continually supplied with it. It should be filed for him, and perhaps supplied to him in digest form at his request or at preestablished intervals. There is nothing to be gained, and much to be lost when time and effort are spent preparing, distributing and receiving information that is not going to be given a useful response.

CASE IN POINT

The quality control procedures applied to glass containers and closures used to package foods are important, not only for cost control reasons, but also because of hazard-to-health reasons. In the plant of one northeastern food processor, individual containers are inspected before, during and after filling. The inspectors make notations of all causes for rejection. If a single container shows multiple defects, all of the defects are noted. The purpose of gathering the detailed information is to identify vendors with specific defects, especially those that tend toward the limits of acceptability; that tendency warns of a potentially serious condition.

Each day, each inspector prepares several pages of notations. Copies of all of the daily reports are sent, once each week to the purchasing agent. The copies are intended to furnish him the information he needs for working with the vendors. The purchasing agent's reaction is, in his own words: "I know that somewhere in all of these pieces of paper, there is information that I should be putting to good use. There is so much data, I'm afraid that I'm overlooking something important. I just hope that someone else is also examining these reports, determining what actions I should be taking and telling me what they all are." The fact is that the quality control staff were informing him, in an informal way, of the critical conditions in addition to supplying him with the copies. Nevertheless, he was uncomfortable with receiving so much information because he felt that he should be doing more to try to assimilate it and he didn't have the time for that.

He felt much relieved when copies of the daily reports were replaced by a weekly digest. The quality control staff used the more formal digest to advise him of the critical conditions, instead of the informal reporting that they had practiced previously. The formal digest contains a summary analysis in which the average frequency of occurrence is shown for each defect, together with the acceptable limits, with special notation of those items that are tending to go toward the limits, or are otherwise critical. The purchasing agent has much less data to examine and, at the same time, the information that he should be using in discussions with vendors is highlighted. As an aside, less paper is being used for copies.

There was a similar situation in another quality control activity, this time in the confection industry. In this case, the director of quality control was being supplied each day with copies of all test log sheets that showed entries from the testing activities of the previous day. This practice was based on the thinking that, with a minimum amount of effort of the testing staff, the director was being supplied with all of the information that he needed to stay abreast of the conditions in the plants throughout the country. In actuality, he was being glutted with information that required no further action from him or his staff. He had to examine all of the data to determine which required attention, and to what degree. He was unable to carry out his laborious task every day and at the same time give attention to other important matters.

His subordinate managers were shown that the situation involved several opportunities for improvement. The procedure was changed so that its primary thrust is directed toward furnishing the director with daily summary reports from each plant that read: "All conditions were found to be under satisfactory control except: ..." The exceptions are described in detail, showing the specific out-of-control conditions, corrective actions that are being taken, and the expected time for the situation to be brought back under control.

The new procedure focuses the director's attention directly on the critical conditions, and at the same time, assures him that everything else is under control. The change also yields a marked reduction in the amount of paper used for copies. And, there is another change of more important significance. The subordinate managers see the daily summaries before the director does. Many of them supervise the preparation for their plants. This gives them the opportunity for anticipating the questions that the director may ask and allows them to be prepared with answers. The subordinate managers have found that they themselves are being brought into contact with critical situations more directly than previously and are making better use of their time.

In the director's words: "I now feel, for the first time since I've had this position, that my managers and I know what is going on."

After the quantity of data has been reduced to a manageable situation, the job of assuring the reliability of the data is easier.

CONTROL THE QUALITY OF INFORMATION
IN THE COMMUNICATION SYSTEM

Control of the quality of information in the system is probably more important than control of the quantity. Great care must be exercised to insure that the system has "communication authenticity." In other words, no improper information must be permitted to move through the system, whether the information is improper because it is in error, ambiguous or misleading. Constant surveillance must be maintained to insure that improper information is removed from the system.

Improper information will lead to improper behavior and decisions and provide improper guidance to the organization's members. It will also produce a reduction in credibility of the system. When that happens the members of the organization, knowing that some of the information is improper, can justifiably become suspicious of all of the information in the system. It is difficult for the user of information to determine the quality of the information put into the system by someone else. In fact, in many cases he cannot determine the quality although he may identify inconsistencies and raise questions. Responsibility for information quality must lie with the source of information; surveillance of the information quality must be exerted by the source. But if at any point, quality of the information is questionable, steps must be taken immediately to make sure that those questions are removed.

CASE IN POINT

The situation that existed in a multi-plant company that manufactures fittings for pipe and tubing provides a dramatic example of the confusion that can be caused by improper information in the communication system. The condition arose because two different procedures were being used in the analysis of manufacturing costs. The effects could be seen very clearly by comparing the two analyses of one product line, steel fittings. One analysis was in the form of a quarterly cost sheet. The other was a quarterly profit and loss statement.

For both procedures, all costs of manufacturing incurred during any given accounting period were charged into the cost of goods sold during the same period. No recognition was given in either procedure to differences between quantities manufactured and quantities sold. Material purchased was added to simple inventory accounts in terms of weight and dollars. At the end of each month the inventory accounts were reduced by the finished weight of the products sold (and corresponding dollar value) without recognition of scrap, waste or machine reduction of raw material. When scrap and machine reductions were sold, the weight sold was deducted from inventory and charged to material usage, and material cost was relieved in the amount of the salvage value.

Cost sheets were maintained for the products of each line. For the steel fittings line, the factory burden was assumed to be 225% of the direct labor costs. The general administrative and sales costs were calculated as 33⅓% of the total manufacturing costs. Cost sheets for the second quarter of last year showed:

Sales		$109,846.16
Manufacturing Costs		
Materials	$43,729.65	
Labor	5,776.34	
Burden (225% of Labor)	12,996.77	
Total		$ 62,502.76
Gross Manufacturing Profit		$ 47,343.40
General Administrative and Sales		
Cost (33⅓% of Total Manufacturing		
Costs)		$ 20,834.25
Net Profit		$ 26,509.15

Quarterly profit and loss statements were prepared for each product line to show the contribution of each product line to the total profits of the company. Actual factory burden expenses incurred during the quarter were prorated among all of the product lines according to the following indices:

Flared Fittings	1.28
Solder Fittings	1.74
Drainage Fittings	1.89
Wrought Fittings	2.11
Steel Fittings	12.02
P.R. Valves	1.45
L.P. Valves	1.56
	22.05

Administrative and selling expenses, as a single total, were prorated among all the product lines on a sales dollar volume basis. The quarterly profit and loss statement for the second quarter of last year showed:

Sales		$109,846.16
Manufacturing Costs		
Materials	$43,729.65	
Labor	5,776.34	
Burden (Prorated)	65,884.90	
Total	$115,390.89	
Gross Manufacturing Profit (Loss)		$ (5,544.73)
General Administrative and Sales Costs		
(Prorated)		$7,295.84
Net Profit (Loss)		$ (12,840.57)

The differences in results from the two procedures occurred because the procedures had been installed with predominating concern for keeping accounting costs at a minimum. Concern for providing useful control information had been a secondary issue. The confusion arising from the difference in results from the two procedures generated a condition where the information from both were treated with suspicion. Neither report was generally accepted for use as cost controls.

The situation was rectified by discarding both procedures and installing one procedure that contains elements that satisfy all of the individuals who use the information as the basis for making decisions. The new procedure recognizes differences between quantities manufactured and quantities sold. It relates quantities of materials withdrawn from raw material inventories to quantities of products manufactured. It provides a single basis for accounting for factory burden and administrative and sales expense. The new procedure does require more accounting effort than either one of the two procedures it has replaced. But, the new procedure requires less effort than the total for both of the two old procedures. There has been a slight reduction in accounting effort. That is less important than the fact that the confusion that previously prevailed has been eliminated and usable cost controls have been provided. There is now less data and more usable information.

This situation was a dramatic one, and the communication problem was extremely visible. Not all communication problems can be so clearly seen.

DON'T EXPECT THAT POOR COMMUNICATIONS WILL BE CLEARLY LABELED

Frequently, situations requiring improvements in communications display several different types of breakdowns. The best, most permanent correction is made when each individual problem is identified and addressed separately. That calls for a thorough, detailed examination to identify each breakdown, as the following four cases will show.

CASE IN POINT

A project was initiated to improve the utilization of 22 pieces of equipment employed in the automatic assembly of preassembled fastener products. The group of machines required the services of two setup operators and three machine operators. A study of the situation covering a period of one week showed:

Status of the Equipment	Percent of Machine Time
1. Machine running and producing products	46.6%
2. Machine setup, not running, waiting for parts	10.8
3. Machine running, hopper or bowl out of parts	2.1
4. Machine running but "cutting air"	10.6
5. Machine stopped to correct track jam.	14.9
6. Machine stopped to adjust setups or replace dies	3.6
7. Machine down, undergoing setup changeover	1.8

8. Machine down, waiting for setup
   changeover
9. Machine down, waiting for repairs
10. Machine down, no orders
                                                            3.9
                                                            3.9
    Total   1.8
                                                         100.0%

These percentages provided the basis for specific investigations which uncovered individual breakdowns in communications:

— The foreman was not advised of production plans. He scheduled machines as parts became available. He was not able to do any advance planning of schedules for labor assignments or preventive maintenance of the equipment. The people who performed the material and production planning did not know to what extent they were adversely affecting the utilization of the equipment. Items 2 and 3 above show 10.8% plus 2.1%, a total of 12.9% reduction in machine utilization caused by material shortages. To aggravate the situation, overtime was often needed to keep delivery promises.

— The conditions of machine running but "cutting air" and machine stopped to correct track jam, which represent 10.6% plus 14.9% or a total of 25.5%, were generally caused by a material condition. Mixed parts, improperly sized parts, misshapen or misformed parts and dirty parts had all been identified. The supervisors and operators state that they had been complaining about the condition of parts coming to the department for a long period of time. Many individuals were found to have contributed to the poor conditions of parts: machine operators, inspectors, material handlers, stockroom clerks.

This communication system displayed many gaps. It also displayed a major opportunity for a reevaluation of the efforts being made to properly motivate a major portion of the employees, including supervisors. When this opportunity was recognized and used as the primary basis for corrective action, the situation began to improve. It is noteworthy that one motivating device being employed here is frequently found to be very effective, and it is simple. It consists simply of an openly published report (on the bulletin board) of the progress being made in reducing unscheduled downtime.

The communication area that is most generally found to be poor is that of forecasting. Poor quality in this area of communication can be extremely costly in many ways. The extra costs are incurred because of:

— improper utilization of equipment
— improper estimates of labor requirements
— customer complaints about deliveries
— extra efforts exerted to recover from material shortages
— excessive investments in inventories

There are many individual cases where the required corrective action has been the establishment of a clear understanding between those people who are best qualified to prepare the forecast and the people who have to work with the forecast. In some instances there were differences of opinion as to who was best qualified to prepare the forecast. There are companies in which forecasts are prepared by three groups of people: marketing, finance and production. When there are three or even two forecasts, it is difficult for the people involved to communicate among themselves. They cannot properly discuss budgets, capital equipment expenditures, inventories or other cost elements that must be controlled, because each individual's thinking operates from a different base.

The solution to the forecast communication situation has been demonstrated to be very simple. A forecast must be prepared by those best qualified (it's the marketing people's responsibility to be the best qualified). It must be tracked and corrected when the results become available. There must be a basic understanding that nearly every forecast will be wrong. Actual results generally are higher or lower than the forecast. That is why forecasts must be tracked. The difference between actual results and forecasts must be known to provide guidance for adjustments in operating plans. Understanding that there are probable errors in forecasts leads to an understanding that there are also probable risks.

A policy should be established and generally accepted as to whether the risk is going to be one of optimism or one of pessimism. That policy may change from time to time, depending on many considerations. When the error in the forecast is observed, with the nature of the risk being understood in advance, attention is focused on correcting plans according to the error in the forecast. Tracking and correcting the forecast helps minimize the risk. While discussing the nature of the risk to be taken, plans can also be discussed for alternative actions to be taken for alternative actual results. This solution is nothing more than establishing an open communication system where all individuals concerned are kept informed of anticipated results and of alternative plans for adjusting for actual results as they occur.

CASE IN POINT

In a company that manufactures building supplies, only 17% of delivery promises were being met. To rectify this situation, a simplified procedure was established for planning production for periods of two weeks. These plans were made initially without a forecast from the marketing people, but with their knowledge and acceptance. The sales people made delivery promises with the production plans in mind and continually kept the production planning people advised of the promises. The sales people and the production planning people were located in the same room to facilitate communication. When the production planning people observed that delivery promises were approaching the planned production quantities, they informed the sales people that the two week period had been committed. The sales people then added two weeks to the promised delivery dates. The production people always "underloaded" each two-week period, allowing a small cushion of unplanned production time, because they knew there would always be the need to make emergency shipments. After one year of operation, unkept delivery promises were negligible. The situation was solved by establishing good, open communications.

CASE IN POINT

It is purely incidental that the company involved in the next case is engaged in ready-mix and sand and gravel operations. The conditions that were found here and the opportunities that existed might be found in many companies in which a large vehicle fleet is in operation and in which the vehicle drivers come in contact with the customers of the company.

Some of the costs of the poor communications that existed in this situation are readily discernible. Other costs are less easily evaluated, but it will be recognized that these are all important costs and that they can be brought under control through the use of improved communications. One of the communication problems that existed was that, although a large quantity of data was being transmitted throughout the operation, it was not always in the form of useful information.

For example, during the year ending March 31, the total delivery costs equaled 99% of the gross spread (average selling price less average material costs). In the next five months from April to August, the delivery costs ranged from 73% to 110% of the gross spread. This wide range of variance indicates to some extent the magnitude of the opportunities that existed for improving the delivery costs. A proper measuring device was needed for analyzing and controlling these delivery costs. Vehicle operating costs and maintenance costs were being totalled together over varying periods of months. No comparison was being made between either of those costs and the number of hours of operation or the number of miles driven.

changes resulted in changes in reporting procedures. The communication system within the total organization lacked positive direction. As a consequence there was ineffective collection, organization and distribution of data, including duplication of effort and the unnecessary distribution of data. The communications system was excessively costly as well as ineffective.

To be effective, the management of any company requires reliable information covering the utilization of its resources and facilities. For companies with truck operations such as are found in the ready-mix industry, it is essential that the following detailed information is identified by driver and truck:

1. Revenue generated
2. Driver utilization
3. Truck utilization
4. Truck operating costs
5. Truck maintenance costs

For this company, these details are converted in meaningful ratios that are being used to provide guidance for management decisions directed toward improving performance. The ratios help all of the individuals involved to communicate because they are used to describe specific targets and specific performances. Some of the ratios found to be useful for these particular circumstances are:

1. Miles driven per driver per hours worked
2. Income generated per driver per mile driven
3. Operating costs per vehicle per mile driven
4. Maintenance costs per vehicle per mile driven

Working with data from individual drivers and vehicles, the management of this company has so far achieved about 28% improvement in costs.

CASE IN POINT

The visible symptoms of an ailing plant of a multi-plant company included low productivity and a need for improved production control procedures. However, these were only the visible symptoms. Other conditions had to be addressed first before a sound foundation could be established for improvement of costs and schedule performance. The basic problems of the branch plant developed from:

1. The general attitude of the hourly paid people as well as that of the supervisory groups
2. The dominant position of the union in the plant operations
3. Community relations

An especially difficult condition was found to exist at the branch plant in the areas of manufacturing practices and local operating conditions. The interpretation of objectives in these areas by the union and by the hourly paid people was at variance with the thinking of the management at the corporation's home office. The local management found itself in the frustrating position of acting as a message exchange for the two opposing parties. The local management believed that a compromise could be reached but only if those with opposing views were to meet face to face for the purpose of reaching a compromise. Until this communication gap was closed there could be no real improvement made.

The communication system was hazy at all levels of the manufacturing organization. The local operating management had no clear understanding of the policies being generated at the corporate level. This provided them with no sound basis for communicating with subordinates down the line.

The poor quality of the communications with the employees is reflected in the poor quality of communications with the community in general. The plant contributed substantially to the general welfare of the community. The wages paid to the employees are high compared to wages for similar occupations in the area. The company had a good story to tell the employees and the community and had not told it.

It might appear that the local management was primarily responsible for the poor communications situation. In actual fact, the poor quality was due to the remoteness of the home office and the lack of understanding on the part of some individuals in the home office of their proper role in the communications system.

When it was determined that the potential benefits of achieving improvements at the branch plant were in the neighborhood of $2 million per year, a decision was made to take corrective action.

The corrective action can be described in simple terms: Strong efforts were exerted to improve communications. Face-to-face meetings were held between corporate and local union people and compromises were arranged. Corporate policies were examined and clarified, so that they could be understood by local management. Communications regarding corporate policies now flow easily down the line. A basis has been provided for improving relationships with employees and with the community. Improvements are being implemented both in labor utilization and schedule performance.

When information identifying the potential $2 million benefit was introduced into the corporation's communication system, the result was generation of a motivating force affecting all those involved, directed toward realizing that potential.

The general principle of good communications is simple. No group of individuals, even a group as small as two people, can work in concert without good, open communications. All individuals in the group must work diligently and deliberately at establishing and understanding mutual objectives and at determining and understanding how each member of the group is to function in working toward those objectives. They must keep proper, positive signals moving back and forth.

Chapter 4

Keeping Track of Where You and
Your Production/Inventory Control System
Are Going

The timely delivery of a customer's order is the result of an interrelated series or chain of events. The reputation of a company's ability to "deliver the goods" is dependent upon its ability to bond the linkage and ensure that the weakest link is strong enough to endure. The production plan serves as the major network and generates the management thought and decision process on a number of other important factors.

A typical chain takes the following form:

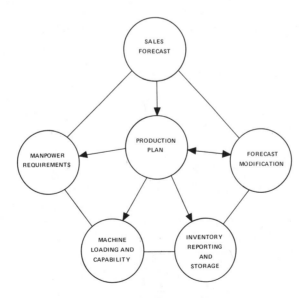

FIGURE 4-1

THE PRODUCTION PLAN

What is the required delivery date? What are the lead times of various material items? How much lead time is required for the final production process? This is key time data required to develop a workable production plan. In addition, it is necessary to know how many of what models or products. And finally, knowledge of equipment and facilities capability must be available. These three basic items of information are necessary to develop a production plan. Simply stated a production plan is:

A breakdown of the model or product requirements into the various components fitted to a time frame that will result in on-time delivery in the shortest time span.

As an illustration, if a particular product had a combination of components requiring a cumulative lead time of 15 weeks it would result in a "planning picture" as illustrated in Figure 4-2. This type of planning picture is the basis for the following monitoring reports:

— Production plan
— Production schedule
— Control by exception techniques
  • Past due order report
  • Shortage report
  • Scrap/rejection report
  • Forecast variance report
  • Inactive inventory report

Envision an automobile trip from Chicago to New York City. A review of maps for possible routes will reveal several alternatives for reaching the intended destination. Eventually a route is selected and this becomes the plan for the trip. Once the trip is underway certain monitoring of progress will be conducted. At a minimum, towns and cities passed along the route would be checked off so that rate of progress can be noted. The fuel supply, highway information signs indicating potential detours and human needs would also be monitored. Adjustments would be made from time to time to ensure maximum effectiveness as the trip progresses. The object in monitoring progress on the trip and making adjustments is to ensure the results achieved are as planned and desired.

And so it is with organizations that desire to control results rather than merely record events. It is necessary to have a plan and monitor results against the plan. As illustrated in the example of the planned trip from Chicago to New York City it is important that all facets be planned and monitored. It is not sufficient to merely note that three-quarters of the fuel supply has been used unless action is initiated to replenish the supply prior to complete exhaustion. In the typical production process, at a minimum, a plan and system is needed for monitoring:

— Manpower
— Materials

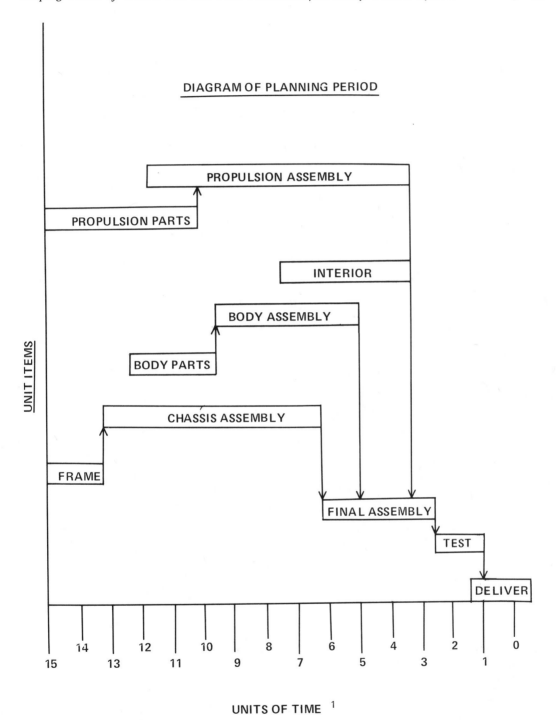

DIAGRAM OF PLANNING PERIOD

UNITS OF TIME [1]

[1] Units of Time = Days, Weeks, Months, Periods

FIGURE 4-2

— Equipment/Process
— Time

The particular techniques used to track progress against the plan are based upon the needs of the plan itself. A complex operation requiring a complex plan will require a wide range of techniques to monitor progress and maintain control. A simple process will require less detail to maintain adequate control.

The planning function in some organizations is minimal or nonexistent. With relatively simple production processes or products, often the sales forecast serves adequately as a production plan. In job shops or custom fabrication operations the actual sales orders received may determine the production plan.

As the product or production process becomes more complex with greater requirements for coordination, more planning will be required for successful accomplishment. Certainly the coordination required and the complexities involved in producing commercial aircraft or automobiles are considerably more intense than those involved in the production of wooden pencils or hula hoops.

The production plan is the basis for generating a schedule, writing work orders, purchasing material, planning production time, determining space requirements for raw material, production capacity, and finished products. Likewise it becomes the framework for the development of basic control systems. In the most simple terms it is a "roadmap"—it provides a route to get from the "drawing board to fulfilling the customer's needs."

Without a production plan there is simply no basis for control. Without a basis for control it will be impossible to know how much time, material, production capacity and manpower is required. Further it will be very difficult to determine accurate costs as well as planned profits.

The steps required in preparing a production plan include:

* *Analyze sales forecast or orders*—digest the sales forecast or orders received. This provides basic product, model, quantity data which determines material, parts, manpower and production requirements.
* *Determine time factors*—ascertain lead times of the various steps in the production process: material, production order requirements and manpower.
* *Analyze facilities and equipment capability*—have basic knowledge of production capability, manpower skills and equipment available for use in developing the production plan.

SOURCES OF DATA FOR THE PRODUCTION PLAN

Product/Model Data

There are basically three sources of information for products or models that are to be produced.

— Sales forecast
— Sales orders
— Inventory plan

Sales Forecast

The sales forecast is a common source of product/model designation which is utilized by many companies for planning purposes. It is an estimate of anticipated sales for a future period of time. Because it is an estimate (based upon various past data and judgment) it is subject to inaccuracies and frequent revision. Most notably it is employed by companies producing a standard line of products with only minimal variations or options available. The food, automotive, pharmaceutical, chemical, and soft goods industries are examples of industries that rely heavily upon sales forecasts for basic product or model data required for the production plan.

Sales Orders

Sales orders are used almost exclusively by custom fabricators and job shops. Typical of these would be printing establishments, tool and die shops, contract sheet metal fabricators, die cast and forging operations and custom plastic molders. The key characteristic is that the parts or products produced are for other companies. In most cases the custom fabricator or job shop would not have any proprietary products of its own. Rather, it is employed on a make-to-order basis by other manufacturers. Sales orders are also used in production planning operations in combination with the sales forecast for products that are basically standard but offering a variety of options. The automotive, light aircraft and machine tool industries use this as a basis for planning. In this instance, the sales forecast provides the basic data for planning and is supplemented by specific sales orders indicating variations required.

Inventory Plan

An inventory plan is basically an extension or variation of the basic sales forecast. Using this concept, a plan indicating the level of inventory desired to be maintained is the basic input for production planning. Industries employing this concept would be proprietary products not distributed on a broad market scale such as specialized equipment, tools and instruments. They would be sold and shipped on an individual order basis but without a waiting period for fabrication. This can be viewed as an addition to the basic sales forecast. The sales forecast indicates we expect to sell X units during a specific period of time. In addition it is desired to maintain a quantity of 4 in stock. The total of X + 4 becomes the total requirements for the production plan.

Many companies use all three sources of input for production planning. Characteristic would be companies producing standard products (can be forecasted) offering options (specific sales orders) with a desired short delivery period (maintain finished goods inventory). Specific industries would include light aircraft, food processing and machine tool.

Time Factors

Production planning involves three time factors.

— Material lead time
— Production lead time
— Sales order lead time

Obviously the first two, material and production lead times, can have a direct effect on the last, sales order lead time. A brief definition of each follows:

— Material lead time is external time required for vendors to deliver orders placed for material and/or parts. It includes ordering time, vendor production time and shipping or delivery time.
— Production lead time is internal time to process materials and parts into the required product(s). It includes preparation/order time, process time, assembly, inspection or test and making ready for shipment.
— Sales order lead time is the time in which the customer desires the product or material or the time sales has established as policy for normal delivery of orders to the customer.

In developing a production plan, each of these factors has an important influence on the operating policies of the organization. For example, if the sales policy is to deliver any order received within a maximum of two weeks and the normal production cycle is three weeks, material lead time four weeks, this will have a direct effect on company operating policy as it relates to production facilities and level of inventory maintained. It will also have far-reaching effects even in the area of hiring, overtime and other personnel-related policies. On the other hand, without a stated sales order lead time with fabrication three weeks and material lead time four weeks, the sales order lead time can be expected to extend to as much as seven or eight weeks for delivery.

To prevent surprises and be able to develop a sound production plan, one that can truly be used as a "roadmap" and one that the total organization believes in, it is important that time factors be acknowledged and treated in an open manner. A company policy must be adopted relative to these factors. This will determine the method of operation relative to sales order lead time, inventory levels provided and the general planning mode.

Facilities and Equipment Capability

What is our company capable of making? What is the rate of production? What must be supplied by other vendors? This is the third key of production planning. Total knowledge of production capabilities is necessary to develop the production plan. Key factors include:

— Size and capacity of equipment
— Tooling capability
— Rate of production
— Skill inventory of personnel
— Types of equipment
— Alternate methods of production
— Availability of subcontractors
— Tolerance and specification requirements
— Finishing requirements
— Special processing

The knowledge and capability of deciding what items will be produced in-house or purchased from a vendor must be available to enable a logical production plan to be developed. Lead times, both internal and external, and other factors affecting the production load should also be available.

These factors all point to a basic conclusion that an intimate knowledge of product make-up as well as manufacturing capability is the key to developing a logical and sound production plan. They are the major ingredients of the production plan and will vary in emphasis and intensity from company to company. Particular factors such as complexities of the product, philosophy of the organization, needs of the market and the relationship of the company to the market all have a bearing on this emphasis.

Production Schedule

The production schedule is the roadmap. It determines the route used to translate the production plan into production for sale. It provides the basis for measuring progress, determining when or if detours occur and forms a basis for decision-making during the production cycle.

Production scheduling is one of the most detailed and demanding tasks in the industrial organization. Performed in an adequate manner either through manual or mechanical (ADP) techniques, successful accomplishment requires the capacity to maintain large amounts of information relative to product, process, production status, and manning in a ready reference format. Some degree of mental recall is also mandatory, in addition to the various forms, reports and other documents used to track progress.

The production schedule itself is a specific plan of work to be accomplished within a given period of time. The period of time may be an hour, day, week, month or some other unit appropriate to the organization's objectives. The basis of the schedule is the production plan translated into specific components that can be charted, measured and against which results can be reported and adjustments made as required. Depending upon the method and techniques employed, it can be a very rigid schedule exerting maximum control in a very structured format. On the other hand, a smaller company or one with very simple planning requirements will need only a guideline to accomplish the work desired.

Rigid scheduling and control requirements generally exist in larger companies requiring complex planning, scheduling and coordinating processes. Operations costing thousands of dollars per hour to operate require a very detailed, well-based plan to reduce the opportunity for significant losses in production. A very rigid production schedule will include exact order sequence to be run at each machine or work center and the specific starting and ending time. This can result in a large organization with the use of sophisticated methods (ADP) of scheduling employed, exerting a major impact on the operation of the facility.

At the other extreme, frequently the schedule is issued as a listing or guide of work or orders to be produced within a desired completion date. In this instance production control has only provided the starting and (hopefully) the ending point. No attempt has been made to establish the route and this likewise will not provide the opportunity to develop checkpoints for monitoring progress. It is not really a schedule and it may or may not represent an actual shop load. It may not truly represent the most urgent production requirements at all. Typically, this type of scheduling operation will exist in smaller companies and often is the result of a listing of promises made to customers. Final scheduling is performed by the foreman and the final control of results is within his province.

Between these extremes lies an infinite range of scheduling and control activities and results. The degree to which the production schedule exerts influence on the production operation is important. *A proper schedule can optimize production and inventory costs by proper sequencing of order quantities and time phasing.* A poor schedule can do little more than provide a means of communication between planning and scheduling and the production operation itself.

Preparing the Production Schedule

Any scheduling system requires basic input data from the production plan consisting of:

— What?
— When?
— How many?

Whether the scheduling system is very basic or the most complex in existence, only the degree of detail varies for the input data. For example, in a very simple system illustrated in Figure 4-3, "the what" is the list of parts on the schedule, "the when" is the due date of each, and "the how many" is the quantity in the column indicated. This example is the entire production control scheduling system utilized by many companies. It is a simple system for a noncomplex production operation that serves the needs of the organization.

PRODUCT/PART	QUANTITY	REQ. DATE	ACTUAL COMP.
Product X	340	11/30	
Part A	340	10/15	
Part B	680	10/15	
Part C	340	10/15	

SIMPLE SCHEDULING FORMAT

FIGURE 4-3

A more complex system will utilize the same components of information but would develop them into a more detailed schedule to achieve a similar objective. Because of the complexities of the production operation it is necessary to break down or subdivide the operations required to produce a part or product and schedule it on a *work center* basis rather than merely a department basis. The following example will serve to illustrate:

1. Secure a detailed breakdown of all parts or products to be produced including quantities and required delivery date of each. The production plan would show this information for hypothetical "product X" as:

SIMPLE SCHEDULE FORMAT

MODEL	NO. UNITS	HRS. REQUIRED	DATE REQUIRED
Product X	340	238	11/30
Part A	340	170	10/15
Part B	680	68	10/15
Part C	340	340	10/15
TOTAL HOURS PLANNED		816	

FIGURE 4-4

In some instances the detailed part/operation planning illustrated in Figure 4-5 is included as part of the overall production planning function.

DETAILED PART/OPERATION PLAN

PRODUCT/PART	OPER. NO.	WORK CENTER	NO. OF UNITS	HRS./UNIT @ WORK CENTER	TOTAL HRS. WORK CTR.	TOTAL HRS. PRODUCT/ PART
PRODUCT X	05	001	340	0.70	238.0	
						238.0
PART A	05	103	340	0.05	17.0	
	10	126	340	0.10	34.0	
	15	210	340	0.15	51.0	
	20	211	340	0.05	17.0	
	25	354	340	0.10	34.0	
	30	599	340	0.05	17.0	
						170.0
PART B	05	354	680	0.07	47.6	
	10	599	680	0.03	20.4	68.0
PART C	05	110	340	0.38	129.2	
	10	126	340	0.07	23.8	
	15	214	340	0.45	153.0	
	20	599	340	0.10	34.0	
						340.0
TOTAL HOURS						816.0

FIGURE 4-5

2. Develop total requirements by part and operation to provide the basic input for work center loading.

3. Develop work center loading based on the breakdown of individual parts required (Figure 4-6). Establish actual starting and completion dates for each operation of each part. In a practical sense, it is necessary to work backward to establish accurate actual start and completion dates. This is particularly necessary to avoid a conflict of two parts at one work center at the same time period.

4. The work center loading/planning sheet forms the basis for the production schedule. The schedule is made up of a balanced work load of jobs based on the requirements developed. There are several areas that cause complications. One is the difficulty of maintaining a balanced work load for the production operation. Note on the sample work center planning sheet Figure 4-6, that one part must be started into the production operation as early as 8/13. The next earliest start is 9/10 and the last part need not be started until 9/21. Another consideration is manpower availability. Seldom do companies maintain sufficient manpower to provide full manning for every work center at all times. It is neither practical nor economical. When the work center planning sheet is converted into a weekly production schedule, Figure 4-7, a completely different view of the problem is revealed. (A balanced work load has purposely not been developed to emphasize the potential complexities of the scheduling problem.) It is obvious that this wide range of manpower/equipment requirements would be virtually impossible to plan around for the short term. As a practical approach, a second shift might be employed, a level at some point between the two extremes established, subcontracting, or a combination of techniques employed to level the work requirements. Although the example is limited in scope, it does illustrate not only some of the difficulties involved in developing balanced work loads but attendant to that the potential costs that may result from the development of a poor schedule.

Summary—Production Planning and Scheduling

The production schedule, whether a simple listing of work to be performed or a detailed plan part by part, operation by operation, is the basic means for monitoring production activities. Progress is checked and results reported based upon the planning or production period. As long as results achieved are as anticipated, no action need be taken. However, if results are less than expected, or production is behind schedule, changes must be initiated. This may consist of increasing production capacity with additional manpower and/or machine hours or a revision to the production schedule may be made. On the other hand, if production is ahead of schedule, a reduction in capacity or rate may be initiated to achieve the planned results. Regardless of the circumstances, monitoring production activities with the production schedule becomes the key to successful fulfillment of the plan. It is the method by which control is exercised over the production operation.

In addition to the production report, there are other reports used to monitor the results of the production operation from other standpoints.

WORK CENTER LOADING/PLANNING SHEET

WORK CENTER	PRODUCT/PART	OPER. NO.	NO. OF UNITS	HRS./UNIT @ WORK CENTER	TOTAL HRS. WORK CTR.	GRAND TOTAL HRS. AT WORK CTR.	REQ.'D START DATE	REQ.'D COMP. DATE	ACTUAL START DATE	ACTUAL COMP. DATE
001	Product X	05	340	0.70	238.0	238.0	10/15	11/30	10/15	11/30
103	Part A	05	340	0.05	17.0	17.0	9/15	9/16	9/10	9/12
110	Part C	05	340	0.38	129.2	129.2	8/13	9/ 4	8/13	9/ 4
126	Part A	10	340	0.10	34.0		9/17	9/22	9/12	9/18
126	Part C	10	340	0.07	23.8	57.8	9/ 5	9/ 7	9/ 5	9/ 7
210	Part A	15	340	0.15	51.0	51.0	9/23	10/ 2	9/18	9/26
211	Part A	20	340	0.05	17.0	17.0	10/ 2	10/ 4	9/27	9/28
214	Part C	15	340	0.45	153.0	153.0	9/10	10/ 8	9/10	10/ 8
354	Part A	25	340	0.10	34.0		10/ 5	10/10	10/ 1	10/ 5
354	Part B	05	680	0.07	47.6	81.6	10/ 4	10/11	9/21	10/ 1
599	Part A	30	340	0.05	17.0		10/11	10/13	10/ 8	10/ 9
599	Part B	10	680	0.03	20.4		10/12	10/14	10/ 4	10/ 5
599	Part C	20	340	0.10	34.0	71.4	10/ 9	10/15	10/ 9	10/15
	GRAND TOTAL					816.0				

FIGURE 4-6

91

WEEKLY PRODUCTION SCHEDULE

PRODUCT/PART	WORK CENTER	OPER. NO.	NO. OF UNITS	HRS./UNITS	TOTAL HRS. REQ'D.	NO. UNITS SCHEDULED	NO. HRS. SCHEDULED	UNITS COMPLETED TO DATE
Part A	126	10	110	0.10	11.0	110	11.0	230
Part A	210	15	340	0.15	51.0	194	29.0	
Part C	214	15	251	0.45	113.0	89	40.0	39
Part B	354	05	680	0.07	47.6	570	40.0	
						TOTAL HOURS SCHEDULED	120.0	

FIGURE 4-7

92

Minimize Input—Maximize Output

Although practiced by only a few companies, the technique known as *control by exception* is the most economical technique available for maintaining control of production operations. Control by exception or *exception reporting* is exactly what it means, only deviations from the plan are reported and acted upon.

From a standpoint of benefits, it should be readily recognized that there is no benefit to be gained from merely reporting that everything is on schedule and no problems exist. This may be a slight exaggeration since a certain comfort (benefit) is derived from knowing everything is on target. At the other extreme is the organization that reports the completion of each part or milestone on the production schedule and thereby consumes an excessive volume of time and energy plotting routine data that does not contribute to overall progress or the ability to make decisions on a more sound basis.

Lack of confidence is perhaps more readily understood. There is a certain mystique associated with the thought that only exceptional items will be noted and that we do not keep track of routine occurrences. What is not recognized is that those items not reported are essentially noted by their absence. Their status has been noted by being on schedule.

More likely the reason so few organizations utilize control-by-exception concepts is the lack of understanding as to what it really consists of and the knowledge required to implement it on a systems basis. The basic ingredients of control by exception and the development of a systems approach to obtaining benefits utilizing these concepts can be installed in most organizations and require minimal records and efforts.

EXCEPTION REPORTS

There are several key reporting mechanisms commonly used to control production and inventory activities via the exception principle. Individually, some of them are used in varying degrees by many organizations. Collectively very few companies utilize all reports, hence, do not achieve the total benefits available. The basic exception reports required include:

- Past due order report—sales
  Past due order report—production
- Shortage report
- Scrap/rejection report
- Forecast variance report
- Inactive inventory report

Past Due Order Report—Sales

Every company strives to achieve on-time shipment of orders to its customers. It is one of the best ways to develop and maintain good relationships with customers. In a practical sense it is recognized that there will be occurrences when orders will not be shipped on time. When this occurs, management must know what orders have not been shipped, the reasons they were not shipped on time and the rescheduled shipping date. This information is typically presented to sales management via the past due sales order report as illustrated in Figure 4-8.

PAST DUE SALES ORDER REPORT

Period End: _____
Date Issued: _____

Order No.	Customer Name	Sched. Ship Date	Resched. Ship Date	Reason for Delay

FIGURE 4-8

This is a basic exception report used to communicate information to the sales department regarding the orders that were not shipped as planned. Sales may then take action by advising the customer of the status of his order, provide an alternate means of fulfilling the requirements of the customer, or may take no action.

A minimum amount of key information has been provided concerned with orders in a critical status situation resulting in optimum use of a control mechanism.

Past Due Order Report—Production

Complementary to the past due sales order report is a similar report for production work orders. At established intervals, which are usually related to the production planning period, a summary of past due production orders is produced. Information comparable to that required for sales orders is recorded as well as specific data relative to the production process.

This past due order report provides a capsule summary of data concerned with work orders that were not completed as scheduled. It provides a basis of review for production scheduling personnel relative to the effects it may have on the overall production plan. Adjustments may then be made in the production process such as temporarily increasing the scheduled output through use of additional shifts or manpower. The use of overtime may also be considered. In some circumstances even subcontracting may be required. And in an extreme situation, the only alternative may be to revise the schedule completely.

As with the past due sales order report only those key exceptions need be noted. Depending upon the complexities of the system employed, the production past due order report may be as simple as a marked-up copy of the current production schedule or as complex as a sophisticated computer-produced document. Between these extremes is an infinite variety of methods to provide the means to analyze and act on past due production orders. Generated as a special report, a typical format is illustrated in Figure 4-9.

LATE ORDER REPORT

Period End: _____
Date Issued: _____

Order No.	Part No.	Description	Order Qty.	Due Date	Resched. Date	Comment

FIGURE 4-9

Shortage Report

The shortage report is another method of control by exception. Typically the shortage report reflects a deficiency in inventory and includes raw material, purchased and manufactured parts and finished products. Generally a separate report will be created for the various categories or classifications of shortages.

Regardless of the category of shortage being reported, basic information is required for all circumstances. Included will be the part number designation, description, inventory on hand, date and quantity required, status of the item as to date of anticipated availability, quantity to be available, reason for delay and any alternative information to alleviate the shortage.

Although the shortage report has been defined as reflecting a deficiency in inventory, this deficiency may be related only to the planned inventory and may or may not be a true physical outage.

The philosophy and policy of the individual business enterprise will determine the basis for the generation of a shortage report. This may range from the one extreme of a complete physical lack of parts, material, or product to merely having arrived at the minimum level of inventory desired.

In summary, the shortage report is used to establish the status of shortage to provide production and inventory control personnel the opportunity to make decisions based on the data available. An illustration of a typical shortage report is shown in Figure 4-10.

SHORTAGE REPORT

Period End: _____
Date Issued: _____
Issued By: _____

PART NO.	DESCRIPTION	ORDER NO.	DUE DATE	ORDER QTY.	RESCHED. DATE	QTY. ON HAND	QTY. REQ'D.	STATUS

FIGURE 4-10

Scrap/Rejection Report

Although the scrap/rejection report may often be separate documents issued by quality control, the function served is very similar. The information conveyed is the unavailability of particular material for use as planned. In the case of material scrapped, it is totally lost while rejected material may have value after rework, repair or alteration. The purpose is to report exceptions to the planned status of material. In another manner, it is a signal to production and inventory control that an unplanned situation has occurred and attention is required. The next step will include an evaluation of the remaining balance along with the requirements. The results of this appraisal will frequently lead to the item appearing on the shortage report.

The basic information contained on scrap or rejection reports is primarily concerned with the loss involved, since that is the main purpose (see Figure 4-11). Seldom will information concerning replacement be included since this is primarily a quality control report. Although this is another form of control by exception, the greatest value to production inventory control lies in its message that "all is not as planned—a deviation, requiring action, has occurred."

SCRAP/REJECTION REPORT

Period End: _____
Issue Date: _____
Issued By: _____

PART NO.	DESCRIPTION	ORDER NO.	QTY.	VALUE	DISPOSITION

FIGURE 4-11

Forecast Variance Report

A forecast is basically an estimate of the future based on data from the past (if available) and market data obtained by research or other means all modified by the judgment of marketing personnel. By its very nature, it is frequently very fragile in its accuracy and reliability. The recent history of the Ford Motor Company with the original Mustang and the Edsel are examples of contrasting forecast disasters. In the case of the Mustang, demand exceeded original forecasts resulting in delayed deliveries. Substantial revisions to production plans for increased output were required almost immediately upon introduction. The story of the Edsel is too well-known to relate, other than to note the extreme contrast to the production problems of the Mustang. There are, of course, numerous products in the marketplace that are very stable that are not faced with the extremes experienced by Ford.

FORECAST VARIANCE REPORT

PRODUCT CODE	DESCRIPTIONS	QTY. FCST.	QTY. CONSUMED	QTY. ON HAND	QTY. ON ORDER	TOTAL AVAIL.	OVER FCST.	UNDER FCST.	ACTION/DISPOSITION

FIGURE 4-12

Those products that are faced with significant variations (± 25%) from forecast require a means to monitor inventory levels and production plans. This is the main purpose of the forecast variance report, Figure 4-12. This report lists only those products or parts with unusual deviations from the forecast. Either type of variance, positive or negative, can be equally significant depending upon particular circumstances. In some respects unusual increases in requirements may be a greater problem because of the voids that often result in the supply line. Lead times for parts and materials may significantly affect the ability to maintain adequate supplies and may result in a complete cessation of production.

A reduction in demand, on the other hand, creates a surplus situation. The immediate effect is a build-up of excessive inventory; stock levels exceed the maximum established and a cutoff in orders is effected.

It is for these circumstances that the forecast variance report is provided. The primary purpose is to inform management of significant deviations (exceptions) from plan. It provides the necessary information required to monitor inventory/sales trends enabling improved decisions to be made. Typical information included is forecast quantities, levels of usage, current inventory on hand and on order. In addition, a revised forecast quantity or disposition action recommended may also be included. Key decisions that can be affected by the information include actions concerning production, inventory, purchasing, manpower, finance, and construction plans. Although one of the least used exception reports, it is perhaps one of the most valuable tools or guides in the overall operation of a business.

Inactive Inventory Report

This inventory report is intended to advise of the status of inactive items of raw, semifinished and finished goods inventory. It is an exception report signaling the inactivity of inventory and is requesting that a decision be made regarding disposition. The report is usually generated on an annual basis and is tied to the fiscal year. The objective is to illuminate and examine those items of inventory that might qualify for possible purging from stock.

Typical information contained on the report includes description, part number designation, quantity in stock, data and quantity of last transaction, history of usage, where used or for what it is used, original cost, current value, and recommended disposition. Armed with data, management is then provided adequate information on which to base a sound decision.

There are a number of reasons why inventory becomes inactive and must be disposed of in an effective manner. Primary reasons include obsolescence, change in design, model change, and change in the market itself. The need for periodic purging of all levels of inventory is significant for a number of reasons. First there is the basic space consumed by the material in storage, next is the monetary investment that is being absorbed, and finally there is the direct costs such as taxes commonly paid on an annual basis. In all instances, costs are involved.

Points to Remember

The key to production and inventory control reports is to ensure an awareness of significant check points. The missing of a single check point may not be too significant by itself. The impact and cost effect it may have on the total organization could be multiplied several times.

Exception reports provide the most economical means for communicating important data at key time intervals to those concerned with decision-making. A summary of key objectives that are produced as a result of the use of exception reports include:

— Basic communication of status has been provided.
— Volume of data has been reduced to a minimum.
— Data is presented in a concise format.
— Actions can be taken to suit requirements.
— *Major* economics of operation have resulted.

Installation of a system of exception reporting improves the ability to note significant check points in a timely manner and simplifies the process required for "keeping track of where you are going."

Chapter 5

Putting Your Labor and Material Costs
in Their Proper Perspectives

The task of controlling production and inventory costs has the same problem as any other complex task. The problem is making certain that efforts are being exerted where they gain the greatest return. In a production and inventory system there always is a large number of cost elements with a complex set of interrelationships. There seem to be two attitudes about how to do the job, almost exactly opposite in philosophy, both described by old, wise sayings: "Take care of the pennies, and the dollars will take care of themselves." And, "Don't trip over dollar bills while trying to pick up pennies."

The task is further complicated by the large variety of reports that are in common use in industry. The array of possibilities can be very confusing.

This chapter has one principal theme: *Guide the use of control effort to reap the greatest possible gain.* For the greatest usefulness, any cost control reporting structure should be designed or selected to clearly identify the cost elements of greatest significance. The design or selection of a cost reporting system is somewhat subjective, in that it must be specifically meaningful to and comfortable for the individuals who are to work with it. Several alternative structures will be presented here to demonstrate what is being used, and how effectively each serves its purpose. There will be a differentiation between "controllable" and "uncontrollable" costs, and an explanation of why that differentiation helps guide the use of control effort. All of these considerations will continue to focus on the main theme: getting the greatest return for the efforts exerted for controlling and reducing costs.

CONSTRUCT A COST PROFILE TO IDENTIFY WHERE TO FOCUS CONTROL

A cost profile is a format for presenting cost data. The format is designed to present the data for use as a guide for action toward cost improvement. It is a listing of cost elements, ranked in descending order of value, so that emphasis can be given to those elements of highest value. The elements of highest value are those for which cost control is most important and those that should be given first attention for reduction. Therefore, a properly constructed cost profile provides good guidance for both cost control and cost reduction programs.

Construction of a cost profile is neither difficult nor is it automatic. While constructing a cost profile, it is important to keep in mind that its purpose is to identify those cost elements of highest value so that they can be given proper attention.

The scope of a cost profile can be either all of the products of an entire company or product group or even individual products. Regardless of its scope, the cost profile must be based on the cost data generally accepted by the management of the company. Discussion based on data not generally accepted will be directed toward critical evaluation of the data rather than toward constructive utilization of the information. This misdirection of focus defeats the purpose of the cost profile.

CASE IN POINT

Preparation for construction of the cost profile starts with two steps. First, set up five categories of cost:

- Burden
- Labor
  - Direct
  - Indirect
- Materials
  - Direct
  - Indirect

Second, divide the total costs (whether for the whole company or for a product) among the five categories. Be certain to account for all costs. Table 5-1 shows what resulted when these two steps were taken for the cost elements of a chemical manufacturing plant.

DEVELOPMENT OF A COST PROFILE

From A Chemical Manufacturing Plant of an International Company

Annual Cost in Dollars

Burden	Labor		Materials	
	Direct	Indirect	Direct	Indirect
$2,208,300	$747,200	$634,000	$11,111,600	$508,400

TABLE 5-1

The next step is to rank the categories in descending order of value. This has been done in Table 5-2. Examination of Table 5-2 leads to the suggestion that direct materials are going to be a more fruitful area for cost reduction efforts than direct labor or indirect labor. In fact, at this stage, burden seems to be more important than either direct or indirect labor. It becomes apparent, therefore, that through the development and construction of the cost profile it is easy to determine which is the more important: material cost or labor cost.

Cost Element	Product Group		Total Plant
	Resins	Specialties	
1. Direct Materials	$ 9,083,200	$2,028,400	$11,111,600
2. Burden	1,370,400	837,900	2,208,300
3. Direct Labor	531,800	215,400	747,200
4. Indirect Labor	378,300	255,700	634,000
5. Indirect Materials	290,700	217,700	508,400
Total	$11,654,400	$3,555,100	$15,209,500

TABLE 5-2

Continuing with the development of a cost profile, we arrive at a further breakdown of the five major groups similar to that shown in Table 5-3. It should be noted that there are still large clusters of costs even though the clusters are becoming more and more specifically identified. The breakdown includes a separation of costs for the two product groups: Resins and Specialties. These two groups represent not only different products, but also two individual groups of equipment and operators.

It can be seen from the example that the detailing of the cost elements is not too difficult to accomplish. The task will be carried out with greater ease, perhaps, if it is understood that its purpose is to provide assistance in determining where to focus attention.

To help in that determination one other aspect has been added to our considerations, as shown in Table 5-3. A judgment has been made as to which of the individual cost elements shown are controllable or uncontrollable. The term "uncontrollable" is a matter of judgment because some of the elements that have been designated in that fashion might in reality be controlled. One such cost element would be depreciation. If the management of the company were to elect to eliminate some pieces of equipment this would then reduce some of the depreciation shown in the financial accounting. Such action, of course, is generally of major consequence.

It has been judged, therefore, that the depreciation cost element is uncontrollable. Similar discussion could take place with regard to taxes and insurance. Those two elements also might be reduced through management action. Because reduction in those two cases would also be major steps, they have been judged to be uncontrollable. The use of the designations controllable and uncontrollable is a continuation of the practice of restricting attention to those items that warrant major cost control and reduction efforts.

The procedure now becomes more selective as to the cost elements that are to be considered. Attention will be focused only on controllable elements. Elements that are uncontrollable will be ignored. Further, the number of items to be given attention will be

DEVELOPMENT OF A COST PROFILE

Cost Elements		Annual Cost in Dollars			Controllable	
		Product Groups		Total Plant	No	Yes, By
		Resins	Specialties			
1. Direct Materials						
a. Annual Contracts		$5,312,000	$1,406,700	$6,718,700		Purchasing (Price); Operating Department and Plant Control Laboratory (Yields), Process Development Laboratory (Value Analysis)
b. Open Market Replenishment		3,000,800	372,200	3,373,000		Purchasing (Price); Operating Department and Plant Control Laboratory (Yields), Process Development Laboratory (Value Analysis)
c. Shipping Containers		360,000	159,000	519,000		Marketing (Specification), Purchasing (Price), Operating Department and Plant Control Laboratory (Yield)
d. Materials from corporate overseas plants		410,400	90,500	500,900	X	
Total		$9,083,200	$2,028,400	$11,111,600		
2. Burden						
a. Depreciation		$303,000	$257,400	$560,400	X	
b. Plant Control Laboratory	Note 1	244,300	127,100	371,400		Operating Department and Plant Control Laboratory
c. Energies	Note 2	196,000	124,800	320,800		Operating Department
d. Process Development Laboratory -	Note 1	170,000	85,000	255,000		Administrative Management and Process Development Lab
e. Operating Supervision	Note 1	131,400	66,000	197,400		Operating Department
f. Administrative Management	Note 1	77,900	38,900	116,800		Administrative Management
g. Taxes and Insurance	Note 1	75,000	37,500	112,500		
h. Corporate Charges	Note 1	67,100	33,500	100,600	X	
i. Waste Treatment	Note 1	52,100	26,100	78,200	X	Operating Department and Maintenance Department
j. Warehouse Operating Expense		21,800	27,800	49,600		Warehouse Supervision
k. Cafeteria	Note 1	21,300	9,300	30,600		Administrative Management
l. First Aid	Note 1	10,500	4,500	15,000		Administrative Management
Total		$1,370,400	$837,900	$2,208,300		

Note 1 - Allocated to Product Group
Note 2 - Metered per Product Group

TABLE 5-3

104

Cost Elements	Product Group Resins	Product Group Specialties	Total Plant	No	Yes, By
3. Direct Labor					
a. Basic Wages	$ 349,100	$ 151,300	$ 500,400		Operating Department
b. Benefits	101,200	40,900	142,100	X	Operating Department
c. Overtime	42,200	10,400	52,600	X	
d. Shift Differential	21,800	5,200	27,000	X	
e. All other expenses	17,500	7,600	25,100		
Total	$ 531,800	$ 215,400	$ 747,200		
4. Indirect Labor					
a. Plant Maintenance—Wages	$ 239,900	$ 170,200	$ 410,100		Operating Department and Mt. Dept.
b. Plant Maintenance—Benefits	56,600	40,300	96,900	X	
c. Outside Contractors Note 3	23,900	15,000	38,900		Operating Department and Mt. Dept.
d. Materials Handling—Wages	46,600	24,400	71,000		Operating Department and Mt. Dept.
e. Materials Handling—Benefits	11,300	5,800	17,100	X	
Total	$ 378,300	$ 255,700	$ 634,000		
Note 3 – Supplements Plant Maintenance					
5. Indirect Materials					
a. Operating Supplies	$ 153,500	$ 166,300	$ 319,800		Operating Department
b. Maintenance	137,200	51,400	188,600		Operating Department and Mt. Dept.
Total	$ 290,700	$ 217,700	$ 508,400		
6. Grand Total	$11,654,400	$3,555,100	$15,209,500		

TABLE 5-3 continued

restricted. In Table 5-4, five items represent 79½% of all the cost for resins, and five items represent 64% of all the costs for specialties. The ten items represent 75% of the total cost of the entire plant.

Detailed examination of Table 5-4 brings some interesting thoughts to mind. A reasonable target of 1% reduction of the costs that are shown in that figure would yield about $100,000 a year in savings. A reduction target of 5% would result in savings of $560,000 per year. It seems wise then to concentrate on achieving some of the potential identified so far rather than to look any further. It also seems reasonable that any total expenditure that is less than $100,000 per year should not now be considered as a suitable area for much effort, at least until good effort has been put in those items that are above $100,000. This value then, $100,000, becomes the criterion for discriminating between cost elements that are to be given attention and those that are not to be given attention.

COST PROFILE		
COST ELEMENTS	**Annual Cost in Dollars**	
	Resins	**Specialties**
1. Direct Materials - Annual Contracts	$5,312,000	$1,406,700
2. Direct Materials - Open Market Replenishment	3,000,800	372,200
3. Resins - Shipping Containers	360,000	
Specialties - Maintenance Wages		170,200
4. Resins - Direct Labor Wages	349,100	
Specialties - Operating Supplies		166,300
5. Resins - Plant Control Laboratory	244,300	
Specialties - Shipping Containers		159,000
Total: five items	$9,266,200	$2,274,400
% of Grand total cost of product group	79.5%	64%
Total: ten items	$11,540,600	
% of Grand total costs of entire plant	75%	

TABLE 5-4

The cost profile has served its screening function. It has helped in an examination of all costs and in identification of those of major value. It has focused attention on the ten clusters of costs that include 75% of all the costs of the plant. These costs represent the area of greatest probable potential as cost reduction opportunities.

(Table 5-5 is a listing of cost elements applicable to most companies and industries.)

Cost profiles can serve another function for management. They can help implementation of the management-by-exception principle. Because they identify the costs of greater importance, they might be used to identify the cost elements to be

SUBDIVISION OF MAJOR COST GROUPS		
Burden	**Labor**	
Factory Costs	Direct	Indirect

Salaries - Supervision
Salaries - Clerical
Space
Utilities
Equipment Depreciation
Stationery
Inventory Carrying Costs
   Purchased Materials
   Work-in-Process
Engineering
	Parts Manufacture
	Subassembly
	Finishing
	Assembly
	Final Production
	Packaging
	Rework
	Scrap
	Overtime
	Other Employee benefits
		Materials Handling
		Receiving
		Warehousing
		Shipping
		Maintenance
		Indirect Manufacturing
		   Operations
		Security
		Inspection
		Overtime
		Other Employee benefits

Sales Costs	**Materials**	
	Direct	Indirect
Salaries - Supervision Salaries - Salesmen Salaries - Clerical Space Utilities Advertising Stationery Inventory Carrying Costs Finished Goods	Raw Materials Purchased Components Purchased Processing Packaging Materials Loss in Yield Scrap	Tools Finishing Supplies Cleaning Supplies Maintenance Supplies Shipping Supplies
Administrative Costs		
Salaries - Supervision Salaries - Clerical Space Utilities Stationery Employee Benefits		

TABLE 5-5

reported in a cost control reporting system. Only the important elements would be reported in detail. All other cost elements would be reported as a total of other cost elements. One of the other cost elements would be reported in detail if it exceeded its target by some important, preestablished amount, for example, 30% or $1,000. Following this principle would prevent the details of small valued cost elements from drawing attention away from those elements that are worthy of the attention. The fewer the items of data included in a report the easier it is to find the data that must be found.

At this point thought should be given to consideration of "loss of income caused by machine downtime" as a cost. It may not represent an out-of-pocket expense or cost, but in some plants it represents a loss of income in-to-pocket. If machine downtime represents an important loss to a company, "loss of income caused by machine downtime" must be included in the construction of the cost profile.

Having constructed the cost profile and having identified the major cost elements to be controlled, the next step is to establish the control mechanism.

PREPARE TO FOCUS COST CONTROLS AND TRACK YOUR CONTROL EFFECTIVENESS

The preparations for a cost control program include establishing targets for costs and providing for tracking actual performance against the targets. The most visible part of a cost control program is a structure of reports that are published periodically: weekly, monthly, or even daily in some cases. Sometimes reports are prepared only on demand, when it has been determined that a specific situation is sufficiently out of control to warrant a specific investigation in depth. In the reports, targets and actual performances are compared to show whether and to what degree objectives are being met.

There are four major approaches to cost control reports that cover both labor and materials. These reports are in general identified by the way the targets are established. The four approaches covering both labor and materials are:

— Budgets
— Standard costs
— Job estimates
— Control ratios

Variances

In any type of cost control report in which a target condition and an actual condition are compared, the difference between the target and the actual condition is frequently called the variance. The variance may be either favorable or unfavorable. The causes for both unfavorable and favorable variances should be investigated to provide guidance for improved performance. Unfavorable variances can lead to information about what is being done improperly and what therefore should be corrected. Favorable variances can lead to information about what is being done properly and should therefore be given broader application, if possible.

The purpose of reporting the variances between standard (target) and actual condition is to show clearly whether or not a situation is under control. Therefore the variance can act as a guide to indicate if corrective action should be taken. To serve that purpose properly a variance must be a reasonably factual representation of the condition that it is measuring. A variance must be unfavorable only when the conditions it is measuring are truly out of control. A variance must be favorable only when the condition is really under good control. When the factual representation is absent, even if only part of the time, those individuals who look to the variances for guidance lose confidence in it and ignore it, even when the representation is factual. They ignore it because they do not know when the representation is factual or not.

CASE IN POINT

The need for emphasizing factual representation may be demonstrated by an extreme example of a not infrequently observed cost account situation. If the cost of grass cutting for a factory is budgeted over all of the twelve months of the year, there will be a favorable variance for that cost account during the winter months because no actual expenses will be incurred for that item. On the other hand, during the summer months, when the expense is incurred, the account will show an unfavorable variance.

All variances for this account are meaningless; that is very obvious. There are other situations, however, that are much less obvious.

Budgets

Budgets are reports that cover whole plants, or departments or cost centers. There are generally two types of budgets in use: fixed and variable. Most frequently budgets are constructed to cover a twelve-month period. They are based on anticipated activities that principally come from sales forecasts. In the case of the fixed budget, the values of the budgeted item remain constant throughout the year without consideration being given to differences between actual activity and anticipated activity. In the case of variable budgets, the difference between actual activity and anticipated activity is taken into account and some factor is then applied to the budgeted values of the cost elements. The cost elements covered by budgets are frequently related to the financial expense account structure.

CASE IN POINT

A typical monthly budget report format is shown in Figure 5-1. It should be noted that all values in budgets are given in dollars.

There are some interesting aspects to the data that was entered monthly into the specific report that Figure 5-1 represents. They are interesting because, although the entries are valid from a financial accounting viewpoint, they require considerable interpretation to become useful to any degree for the job of controlling costs. They are not factual representations of conditions. The actual data has been omitted from the format because their numerical values are not important. It is important to understand the reasons why the values are not factual:

1. *Sales.* Monthly sales might vary as much as 100% during the year. In some

MONTHLY OPERATING STATEMENT

_____ FOUNDRY DIVISION

FOR MONTH _____ , 19 ____

ITEM	THIS MONTH			YEAR–TO–DATE	
	ACTUAL	BUDGET	VARIANCE	ACTUAL	BUDGET
INCOME: NET SALES					
PLUS DIVISION CREDITS					
TOTAL OPERATING INCOME					
OPERATING COST: SALABLE LABOR					

BURDEN LABOR
    Receiving, Material Handling
    Molding-Indirect, Coremaking-
    Indirect, Shakeout, All others					

BONUS LABOR
    Holiday Pay, Overtime Premium,
    Shift Bonus					

VACATION RESERVE					
OTHER PERSONNEL EXPENSE					
SALARIES					
MATERIALS					
MAINTENANCE Machinery and Equipment					
Flasks					
Manufacture of Flasks					
All others					
SUPPLIES Misc. Shop Supplies					
Mold & Core Sand					
Core Oil and Binders					
All others					
TAXES Real Estate and Personal Property					
POWER					
DEPRECIATION–BUILDINGS					
DEPRECIATION–MACHINERY & EQUIPMENT					
TOTAL MANUFACTURING COSTS					
ADMINISTRATIVE EXPENSES					
SELLING EXPENSES					
CORPORATE CHARGES					
TOTAL EXPENSES AND CHARGES					

FIGURE 5-1

months products were accumulated in inventory in preparation for large shipments in the following months. To further complicate the situation sales were not reported when shipments were made, but when customers paid their invoices. That means that reported sales did not reflect actual quantities produced, or plant activity, for the month.

2. *Direct Labor Costs.* These costs were included as they were paid each month. That could occur three, four, or five times in one month, depending on the number of paydays and on vacations. The reported data did not necessarily reflect the actual labor costs for the month.

3. *Burden Labor Costs.* These items were paid monthly, semimonthly or biweekly according to the levels of positions in the organization. To complicate things still further, biweekly salaries were paid once, twice or three times a month depending on the number of paydays and vacations in the month. There was not necessarily any real relationship between these reported costs and the activities they were supposed to represent.

4. *Materials.* These costs were reported as vendor invoices for purchases were paid, not as the materials were used. Material usage was not necessarily reflected according to those reported costs.

The example just discussed was a fixed budget. The budget itself was developed by dividing a one-year budget by twelve. Because of the ambiguities related to the reported sales and costs trying to vary the budget according to activities would be exceedingly difficult, if not impossible.

In a variable budget, the variances are more meaningful than for a fixed budget. The budget values more closely describe what the conditions should have been than they do in a fixed budget. With variable budgets, the variances very closely represent the difference between "what should have been" and "what actually was," providing of course that proper factors are used in establishing the variable budget.

Standard Costs

Another form of cost control involves the use of standard costs. Standard costs·are developed for individual products and are targets for both labor and materials based on:

1. Engineered ·standards for labor.
2. Specific recipes, formulations for materials, or bills of materials.
3. Estimates for both labor and materials.
4. History for both labor and materials.

Standard costs for labor may be shown either in dollars or man-hours. If they are shown in terms of man-hours, the job of comparing year-to-year standard labor costs is facilitated because the dollars per hour do not have to be taken into account. This is important because the dollars per hour may change during a given year or from year to year. Similarly, standard costs for materials can be shown either as dollar values or quantities. If quantities are used, as in the case of man-hours for labor, comparison from year-to-year is facilitated. This is especially true of materials because the price for any given material might vary significantly during a single year and would probably be outside of the control of the operating people.

Standard costs covering both labor and material are generally established for products that are standard to a company, for example, those products that are carried in inventory. A standard cost is generally set up once, or occasionally with some companies twice, during a given year.

CASE IN POINT

Typical formats used for presenting standard costs for specific products are shown in Figures 5-2 and 5-3. These formats are for products of a company manufacturing components for audio systems. Figure 5-2 represents a part. The format shows the raw material used and the costs added by each processing step. Figure 5-3 represents an assembly of parts. It shows the parts, together with their costs, that are introduced at each assembly step.

Variances for standard costs are determined in various ways. In many cases the method used for determination of variance will depend on the costs and problems related to labor-time and production-count reporting. If an operator does the same operation on a single product for an entire day, there is no real difficulty in gathering information about the actual number of pieces processed daily. The actual labor-hours per piece can be determined directly. If he does the same kind of work with several different products during each day, his reporting can be handled in two different ways. He might be asked to report the time spent and the quantity processed for each product, so a variance can be determined for each individual product. On the other hand, he may be required to report the number of each product processed over the entire day. If the latter practice is used, the operator saves time spent on reporting. The variance is determined by comparing the total time that should have been spent to process to the sum of the quantities actually processed. The variance between time that should have been spent and the length of his day will give an overall variance that can be applied to the individual products. An arc welding operation on three products may be used as an example:

Product	Welding Minutes Per Unit of Product (Standard)	Number Welded That Day	Minutes It Should Have Taken
A	5	40	200
B	16	12	192
C	21	7	147
		TOTAL	539

539 Standard Minutes Produced
Less: 480 Actual Minutes

59 Minutes - Favorable Variance

$$\frac{59 \text{ Variance Minutes}}{480 \text{ Actual Minutes}} \times 100 = 12.3\% \text{ Favorable Variance}$$

TYPICAL STANDARD COST DEVELOPMENT

Price Part Route Sheet

Material __Cold Rolled Steel__
Spec. __SAE 1050 Annealed__
WIDTH __1-½ + 1/64__ Thick __.020 + .002__ Form __By VL 5/6/__

Company No. _____
Usage Per M __5 lbs.__
Model Group __101__

Part Name __Mounting Bar-Right (Less Finish)__
Used In App'd By DC 5/6
Dist. Class __2A__
Chk'd By DR 5/13

Issue No. __5__
Part No. __53A134__
Sheet 1 of 1

Operation No.	Dept. and Group No.	Description of Operation	Tools and Instructions	Individual Operation			Cumulative Total		
				Hours Per M	$/M Mat'l	$/M Labor	Hours Per M	$/M Mat'l	$/M Labor
11	09-4, 5 —or— 24	Purchase complete, less heat treatment and finish. (Opt'l) / Stamp complete, as above (standard)	T-3558 Progr. Die	5.5	.85	13.97	5.5	.85	13.97
	14	Inspect		–	–	–	5.5	.85	13.97
60	33	Degrease		0.1	–	.85	5.6	.85	14.82
	14	Inspect		–	–	–	5.6	.85	14.82
50	24	Purchase heat treatment and descaling		–	1.36	–	5.6	2.21	14.82
	14	Inspect	Parts must be free of scale	–	–	–	–	–	–
30	33	Oil Dip		0.2	–	.55	5.8	2.21	15.37
	14	Inspect		–	–	–	5.8	2.21	15.37
22	22	Place in Stock		–	–	–	5.8	2.21	15.37

FIGURE 5-2

TYPICAL STANDARD COST DEVELOPMENT

Assembly Route Sheet

Drawing Nos.		Model Group 274		Assembly Name: Speaker		Assembly No. 98-2352					Issue No. 6		Sheet 1 of 3		

		Prepared by DR		Approved by SL 1	Typed by CS	Checked by DR	Distr. Class 1	This copy for							

Oper. No.	Dept. No.	Qty.	Part Number	Description of Operation	Tools and Instructions	Used in Set-up Mins.	Prod. Per Hour	Individual Operation Hours per M	Individual Operation $/M Material	Individual Operation $/M Labor	Cumulative Total Hours per M	Cumulative Total $/M Material	Cumulative Total $/M Labor
10	05	2 1	34A72 33B366	Load insulator on punch, position back plate on anvil. Press insulator into back plate. Repeat for other side.	T-2028 Assembly Fixture Arbor Press	2.0	152	6.6	21.67 1.43 23.10	16.76	6.6	23.10	16.76
20	05	Line 10 1 2 2	30A369 56-23	Load eyelet and terminal onto pin in die. Position back plate onto locators and eyelet. Clinch eyelet, repeat for other side.	5-2700 Riveting Die Air Press with 5'' Cylinder; Use 60 lbs. pressure indicated in gauge.	5.0	102	9.8	1.93 2.63 4.56	24.89	16.4	27.66	41.65
30	05	Line 20 1 1	35-114A 17-90	Cement screen to back plate. Allow to dry 12 hours minimum.	Hypo; Et-2162 Cementing Fixture Et-2163 Nylon Roller	3.0	60	16.7	.67	42.42	33.1	18.33	84.07
40	05	Line 30 1		Test acoustical resistance of screen	Pt-265-3 Manometer Fixture T-2742 Standard #8	1.0	263	3.8		9.65	36.9	28.33	93.72
	48			Inspect	Pt-265-3 Manometer Fixture; Ohmmeter								
50	05	Line 40 1 1	31A630	Stake Line 40 assembly to outer pole piece	T-4052 Staking Die Denison Hyd. Press set to 2 ton on pressure gauge	10.0	333	3.0	4.21	7.62	39.9	32.54	101.34
60	05	Line 50 1 1 1 - 1	90A182 33A427 17-21 66A26	Place line 50 assembly on centering fixture. Apply cement to rim of back plate with hypo, assemble diaphragm on back plate, inserting coil leads through terminals. Place front plate on diaphragm. Place weight on assembly.	T-2898 Centering Fixture (4) and Weights (24) ET-1982 Rotating Base Hypo; NOTE: Clean weights	4.0	41	24.6	9.63 7.41 3.92 20.96	62.48	64.5	53.50	163.82

Revisions: Added operation 91; was part of operation 60.

Reasons: To eliminate unnecessary unloading for inspection

Notes: Use ET-2184 tool for disassembly

FIGURE 5-3

The 12.3% favorable variance can be applied to each product to determine the variance minutes for each. The result would be:

Product	Standard Minutes Per Unit For Welding	Variance Minutes For Day of Report
A	5	0.61
B	16	1.97
C	21	2.59

It might be argued that this practice results in an obscuring of differences among the variances for individual products. On the other hand, sometimes the variances occur because of some factor other than the individual products; for example, it might be due to equipment failure. To apply a variance to a product that just happens to be undergoing processing when the equipment fails may lead to improper conclusions. If all the time standards for the welding operations have been established according to a logical plan, then individual standards are all subject to the same logic. Therefore, the variance may just as well be applied to the total result of the logic as to individual standards.

One other point can be raised about the desirability of using the overall approach taken in the previous example. It can be costly for a plant to have its operators spending effort on time and production-count reporting. A 480-minute day can become a 440-minute day, after two 10-minute coffee breaks and two 10-minute washups are taken out. If 10 minutes more are spent on reporting, that is 10 minutes or 2% out of 440 minutes. Some thought has to be given to the benefits to be gained from increasing the labor cost by 2% before that is adopted as practice. More reporting does not necessarily guarantee accurate reporting. Experience has shown that often the individual times reported by operators for individual jobs do not agree with the times actually observed. When that happens the sought-for detailed accuracy is lacking.

The variances that come from the condition when one operator does several different processing steps on several products can be examined in much the same way as an operator doing the same process to several products. Benefits expected to be gained from detailed reporting should be evaluated against the value of striving for precision and the real probability of achieving it.

Job Order Estimates

Job order estimates are somewhat similar to standard costs. They indicate the cost of both the estimated labor and material expected to be used in the completion of the job. As in the case of standard cost, job order estimates may be based on engineered standards and fixed recipes and formulas. In the case of a job order estimate, however, one estimate is generally made for each job and it may be used again only if that same job is repeated. Costs are recorded by job order and actual costs and the estimated costs are easily compared for each job order.

The format for job order estimates might follow the format shown in Figures 5-2 and 5-3—the format used for standard costs. The job estimate would show the customer and the order number, the product, quantity and all other important data. If the format followed is that used for standard costs, it could help insure that all of the materials that are needed for the job are introduced at the proper point in the process. It could also be used to specify the equipment on which the estimate was based and even permit the use of job standards, whether they be engineered standards or estimated standards. The reporting of the production time and the materials consumed for the job could be given by operation number, just as for standard costs, so that comparisons could be made in detail of the costs as they accrued. In this way, variances can be readily determined to any necessary degree.

Ratios

A variety of ratios are used for cost control. Occasionally, they are identified as indexes.

Labor performance and utilization are often measured by percentages:

1. Performance while on Standard

$$= \frac{\text{Standard Hours Produced}}{\text{Actual Hours on Standard}} \times 100$$

2. Percent Coverage by Standards

$$= \frac{\text{Actual Hours on Standard}}{\text{Total Actual Hours Worked}} \times 100$$

3. Percent Lost Time

$$= \frac{\text{Total Hours When No Work Was Done}}{\text{Total Hours Worked}} \times 100$$

4. Percent Material Handling

$$= \frac{\text{Total Material Handling Hours}}{\text{Total Actual Hours Worked}} \times 100$$

CASE IN POINT

Figure 5-4 is a report that employs those labor percentages. It represents a housewares factory. The material handling item is reported regularly because it is such an important part of the costs of that operation and it is a cost that adds no value to the product.

An index is also shown in Figure 5-4. Frequently an index is a simple ratio rather than a percentage. The index in Figure 5-4 is called Cost Per Standard Dollar (CPSD). For this particular company this index is used to add to the labor that is covered by standards, the labor that is not covered by standards. If the CPSD is $1.10, that means that the total labor in the plant can be calculated by multiplying the labor that is covered by standards by $1.10. If the total labor covered by standards costs $2,000 per week, the costs of all labor that is covered by standards plus that not covered by standards would be $2,000 x $1.10 CPSD or $2,200 per week. The CPSD can be applied to individual products, also. If the standard labor cost of a product is $4.15, and if the CPSD is $1.19, the total labor cost of the product can be calculated as: $4.15 x $1.19 CPSD = $4.94.

By showing consecutive weeks, the report (Figure 5-4) facilitates comparison of data on a week-to-week basis. Progress or lack of progress can be seen easily. For example, the low coverage with standards of 60% is very visible. It is easy to see that unmeasured hours are split fairly evenly between direct and indirect labor. Coverage to such a low degree signifies loss of the control that could be supplied by standards. Even though it may be not practical to be precise, nonrepetitive labor such as setup and material handling can both be covered with good, useful standards. The setup labor is especially important because of its use in calculating economical order quantities used for inventory control. To help in understanding the data in Figure 5-4, the source and derivation of the information in all of the columns has been shown in the body.

Some labor performance reports have been found to contain numerous breakdowns. The additional breakdowns have been provided in an attempt to itemize all the possible causes for lost time and for indirect labor. The objective is commendable; an attempt is being made to provide guidance toward better control of costs. Unfortunately, the activity is self-defeating. A single report may contain so much information that it is difficult to read or it takes a great deal of effort to read. When that happens, it is skimmed or may not be read at all.

Other undesirable conditions have been observed relative to performance reports. Sometimes more effort is put into the preparation or discussion of the reports than in using them for controlling and reducing costs. Reports do not represent the objectives themselves. Emphasis must be placed on cost control and reduction not on the preparation of reports.

When the coverage is low as shown in Figure 5-4, in the 60% range in this particular case, it is very often found that the measured hours worked are not reported to be as large as they actually are. The effect of such reporting is to reduce the number by which the measured hours produced is divided to obtain the performance while on standard. If the measured hours worked are reported to be smaller than they actually are, then the performance is misleadingly reported to be higher than it actually is. For example: Assume an eight-hour day, four hours actually spent on measured work, four hours on unmeasured. During the four hours spent on measured work 3.85 hours of standard work was produced. The condition really should be decribed:

$$\frac{3.85 \text{ Standard Hours Earned}}{4.00 \text{ Hours Worked on Standard}} = 96\% \text{ Performance}$$

$$\frac{4.00 \text{ Hours Worked on Standard}}{8.00 \text{ Total Hours Worked}} = 50\% \text{ Coverage}$$

If the report showed 3.5 hours on measured work, 4.5 on unmeasured, the condition would be described:

$$\frac{3.85 \text{ Standard Hours Earned}}{3.50 \text{ Hours Worked on Standard}} = 110\% \text{ Performance}$$

$$\frac{3.5 \text{ Hours Worked on Standard}}{8.0 \text{ Total Hours Worked}} = 44\% \text{ Coverage}$$

HOUSEHOLD WARES - MANUFACTURE, FINISHING AND ASSEMBLY

Department ___Total Plant___

Week Ending	Unmeasured Hours					Lost Time (No Work)	Measured Hours	
	Direct Labor		Indirect Labor					
	Setup	Day Work	Material Handling	Other	Total		Worked	Produced
	A	B	C	D	E	F	G	H
8/11	98.5	473.8	602.1	1,030.5	2,204.9	113.0	4,259.4	4,582.1
8/18	107.3	241.2	500.1	909.8	1,758.4	178.7	3,775.2	4,568.0
8/25	141.3	580.5	637.2	713.3	2,072.3	202.4	4,052.4	4,800.5
Source of Data	From Employees' Production Cards				Columns A + B + C + D		From Employees' Production Cards	Calculated by payroll from production count

Cost Per Standard Dollar $= \dfrac{\text{Total Hours Paid}}{\text{Total Hours of Work Produced}}$

FIGURE 5-4

The improper reporting is especially important if the operator is working on an incentive. The solution is to increase work measurement coverage so that the labor costs can be kept under control.

Ratios are also used in determining performance in the use of material.

In a small gray iron foundry where the mix of purchased materials does not vary greatly, a material-price variance is used to determine performance in the use of materials. The material-price variance is derived:

$$\frac{\text{Estimated Cost Prices x Actual Quantities of Materials Used During the Month}}{\text{Actual Cost Prices x Actual Quantities of Materials Used During the Month}}$$

Both the numerator and the denominator are the sums of the individual calculations for each material used. This index is an accurate indicator, properly weighted by quantities, of the estimated vs. actual prices. The index can be modified to cover both the money spent and the yields:

LABOR PERFORMANCE REPORT

Operation:_____All_____

Total Hours Worked	Bonus Hours Earned	Percent					Cost Per Standard Dollar
		Performance While On Standard	Coverage	Lost Time	Material Handling	
I	J	K	L	M	N	O
6,577.3	322.7	107.6	64.8	1.7	9.2	$1.11
5,712.3	792.8	120.7	66.1	3.1	8.8	$1.11
6,327.1	748.1	118.5	64.0	3.2	10.1	$1.11
From Employees' Production Cards	Column H - G	Column H ÷ G x100	Column G ÷ I x100	Column F ÷ I x100	Column C ÷ I x100	See Below

$$= \frac{\text{Column I + J}}{\text{Column H} + 0.75^* \text{ (Column E)}}$$
* Unmeasured work is assumed to be 75% productive

FIGURE 5-4 (continued)

$$\frac{\text{Estimated Cost Prices x Standard Quantities Used During the Month}}{\text{Actual Cost Prices x Actual Quantities Used During the Month}}$$

It might be argued that putting both material costs and yields into one index will obscure the separate effects of each. The response to that is that if the magnitude of each individual factor, price and yield is important, it should be treated individually; both prices and yields should be considered, rather than prices alone.

A more refined measurement of material costs is shown in Figure 5-5 where the raw material analysis form for the month, and for six months, reports dollar variances for:
— Raw material price variances
— Raw material yield variances
— Product yield variances
— Other raw material with tools given for the results of all four.
The data shown in Figure 5-5 is for a company manufacturing confections. The

MANUFACTURING COST PERFORMANCE REPORT

DIVISION: ___CONFECTION___   PLANT: _____

SCHEDULE B- RAW MATERIALS ANALYSIS

MONTH: August DOLLAR VARIANCE (a)	COST ITEM	EIGHT MONTHS DOLLAR VARIANCE (a)
$ 3,000 (b)	RAW MATERIAL PRICE VARIANCES	$ 20,900 (b)
(600) (c)	RAW MATERIAL YIELD VARIANCES	4,600 (c)
(3,200) (d)	PRODUCT YIELD VARIANCES	(9,200) (d)
(3,500) (e)	OTHER RAW MATERIAL VARIANCES	3,300 (e)
$ (4,300)	NET VARIANCES - SCHEDULE A	$ 19,600

(a)   VARIANCE - ACTUAL OVER STANDARD IN BRACKETS

(b)   DETAILS IN SCHEDULE D-1

(c)   DETAILS IN SCHEDULE D-2

(d)   DETAILS IN SCHEDULE D-3

(e)   DETAILS IN SCHEDULE D-4

FIGURE 5-5

format would be very suitable to other companies where material costs per unit are more important than the labor costs.

When it comes to ratios, percentages and indices, variances are sometimes shown differently from the methods discussed earlier. The differences occur because these measurements are fractions: two items have already been compared by means of the arithmetical procedure of division.

An illustration might clarify this. Suppose a target for labor performance is established at 100%. Suppose the actual performance is found to be 80% using engineered labor standards. When the actual performance reaches 100%, the change can be thought of in two different ways. In one way:

                    100% Actually achieved now
          Less: 80% Actually found earlier
    Results in: 20% Actual improvements

Looking at it another way:

                    Starting Performance   80%
                    Improvement   20%
                    To Reach a Performance of 100%

$$\frac{20\% \text{ Improvement}}{80\% \text{ Start}} = 25\% \text{ Improvement over starting performance of } 80\%$$

To determine which is the correct way of looking at it:

@ 80% Performance the labor costs were:

$\frac{100\%}{80\%}$ = 125%, or 1.25 of what they should have been.

@ 100% Performance the labor costs are what they should be:

25% Lower than they were

This came about because the original 80% performance was calculated:

100 Standard Hours Were Earned Based on the Quantity
Produced = 80% Performance
125 Actual Hours were Spent Producing That Quantity

The proper way of looking at variances for these types of factors is a matter of how the variances are to be used. No general rule can be given except: Remember that these factors are the result of an arithmetical division operation, and the results of that arithmetical operation have mathematical properties that differ substantially from the results of the arithmetical multiplication operation.

Budgets, standard costs, job estimates, control ratios are sometimes used independently of each other and sometimes used to support each other. When they are used to support each other, they form a unified cost control system.

Mill Operating Cost Control

A report structure that combines many of the features of budgets, standard costs and ratios is called Mill Operating Cost Control. The MOCC is directed toward control of three aspects of costs:

— Productivity
— Spending
— Yield

The program is limited primarily to controllable costs at the department head level. Such expenses as taxes, depreciation, insurance and net material cost are not included. Control of other expenses such as plant administration expenses and maintenance overhead are sometimes included but when they are, they are restricted to top levels of responsibility.

Under certain circumstances excess costs are shown even though they may not be immediately correctable by the department head. This is done when it is desirable to indicate to the top management where there are work centers with improper operating practices or improper conditions such as low work load or line balance problems.

The productivity phase measures the utilization of machines, equipment, operating crews and individual employees.

Production standards are developed on a time basis per major operating variable such as production volume or product mix. Standard hours are computed either daily or weekly, and also monthly for each cost center and compared with actual hours. This comparison is expressed as a percent performance or productivity similar to the comparisons in Figure 5-4.

The spending phase provides the basis for comparing actual costs to predetermined standard costs for each item of controllable expense in each department by cost center. The nature and extent of variances from standard direct supervisory attention to the areas where corrective action is indicated. The effectiveness of control exercised is measured in terms of Cost Per Standard Dollar or CPSD. The Cost Per Standard Dollar is the ratio of total actual costs to total standard costs, $\frac{\text{Total Actual Costs}}{\text{Total Standard Costs}}$ expressed an an index. Labor controls in the spending phase are limited to standard work force variances i.e. to instances when the actual size of the work force differs from the standard size of work force.

The yield phase provides the basis for comparing actual with standard yields for various products and operations. The yield percentages are converted into actual and standard costs of material loss and the amounts are compared to determine the dollar variances. Yield Costs Per Standard Dollar are also computed as a means of determining the effectiveness of the control exercised over the materials.

The techniques that are used to develop cost standards include:

Productivity	—	Time study
		Standard data
		Past history analysis
		Work sampling
Spending	—	Past history analysis
		Work sampling (standard forces)
		Engineered calculation
Yield	—	Past history analysis

The three performance indices that are of major interest are:

1. Productivity performance is derived by dividing the standard hours allowed by the actual hours times 100:
$$\frac{\text{Standard Hours Allowed}}{\text{Actual Hours Used}} \times 100$$

2. The Spending Cost per Standard Dollar is calculated by dividing the actual expense by the standard expense:
$$\frac{\text{Actual Expense (\$)}}{\text{Standard Expense (\$)}}$$

3. The Yield Cost Per Standard Dollar is determined by dividing the actual cost of loss by the standard cost of loss:
$$\frac{\text{Actual Cost of Loss (\$)}}{\text{Standard Cost of Loss (\$)}}$$

CASE IN POINT

A typical monthly operating cost report is shown in Figure 5-6.

The format of Figure 5-6 is very similar to that of a budget because it shows actual expense and the cost per standard dollar for the current month and the average for the year

MONTHLY OPERATING COST REPORT

MONTH OF _____September_____ 19 XX

COST CENTER _____Rolling Mill (650.0)_____

DEPARTMENT _____Rolling Mill_____

PRODUCTION

This Month _____34534_____

Year to Date _____359920_____

Units _N.T. 4-Hi Production_

ACCOUNT		ACTUAL EXPENSE	VARIANCE	COST PER STANDARD DOLLAR	
NO.	DESCRIPTION			CURRENT MONTH	AVERAGE YEAR TO DATE
110	Administrative Salaries and Wages	$ 14,294	$ -0-	$1.00	$1.00
120	Producing Labor	46,992	(2,448)	1.05	1.01
130	Service Labor	353	-0-	1.00	1.00
170	Premium Pay	860	(601)	3.32	2.60
	TOTAL LABOR	62,499	(3,049)	1.05	1.01
210	Assigned Maintenance	32,066	(3,949)	1.14	.94
220	Distributed Maintenance				
230	Refractory Materials	347	1,040	.25	.25
240	Maintenance Material	47,202	(24,647)	2.09	1.17
270	Repairs to Tools	203	-0-	1.00	1.00
280	Repairs Due to Damages				
290	Contract Work - Outside Companies	780	-0-	1.00	1.00
	TOTAL REPAIRS TO PLANT & EQUIPMENT	80,598	(27,556)	1.52	1.05
310	Gases	21,149	(1,428)	1.07	1.08
320	Liquids				
	TOTAL FUEL	21,149	(1,428)	1.07	1.08
410	Water	9,996	(1,846)	1.23	1.18
420	Steam	336	(6)	1.02	1.31
430	Cold Blast				
441	Electricity - Demand	12,873	-0-	1.00	1.00
442	Electricity - Usage	11,425	1,257	.90	.99
450	Compressed Air	889	(306)	1.52	1.61
460	Oxygen - Acetylene System	2,446	(1,536)	2.69	2.31
	TOTAL UTILITIES	37,965	(2,437)	1.07	1.08
510	Processing Supplies				
520	Chemicals and Re-agents				
530	Lubricants and Coolants	5,800	(638)	1.12	1.14

FIGURE 5-6

123

MONTHLY OPERATING COST REPORT (continued)

ACCOUNT		ACTUAL EXPENSE	VARIANCE	COST PER STANDARD DOLLAR	
NO.	DESCRIPTION			CURRENT MONTH	AVERAGE YEAR TO DATE
560	Operating Accessories	-0-	1,004		1.02
570	Small Tools and Supplies	5,025	(3,144)	2.67	.79
580	Shipping Supplies				
590	Miscellaneous Supplies	1,686	(181)	1.12	.79
	TOTAL OPER. SUPPLIES & ACCESSORIES	12,511	(2,959)	1.31	1.01
610	Property Servicing	221	358	.38	.39
620	Relocating & Re-arranging Existing Fac.				1.00
630	Transportation	2,797	(743)	1.36	1.15
640	Interdepartmental Services	2,904	573	.84	.81
650	Intradepartmental Services				
690	Purchased Services	557	(48)	1.09	1.12
	TOTAL SERVICES	6,479	140	.98	.92
720-30	General Expense	$ 107	$ -0-	$1.00	$1.00
	TOTAL CONTROLLABLE SPENDING	221,308	(37,289)	1.20	1.04
Productivity Variance			(11,148)		
	CONTROLLABLE COST ABOVE	221,308	(48,437)	1.28	1.08
Net Yield Loss		282,271	(5,884)	1.02	1.03
	TOTAL CONTROLLABLE CONVERSION COST	503,579	(54,321)	1.12	1.05

	ACTUAL EXPENSE	STATISTICS	STD.	ACT.
Maintenance Overhead	32,082			
Maintenance Sub-Standard Labor Cost	14,430	STATISTICS		
810 Works Administrative Expense	27,937			
820 Department Administrative Expense	11,949	Operating Hours	289.7	327.0
840-60 Provision for Replacement	41,283			
640 Shipping Department Expense	3,165	Productivity %	100.0	88.6
640 Inspection Department Expense	668			
870-80 Depreciation, Insurance and Taxes	88,614	Yield %	82.43	82.06
Other Uncontrollable	4,246			
		Manhours Per N.T.	.475	.500
TOTAL CONVERSION COST	727,953			
		Conversion Cost N.T.		$21.08
NET MATERIAL COST	1,577,600			
TOTAL OPERATING COST	2,305,553			

FIGURE 5-6 (continued)

124

ROLLING MILL
DAILY PRODUCTIVITY PERFORMANCE

DATE 9-2

TURN	CREW	PROCESSING			INCIDENTAL WORK			DELAYS			TOTAL		
		Act. Hrs.	Std. Hrs.	% Perf.	Act. Hrs.	Std. Hrs.	% Perf.	Act. Hrs.	Std. Hrs.	% Perf.	Act. Hrs.	Std. Hrs.	% Perf.
2-HI MILL													
A	2-3	8.00	8.63	107.9	-	-	-	-	.26	100.0	8.00	8.89	111.1
B	2-2	8.00	7.10	88.8	-	-	-	-	.21	100.0	8.00	7.31	91.4
C													
Day Total		16.00	15.73	98.3	-	-	-	-	.47	100.0	16.00	16.20	101.3
Month to Date		16.00	15.73	98.3	-	-	-	-	.47	100.0	16.00	16.20	101.3
Best Month		/////		99.7	/////		-	/////		429.3	/////		101.9
4-HI MILL													
A	4-1	8.00	6.99	87.4	-	-	-	-	.35	100.0	8.00	7.34	91.8
B	4-3	7.75	7.70	99.4	.25	.38	152.0	-	.39	100.0	8.00	8.47	105.9
C													
Day Total		15.75	14.69	93.3	.25	.38	152.0	-	.74	100.0	16.00	15.81	98.8
Month to Date		15.75	14.69	93.3	.25	.38	152.0	-	.74	100.0	16.00	15.81	98.8
Best Month		/////		102.9	/////		107.6	/////		164.8	/////		104.8
TOTAL ROLLING MILL													
Day Total		/////		95.8	4-HI ONLY		152.0	/////		100.0	/////		100.1
Month to Date		/////		95.8	4-HI ONLY		152.0	/////		100.0	/////		100.1
Best Month		/////		101.4	4-HI ONLY		107.6	/////		134.4	/////		102.4

FIGURE 5-7

to date. All of these Costs Per Standard Dollar are based on the actual production from the plant. This, in effect, is a variable budget based on activity. Figure 5-6 represents the final monthly report. The subordinate reports that are the basis for that monthly report are published daily and weekly to provide the operating people with information to be used in the control of their costs.

One of the daily reports covers labor productivity. A typical report for one department is shown in Figure 5-7. It can be seen that the information in this report is very similar to the information shown in Figure 5-4. The example here is a rolling mill department of a steel mill. In this particular case all work is covered whether it is processing or incidental. Even delays are covered by work measurement standards so that 100% of the time spent by the labor at that rolling mill is accounted for under work measurement. Figure 5-8 shows a summary of all of the production departments of the steel mill.

In the process industries, which include steel mills and chemical plants, the maintenance departments represent sizable portions of the labor employed. Therefore, control of the performance of maintenance labor is important. Figure 5-9 shows a weekly performance report for the maintenance department. Again, it can be seen that the format is similar to that employed in Figures 5-4 and 5-7. The weekly maintenance productivity

DAILY PRODUCTIVITY REPORT

EQUIPMENT OR WORK GROUP	PERCENT OF PRODUCTIVITY							
	DAY			MONTH TO DATE			BEST MONTH	
	Melting	Delay	Total	Melting	Delay	Total	%	Mo. & Yr.
COKE OVENS								
BLAST FURNACE								
OPEN HEARTH								
Furnace No. 1							103.0	8-75
Furnace No. 2	96.7	104.5	97.5	95.6	116.9	97.6	108.5	7-76
Furnace No. 3							108.9	6-76
Furnace No. 4	110.6	150.9	113.4	109.6	154.4	112.7	105.0	4-75
Furnace No. 5	100.9	125.6	103.2	96.0	133.6	97.7	107.6	2-76
Total Open Hearth	103.5	127.2	105.5	97.9	119.8	99.9	105.3	2-76

EQUIPMENT OR WORK GROUP	A Turn	B Turn	C Turn	Total	Proc.	Incid. Work	Delay	Total		
ROLLING										
Rolling Mill	88.3	79.0	Down	83.6	75.5	108.8	31.1	69.6	102.4	4-76
Rod Mill										
E. W. PIPE MILLS										
No. 1 Welding	28.5	63.4	60.5	50.8	101.8	72.0	21.2	55.0	81.2	12-75
No. 1 Cutoff & Threading	55.9	42.1	73.8	57.3	86.3	77.4	24.1	71.2	81.9	8-76
No. 1 Testing	87.0	69.3	107.6	88.0	84.2	80.9	35.3	69.9	63.7	6-76
No. 2 Welding & Stretch Reducing	115.8	36.3	72.1	74.7	82.8	60.7	56.3	75.1	79.5	7-76
Tubing Cutoff & Threading	Down	72.6	70.9	71.7	70.1	-	65.7	69.5	71.2	3-76
No. 2 Cutoff	65.3	62.4	47.7	57.7	81.2	71.4	63.3	79.8	71.9	9-76
No. 2 Threading	Down	Down	Down		67.4	72.0	75.8	68.0	72.3	9-76
No. 2 Testing	70.9	78.6	75.5	75.8	80.0	97.7	62.8	77.0	73.8	9-76
Std. Pipe Finishing										
Roll Shop	-	-	-	65.8	-	-	-	62.0	63.3	9-76
SPIRAL WELD PIPE MILL										
Manufacturing										
Finishing										
CAST IRON PIPE FOUNDRY										
Pipe Casting	Down	84.3	87.3	35.8	85.3		82.2	85.0	87.2	1-76
Cement Lining	Down	97.0	96.4	96.7	98.4		59.0	93.1	102.6	6-76
Core Making	Down	72.2	67.4	69.8	94.9		19.3	.65.2	67.9	6-76
Ingot Mold Foundry	Down	91.8	Down	91.8	94.0		77.2	92.0	93.7	3-76

FIGURE 5-8

126

SHIPPING & SERVICES										
Gentry Cranes	55.8	63.3	70.5	63.4	64.9		66.8	65.1	˙68.4	4-76
Fork Trucks	Nonstandard Operation									
Ross Casters	Nonstandard Operation									
C.I. Pipe Loco. Crane	Down	85.3	74.2	82.0	75.2	86.3	68.9	75.8	71.0	9-76
Warehouse										
Switch Engines	-	-	-	54.3	-	-	-	60.3		
Loco. Cranes										
MINING & BENEF										
Mining & Loading	Down	73.4	Down	73.4	74.6		54.6	71.8	73.8	8-76
Hauling	Down	81.4	Down	81.4	91.9		33.9	82.3	81.8	8-76
Primary Treating & Milling	Down	91.1	Down	91.1	90.0		34.1	77.6	83.8	8-76
Calcining Plant	121.3	106.3	126.9	118.1	82.2		119.7	89.2	95.0	3-76
Sintering Plant	Nonstandard Operation			Major	Changes	in	raw	materials		

FIGURE 5-8 continued

MONTHLY MAINTENANCE PRODUCTIVITY REPORT

DEPT.		PERCENT OF PRODUCTIVITY						
NO.	AREA OR CRAFT	REFERENCE		PREVIOUS	CURRENT MONTH		BEST MONTH	
		%	Mo. & Yr.	MONTH %	%	No. of Empl.	%	Mo. & Yr.
MECHANICAL MAINTENANCE								
241.0	Machine Shop	56.3	Dec. '75	67.8	71.7	39	73.1	Apr. '76
241.2	Tool Grinding	58.8	Dec. '75	85.3	81.6	10	85.7	Jun. '76
244.1	Mechanical Repair	31.0	Jan. '76	59.4	58.9	46	59.4	Aug. '76
245.1	Fabrication - Shop Work	61.0	Jan, '76	86.5	77.9	24	89.4	Apr. '76
	- Field Work	36.2	Dec. '75	100.9	93.2	11	100.9	Aug. '76
ELECTRICAL MAINTENANCE								
251.0	Central Electrical and							
252.1	Motor Inspection	42.0	May '76	93.3	96.4	29	96.4	Sept. '76
253.0	Armature Shop	71.5	Apr. '76	77.0	83.8	10	89.2	Jul. '76
MASONRY								
281.0	Brick Masons	75.7	Oct. '75	108.3	109.3	17	119.0	Apr. '76
282.0	Mason Laborers	68.6	Oct. '75	106.1	102.6	54	109.0	Apr. '76
283.1	Carpenters	74.3	May '76	115.8	115.9	17	115.9	Sept. '76

FIGURE 5-10

WEEKLY PERFORMANCE REPORT
MECHANICAL MAINTENANCE DEPARTMENT
MECHANICAL REPAIR
CRAFT: MILLWRIGHTS (244.1)

WEEK ENDING	EQUIVA- LENT NO. OF EMPLOY- EES 2 + 4 HR.	TOTAL HOURS WORKED THIS WEEK	HOURS FROM PREVI- OUS WEEKS	HOURS TO NEXT WEEK	ACTUAL LOST TIME HOURS	HOURS ON COMPLETED JOBS (2 + 3) - (4 + 5)	ALLOWED LOST TIME HOURS	HOURS ON UN- MEASURED WORK	HOURS ON MEASURED WORK - 8	STANDARD HOURS PRODUCED	% COVERAGE (9 ÷ 6)	% PERFORM. ON MEASURED WORK (10 ÷ 9)	% PERFORM. OVERALL (8 x 12) * (10 + 7) (5 + 6)
CC L. NO.	1	2	3	4	5	6	7	8	9	10	11	12	13
8- 3	35	1393.0	1259.6	1228.5	30.6	1393.5	1.1	1213.1	180.4	90.4	12.9	52.1	51.0
8-10	31	1253.5	1228.5	1106.5	52.2	1323.3	3.0	1018.0	305.3	217.2	23.1	71.1	68.6
8-17	34	1345.5	1106.5	966.2	38.2	1447.6	9.4	1296.1	151.5	90.5	10.5	59.7	58.8
8-24	47	1883.0	966.2	1137.6	32.7	1678.9	1.3	1281.4	397.5	226.6	23.7	57.0	56.0
8-31	50	2000.3	1137.6	1092.9	60.3	1984.7	12.4	1255.0	729.7	369.9	36.8	50.7	49.8
9- 7	45	1789.0	1092.9	1210.2	51.5	1620.2	9.7	1381.2	239.0	116.3	14.8	48.7	47.8
9-14	38	1504.0	1210.2	1263.5	53.4	1397.3	18.2	1197.2	200.1	131.5	14.3	65.7	64.5
9-21	50	1984.0	1263.5	1185.9	60.3	2001.3	21.0	1601.1	400.2	301.3	20.0	75.3	74.1
9-28	50	2015.0	1185.9	877.2	77.3	2246.4	33.3	1896.0	350.4	229.4	15.6	65.5	64.8
10- 3	55	2187.8	877.2	1004.4	96.2	1964.4	33.5	1562.4	402.0	274.1	20.5	68.2	66.6
10-12	51	2021.8	1004.4	1079.8	66.4	1880.0	20.5	1444.6	435.4	330.4	23.2	75.9	74.4

Sampling - Jan.

Based on Work

$$*\frac{(8 \times 12) + (10 + 7)}{(5 + 6)}$$

FIGURE 5-9

TOTAL WORKS COST PERFORMANCE SUMMARY

DEPARTMENT	CONVERSION COST		VARIANCE				VARIANCE MATERIAL LOSS		OVERALL COST PER STANDARD DOLLAR	NET GAIN OR (LOSS) FROM REFERENCE	
			SPENDING		PRODUCTIVITY						
	TOTAL	CONTROL	C.P. S.D.	AMOUNT	% PERF	AMOUNT	C.P. S.D.	AMOUNT		THIS MONTH	CUMMULATIVE TO DATE
Open Hearth	$ 816,246	500,828	.99	$ 2,119	98.6	$(1,569)	1.09	$(16,007)	$1.03	$ 48,624	$ 905,771
Rolling Mill	727,953	503,579	1.20	(37,289)	88.6	(11,148)	1.02	(5,885)	1.12	35,971	1,088,015
E.W. Steel Pipe Mills	1,804,393	980,002	1.14	(70,457)	73.8	(85,838)	1.08	(30,262)	1.24	110,642	437,448
Spiral Weld Pipe Mill											
Coke Ovens & Coal Chem.										Reference Not Yet Established	
Blast Furnace	188,451	153,971	1.12	(16,931)	-	Not Covered	-	Not Covered	1.12		
Cast Iron Foundries	369,020	216,198	1.12	(18,519)	30.2	(17,327)	1.46	(15,580)	1.31	(4,951)	101,166
Shipping	231,752	132,736	1.05	(5,975)	64.4	(14,306)	-	-	1.18	25,870	384,672
Ore Operations	515,079	263,768	1.00	(33)	81.6	(28,523)	-	(2,061)	1.13	9,337	31,543
Coal Mines											
Utilities											
Mechanical Maintenance*	330,047	239,012	1.09	(10,766)	82.4	(20,008)	-	-	1.15	35,332	237,146
Electrical Maintenance*	122,885	90,825	.94	3,293	100.3	(13)	-	-	.97	19,663	79,845
Mobile Equipment Shop											
Yards & Roads											
Transportation											
Masonry*	81,460	60,931	1.55	(2,130)	106.9	3,476	-	-	.98	16,787	107,305
Inspection											
Combustion & Instruments											
DEPARTMENT TOTALS	$4,652,894	$2,751,082	1.09	(147,085)	80.7	(158,711)	1.08	(69,794)	1.16	225,583	2,948,615
Additional Controllable - Plant											
TOTAL PLANT CONTROLLABLE		$2,751,082	1.09	(147,085)	80.7	(158,711)	1.08	(69,794)	1.16	225,493	2,948,615

*The amounts in these departments are not included in the total because they are reflected in other departments.

FIGURE 5-11

reports are summarized monthly and a typical monthly report is shown in Figure 5-10. Notice that all of the values are "percent of productivity."

The preparation of the monthly operating cost report, Figure 5-6, has its sources in detailed reports that cover cost trends and cost performance as well as the productivity values previously shown. The available data serves as the basis for converting productivity and other phases into total costs in terms of dollars and the result is typified in the cost performance summary shown in Figure 5-11. It should be noted that the report format emphasizes the variances and only three variances are reported for each department: spending, productivity, material loss. It should be noted that the report coverage is plant-wide. The reported variances are related to the phases that we are interested in: spending, productivity, and yield or material loss. This report is designed to call attention to those areas where attention should be given. In other words, the report avoids giving more information than can be easily digested.

Each department can see whether its losses are primarily related to spending, productivity or yield. In the case of the rolling mill, it can be seen that the spending variance is the most important of the three. In the case of the steel pipe mills, productivity is the most important variance with spending second. Material loss is not as important for either one of the two departments. The *variance* for productivity exceeds $158,000 and the

STANDARDS IMPROVEMENT CREDIT

April, 19XX

DEPARTMENT	MOCC PHASE			MONTHLY TOTAL	CUMULATIVE TO DATE
	PRODUCT	MAT'L. LOSS	SPENDING		
Open Hearth	$ 8,965	$ -	$ 3,200	$12,165	$ 89,640
Rolling Mill	12,032	$ 2,029	-	14,061	92,630
E.W. Pipe Mills	9,643	4,320	1,862	15,825	74,960
Spiral Weld Pipe Mill	-	-	-	-	-
Coke Ovens & Coal Chem.	-	-	-	-	-
Blast Furnace	-	-	-	-	-
Cast Iron Foundries	1,642	2,032	2,973	6,647	54,730
Shipping (incl. Yards & Roads & Transportation)	4,690	-	1,800	6,490	38,408
Ore Mining & Benef.	2,893	-	3,200	6,093	41,690
Coal Mines	-	-	-	-	-
Utilities	-	-	2,106	2,106	9,062
Mechanical Maintenance	3,460	-	892	4,352	19,640
Electrical Maintenance	4,167	-	-	4,167	13,841
Masonry	2,640	-	563	3,203	9,327
Inspection	-	-	-	-	-
Combustion & Instruments	-	-	-	-	-
TOTAL	$ 50,132	$ 8,381	$ 16,596	$ 75,109	$443,928

NOTE: Each project will receive twelve months credit only but this credit will continue permanently in the cumulative to date column.

FIGURE 5-12

variance for spending exceeds $147,000 and those two items are out of a *total controllable cost* valued at $2,751,082. The two important variances represent about 10% of the total controllable costs.

The controllable costs are only part of the total conversion cost, but only the items that are controllable are examined.

Figure 5-12 shows a report on the efforts of the various departments to reduce their costs and again it is noticed that most of the effort is put in the productivity and in the spending phases rather than in the material loss phase. Figure 5-13 shows how the yields are reported. The comparison between the actual yields and the standard yields is clearly shown separately from the details. The details for the losses are shown at the bottom half of the report. The reports, all of them in this MOCC structure, have been designed to display a maximum of necessary information in a form that can be read with a minimum of effort.

The monthly operating cost report, (Figure 5-6), highlights the actual expenses and the variance from standards. The Cost Per Standard Dollar values for the current month

ROLLING MILL YIELD STATISTICS
YIELD SUMMARY
MONTH OF SEPTEMBER, 19XX

DESCRIPTION	ACTUAL	STANDARD	VARIANCE
Ingots to 2 Hi Mill (tons)	42,086	42,086	-0-
Material Loss (tons)	7,552	7,395	(157)
Prime Skelp (tons)	34,534	34,691	(157)
% Yield	82.06%	82.43%	(.37)%
Net Material Loss ($)	$282,271	$276,387	$(5,884)
C.P.S.D.	$ 1.02	$ 1.00	$(.02)

MATERIAL LOSS DETAIL

CLASSIFICATION	MATERIAL LOSS			SALVAGE CREDIT			NET
	TONS	COST PER TON	AMOUNT	TONS	VALUE PER TON	AMOUNT	ACTUAL MATERIAL LOSS
Rejected Coils	159	$ 66.76	$ 10,615	159	$ 18.00	$ 2,862	$ 7,753
Scrap	5,940	53.74	319,216	5,940	18.00	106,920	212,296
Scale	1,442	53.74	77,493	1,442	11.00	15,862	61,631
Other	11	53.74	591	-0-		-0-	591
TOTAL	7,552	$54.01	$407,915	7,541	$16.66	$125,644	$282,271

	Month	YEAR TO DATE
% Reject Coils	.46%	.61%

FIGURE 5-13

and for the average year to date are also shown for one rolling mill of the plant. It can be seen that the important variances stand out immediately. The most important variance obviously is for the maintenance materials. It is in excess of $24,000 and the current Cost Per Standard Dollar becomes 2.09. There is an even higher Cost Per Standard Dollar, 2.67, for small tools and supplies, but that variance is $3,000 compared to the $24,000 for maintenance materials. There is also a variance of $2,000 in producing labor, but that is less than 10% of the maintenance materials variance. The final result of that operating cost report is to develop a standard cost per net ton, and for the rolling mill that is $21 per net ton. This, of course, is the one single figure that informs top management whether the costs in that operation are under control or are not.

Cost control reports merely provide a base for cost control. The control of costs comes from application of the information contained in the reports.

USE THE CONTROL REPORTS TO SHOW WHERE TO REDUCE COSTS

Management's real job is cost reduction. And, as each reduction is achieved, the next one must be sought. The question is: Where to seek it? The answer is: Where the greatest potential is.

As mentioned earlier in the chapter, the greatest potential lies in the largest single cluster of costs. The word "cluster" is used here to describe a class of costs that might be approached for cost reduction through a common method or a common class of methods.

A typical cluster of costs might be purchased materials. This cluster can be divided further. For some types of products such as food, beauty and health care items, useful subdivisions are raw materials and packaging materials. Reduction in the costs of raw materials can be sought through:

— Value analysis
— Yields
— Quantity-price breaks

Reduction in costs of packaging materials can be sought through:

— Redesign of packages to utilize cheaper materials
— Reduction in the variety of packaging components and package sizes
— Quantity-price breaks

Reduction of labor costs might be approached by considering all manual assembly operations or all material handling operations, or all machining operations as a single cluster. Cost reduction can be sought through:

— Work simplification
— Mechanical aids
— Automation

Cost reduction programs begin with evaluation. The first evaluation is related to identification of the area of highest potential. The second evaluation is related to the cost of realizing the potential as compared to the value of the potential expected to be realized. The latter evaluation has some traps to be avoided, especially in using the reports to evaluate the expected benefits. For example, evaluation of the benefits expected from the use of highly automated equipment must consider the costs of setups and changeovers as well as the unit cost expected from the use of the equipment. Experience shows that the costs of setups and changeovers are often slighted or even overlooked because of the construction of cost control reports. In those reports, the costs of setup and changeover labor are frequently reported separately from the costs of operating labor, and therefore are not thought of as being related.

Returning to the first principle of a cost reduction program, identification of the areas of highest potential, two procedures may be used with a high degree of effectiveness. One procedure employs the cost profile mentioned earlier. The other uses a process chart.

Put the Cost Profile to Work

In Table 5-4, it was shown that ten cost elements, or clusters, represented 75% of the total costs of the plant. These ten elements are excellent candidates for a cost reduction program. A cost reduction program can be set up by assigning one item each to ten individuals or teams. A program can also be established by assigning all ten, or the five highest valued items of the ten, to a special task force. There is no need to look for the place to start activity; that place has been identified by the cost profile. All efforts can now be directed toward achieving the reductions.

Tracking of achievements can also be done through the cost profile. As cost elements are reduced in value, the cost profile can be revised. In fact, a competition can be set up directed toward lowering the position in the cost profile of individual cost elements. Reducing the cost of an element so that it moves from third to fourth position means that more effective work had been done on the element that moved down rather than on the one that moved up. When the program results in an important revision of the cost profile, the revised cost profile should be used for establishing a new program. In that way, attention will continue to be focused on the most important elements. Cost profiles identify clusters of costs; they do not provide any indication of how the costs are accumulated. A process chart can be used for that purpose.

USE PROCESS CHARTS TO IDENTIFY SOURCES OF COSTS

A process chart can be established from personal knowledge or from standard cost formats. The use of standard cost formats is beneficial because it helps insure that generally accepted values for individual cost elements are being entered into the evaluation of costs versus benefits.

A cost reduction program based on process charts can proceed toward any of several ends. It might be directed toward a single product, to try to increase its profitability or to convert an unprofitable product into a profitable one. Or, it might involve a group of products with similar processing. The same procedure is used in all cases.

A combination process chart and cost sheet was shown in Figure 5-14. It is not important which was in existence first, the process chart or the cost sheet. They are both needed for this procedure. It must be certain that all processing steps are shown and that they are shown in the actual sequence used to produce the product. All the processing steps, and materials added at each, must be shown to account for the total costs. The proper sequence must be shown to account for the accumulation of costs as the processing is carried out.

The accumulation of costs is necessary for placing a value on the product at each step of the process. This information can be used for evaluating the cost of reworking versus the cost of losing a product at any stage. It can also identify where in the processing special care must be taken to avoid losing a product, and how much can be properly spent on providing the special care.

PROCESS CHART   **PARTS FABRICATION**

Raw Material Inventory

Move
Operation #1
Machine
Move
Inspect

Move
Operation #2
Degrease and Plate
Move
Inspect

Move
Operation #3
Polish
Move
Inspect
Move
Parts Inventory

Cost Breakdown Sheet

Operation Number	Costs			
	Labor		Material	
	At Operation	Cumulative	At Operation	Cumulative
1.	$2.16	$2.16	$ .47	$ .47
2.	$ .75	$2.91	$ .003	$ .473
3.	$2.96	$5.87	- - - - - -	$ .473

Total Labor and Material: $6.343

FIGURE 5-14

Cost Breakdown Sheet

Operation Number	Labor At Operation	Labor Cumulative	Material At Operation	Material Cumulative
1.	.54	.54		
A.			.57	
B.			.12	
C.			1.34	
			2.03	2.03
2.	1.53	2.07		
D.			9.53	
E.			.16	
			9.69	11.72
3.	1.36	3.43	- - - - -	11.72
4.	.84	4.27		
F.			.18	
G.			.23	
H.			2.61	
I.			.19	
			3.21	14.93

Total- Labor and Material: $19.20

FIGURE 5-14 CONTINUED

ASSEMBLY

Process Chart

In Figure 5-14 two interesting considerations are shown. The process chart for the part fabrication shows three inspections, but the costs of the inspections don't appear on the cost breakdown sheet. That happens because inspection is an indirect cost and is generally not measured. Three inspections seem to be excessive, although certainly the piece should be inspected before the expensive polishing operation is performed. The cost of the inspection operations should be taken into account. This can be done without too much difficulty. Inspection is an operation that can be measured just as all other operations are measured, even though inspection is an indirect operation.

The assembly process has a similar condition; the first three operations consist of assembling and adjusting. The cost of handling between the three operations has been considered as indirect work, and is not shown on the cost sheet. If the first two assemblies could be combined, one handling could be eliminated. Returning to the piece part fabrication, elimination of one inspection operation would also eliminate one handling. One question that should be answered for these process charts, and for all process charts, is the value of indirect labor operations not normally shown in cost breakdowns.

After the process charts and cost breakdowns have been prepared, the procedure is the same as for cost profiles. The first step is identification of the area of highest value. This might be found to be either material or labor. If it is labor, it might be either direct or indirect.

For the piece part, the operation showing highest direct labor cost is polishing, the next is machining. For the assembly, the second assembly operation is the costliest—direct labor operation. As an alternative, the first and second assembly operations might be considered as one operation with the appropriate value given to the material handling cost now required because of two separate operations. Regarding material, Component D has the highest cost. If indirect labor is insignificant compared to the direct labor, the second assembly operation is the place to start.

The second step in the cost reduction program remains the same as described earlier. It consists of a comparison of the cost of achieving the reduction as compared to the value of the reduction in production costs that are expected.

It should be obvious by this time that one basic difference among cost reduction programs is the method used for identifying the cost elements. After that is done, the next difference is to whom the responsibility for results is assigned. It can be assigned to a group for several projects, or for one major one. Smaller projects can be assigned to individuals. To get results, specific projects must be assigned with definite objectives, especially time objectives. A program has value only if there is clear understanding about:

— What is going to be done
— When is it to be done
— Who is going to do it

NOW, PUT IT ALL TOGETHER

For either cost control or cost reduction activities, the relative significance of a cost is more important than whether it represents a labor cost or a material cost. The construction of a cost profile will provide objective information about the significance of individual cost clusters. It does this by ranking them in descending order of value. The most important costs are immediately highlighted.

Another important consideration is whether or not the cost item is controllable. Cost control and cost reduction efforts should be focused only on controllable costs. Calling attention to uncontrollable costs results in wasted time and loss of attention to controllable costs.

Cost control programs use formal report structures to identify targets and variances. Targets may be budgets, standard costs, job estimates or control ratios. Variances provide information about the differences between target conditions and actual conditions. Both unfavorable and favorable variances provide useful information. Unfavorable variances identify situations where something is wrong and needs to be corrected. Favorable variances identify situations where something is right and should be extended.

Management's real job is cost reduction. Cost profiles and process charts are two formal analyses that show where to focus cost reduction efforts. In all cost control and reduction programs, care must be taken to put effort toward realizing opportunities according to the value of the opportunity versus the cost of realizing it. After all the alternatives have been examined and decisions have been made as to where to focus effort, an organized cost reduction program should be established. For best results the program should have clear understanding about:

— What is going to be done
  • Get the facts
  • Determine alternatives
  • Evaluate alternatives
  • Implement the selected alternatives
— When is each action going to be done
— Who is going to take each action

This approach to a cost reduction program puts it all together: *an organized method for examining data to identify where and how to focus control.*

Chapter 6

Recognizing Your Manufacturing Potentials

and Limitations

It is often difficult to state the capacity of equipment or a production system in precise, specific terms. This is true because the capacity is affected by many factors, each of which is variable to some degree:

— The behavior of the equipment.
— The characteristics of the material being introduced into the equipment.
— Operator skill and/or motivation.
— Temperature and humidity.

These same factors are also the sources of bottlenecks, because a bottleneck occurs when some factor prevents the anticipated capacity from being reached.

The resulting situation, because it is somewhat complicated, requires a thorough analysis for good understanding. The analysis is needed for the establishment of capacity values and for the identification of the causes of bottlenecks, so that the bottlenecks can be properly attacked. It sometimes happens that an action taken to relieve a bottleneck brings undesirable rather than beneficial results. On the other hand, it has been observed that persistent bottlenecks have been broken with ease after the real cause has been identified.

CLEARLY STATE THE CAPACITY VALUES

Care must be taken in discussions of manufacturing bottlenecks to ensure common understanding of the terms used. In describing the operating levels of man/machine/process the terms most often used are those related to capability and capacity. Capability is generally defined as the *theoretical* maximum output or volume, expressed in appropriate units of measure. Capacity is generally defined as the *actual* quantity that can be produced. To be more specific:

— Theoretical Capability: The producing rate per unit of time beyond which the machine or component or process fails or yields reduced benefits. The most common example is the situation in which the mechanical strength of a device is the limiting factor. Other situations in which reduced benefits occur are when increasing the cutting tool speed produces a rough surface that cannot be economically worked further or of the type, in chemical production, where increasing the temperature or pressure has adverse effects on process yield, rather than beneficial effects.

— Rated Capacity: The maximum rate per unit of time at which the machine or process may be operated as a practical producing system without endangering the operator, the equipment or the quality. The rated capacity is established from equipment manufacturers' warranties or from statistical quality control analyses of actual results.

— Deployed Capacity: The rate of output per unit of time, after allowances have been applied for personnel considerations, planned downtime for cyclical maintenance, tool and product changes and policy time.

The differences between these three values are the reserves, with two commonly used terms:

— Critical Reserve: The difference between the theoretical capability and the rated capacity. The availability for use of this reserve is a matter for careful consideration. Its use provides opportunities for unsafe conditions for personnel, excessive damage to equipment with the probability of accelerated replacement, and reduced product yields. Opportunities for improvement are generally difficult to find, or require radical changes for realization.

— Employable Reserve: The difference between rated capacity and deployed capacity. This reserve is generally considered to be available for unexpected demand peaks, for adjusting line balances and for overcoming temporary raw material outages. If the deployed capacity has been established after careful examination of all of the allowances, this reserve should be used only for emergencies and with caution. On the other hand, experience shows that this reserve frequently has opportunities for improvement to be realized by changing the conditions on which the allowances are based.

A summary of the relationships among capability, capacities and reserves is shown in Figure 6-1. The percentages shown begin with the theoretical capability established at the 100% level. The other percentages are based on experience with a variety of companies and industries; they represent values typically found.

RECOGNIZE THE REAL DIFFERENCES BETWEEN CONTINUOUS AND BATCH OPERATIONS

In a continuous operation with all of the components balanced for throughput, the capacity of the operation is determined by the component with the lowest capacity. If

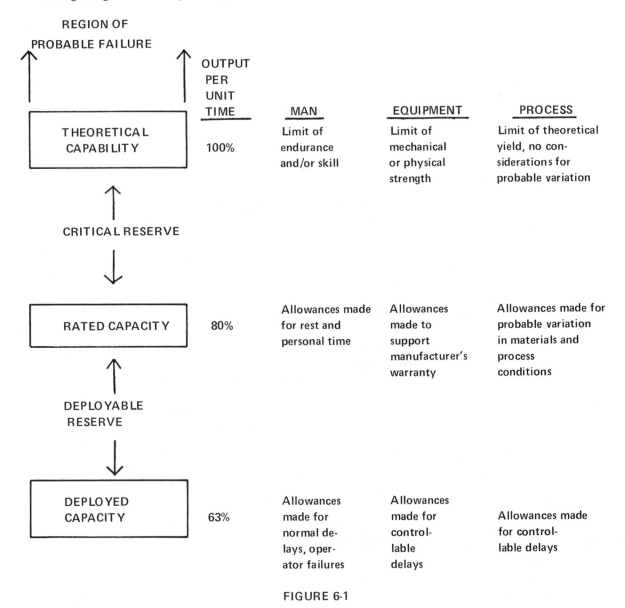

FIGURE 6-1

the capacity of that component is raised, another component becomes the limiting one. Generally, identification of the limiting component is readily made. This condition exists whether the continuous operation consists of a single structure into which the components have been assembled, or whether it consists of an assemblage of independent devices that are located adjacent to one another.

In the latter case, the differentiation between continuous and batch operation becomes vague. If single piece parts or products are continuously being processed, but are transferred from operation to operation, each single unit might be considered a batch. Generally, however, an operation is considered a batch operation if there is a pause between operating steps. It is this break in the continuity of the processing that often hinders the identification of the limiting operation. At times, the limiting factor is not a process operation or a device, but is some other characteristic of the situation. It is at this point that the problem requires thorough analysis and examination to expose its basic cause.

CASE IN POINT

The final assembly of military aircraft is a continuous operation, since a line is set up to produce a large quantity of the same product. The line is not a single structure, but rather is a series of individual operations through which the product moves progressively on its way to final assembly. Nevertheless, it is a continuous process since one product follows immediately behind another product with identical specifications. The aircraft assembly line may be thought of as a continuous process in slow motion.

For one aircraft manufacturer, overall utilization was determined to be about fifty percent of what it should have been on a practical basis. The utilization of facilities can be considered to be the same as utilization of capacity with facilities including both personnel and equipment. The cause of the poor utilization was found to be something other than personnel performance or capabilities of equipment. The source was found to be in the quality of incoming parts, the tooling, and the fact that the assembly practices had not been planned for high volume output.

The situation was corrected by taking several different steps. All drawings for parts were examined for accuracy, needed revisions were made, and actions were taken to ensure that fabricators of parts, consisting of internal departments and vendors, were working with corrected drawings. Inspection of parts received for assembly was made more rigorous.

The tooling and assembly practices had been used for construction of the prototypes. A toolmaker was assigned to the assembly department to revise, or to make recommendations for major revisions of jigs, fixtures and clamps.

The work elements of the assembly operations were analyzed and revised to reflect the high volume conditions. Job standards were installed, and performance records were initiated to provide guidance to crew chiefs for concentrated operator training.

The assembly time was reduced from four hours to two hours per unit. Considering the number of persons required during the assembly time (74 sheet metal workers, electricians and painters), the reduction amounted to a savings of 148 direct labor hours per unit assembled.

Similar conditions can arise in a single-structure, continuous operation typically found in the chemical industry. Care must be taken to establish proper specifications for raw materials, the materials must be rigorously tested before use, and the equipment must be maintained in proper condition to insure that the operation produces at capacity.

The primary difference between continuous operations and batch operations is the break between steps. This break represents the point at which the batch has been completely processed in one operation and is transferred to another operation. The second operation may require the use of equipment that also is used for other products.

Often there is competition among products for the use of equipment. The processing of one product will be delayed when that product must wait for equipment time until the equipment has finished another product. The identity of the equipment that causes the delays may vary from day to day, as the product mix varies.

CASE IN POINT

A midwest producer of chemical products was obtaining an output of 55 percent of expected capacity. In addition, the labor force was judged to be too large, with the estimates of overmanning varying from 10 to 24 percent. Part of the problem was caused by the need to rework a portion of the output. Another part was related to the mixing equipment.

The various mixing operations were examined to determine if:
1. The mixing speeds could be increased.
2. The use of the equipment could be scheduled more systematically to reduce time lost because of crews waiting for mixers.

As a result of the study:
1. Mixing speeds were increased.
2. Two new mixers were purchased and the plant layout changed to accommodate them.
3. Systematic scheduling of the mixers was established.
4. The pressure on operators to vacate the mixers to make room for waiting operators was relieved. Proper time was spent in mixing operations and the product yield improved while the need for rework was reduced.
5. Crew sizes were reduced and labor assignments were changed, resulting in the labor force being reduced from 77 people to 54 people, a 30 percent reduction.

Expected production capacity is being realized and is sufficient for the present and the foreseeable future. The labor cost reduction is valued at $385,000 annually at the present level of output.

It should be noted that the improvements were not achieved solely by the addition of two mixers. Other actions were also taken. The lack of sufficient mixers was only one cause of the bottleneck, although the primary one.

BE SURE TO IDENTIFY THE TRUE CAUSES OF THE BOTTLENECK

Regardless of the type of operation, continuous or batch, mechanical or chemical, whatever the distinctions, ferreting out the basic causes of bottlenecks should include a systematic evaluation of at least four distinct possibilities:

1. The activities that support and provide service to the production operations.
2. Operator methods, skill and performance.
3. Machine and tooling design and performance.
4. Quality of incoming materials and the quality capabilities of the equipment.

The adverse effects on capacity from improper service being furnished by some supporting activities are readily discernible. These include: failure to provide materials, or providing incorrect material so that time is lost because of waiting for replacement material. Also included is the failure to provide proper maintenance of equipment, resulting in lost time because of emergency breakdowns or because of the need to operate the equipment at a lower than planned speed. Production planning and industrial engineering also can influence capacity to a great degree.

CASE IN POINT

The plant of an eastern manufacturer of marking systems occupied two floors. Because of the plant layout, materials moved up and down three times. The operation was considered to be a job shop, so that the runs were short and each customer order was considered a run. The plant was unable to keep up with current needs and future requirements were expected to be 25 percent greater.

During the examination of possible corrective actions, a concept developed whereby the total production process was considered to consist of three parts. Under that concept the customer's special features were isolated into one of the sections, the print section. The other two sections, the base assembly and the final assembly, could be produced in long runs and still accommodate the requirements of individual customer orders. Increasing the size of the runs for the two sections would reduce the number of changeovers and increase the availability of equipment time for producing products. This automatically would increase the plant capacity.

Following through with the new concept, the plant layout was changed, with a great amount of the up and down movement eliminated. The change in layout, with the improved flow of material, freed sufficient space to take care of the expected 25 percent increase in business. The net result of the changes yielded savings amounting to $45,000 annually.

The most frequently observed cases of bottlenecks caused by failure of supporting activities remain those involving the logistics of supply of materials to the operations. There are a wide variety of elements that affect the logistics of supply, including:

— The use of inaccurate, normal values for replenishment or purchasing lead times.
— Abnormal instances of: internal delays, vendor delays, incoming inspection delays, transportation delays, rejection and return of materials to vendors or rework of incoming materials with improper quality, all of which lengthen replenishment or purchasing lead times beyond normal values.
— Careless storage or improper storage conditions that cause deterioration of previously acceptable materials.
— Incorrect or misunderstood production schedules, resulting in inaccurate information of materials required for current or impending production setups.
— Excessive utilization of the deployable reserve, so that materials are consumed at a rate faster than planned or expected.

The total effect of failures in the logistic elements generally is manifested by equipment that has been changed over, but is kept idle waiting for raw materials.

CASE IN POINT

There are many types of industries in which this situation has important consequences. Several pharmaceutical companies have independently resorted to the same procedures to prevent this condition from arising. Packaging production planning is converted to packaging production scheduling only after there has been verification that the materials needed to meet the production plans are available for use. That means that the quantities required are available and are in proper condition. After that determination is made, the materials are brought together to an area and they are "staged" so that the quantities and condition can be further verified. After the second verification, the equipment is set up to use the materials. Experience shows that the materials planning effort is reduced by as much as one-half because of elimination of expediting activities and capacity can be increased by as much as 25 percent through this practice. In addition, the labor lost while packaging line personnel wait for materials or reassignment is completely eliminated.

Another logistical aspect is the planning of labor utilization and equipment. One common example may be found in the situation where the equipment operator has an important influence on the equipment cycle time. It is sometimes found that the value used for planning the capacity of an operation is the same as the standard value used for operator performance measurement or for cost purposes. When that is the case, cognizance is not being given to the fact that the actual value seldom coincides with the standard value. The actual value will nearly always be greater or smaller than the standard value. If the actual value is smaller, the plans will not be met because the actual output will be less than planned. If the actual value is larger, the situation takes a different turn; the actual usage of material will be greater than planned and material shortages may develop. It is, therefore, important that the planning should take actuality into account. To do this, a multiplier factor is generally used to represent the relationship between the actual and standard values that have been derived from actual experience. The multiplier might be a percent cost performance, a percent operator performance, or it might be a learning curve that would show an expected progressive improvement. The application is simple:

Standard Output x Multiplier = Expected Output for Planning

The situation where the operator has an important influence on the equipment cycle time demonstrates this point clearly.

CASE IN POINT

In some sheet metal operations where large sheets are processed in tools set up in large press brakes, the machine cycle time for the press is frequently less than the time spent by the operator in handling the sheet. The operator generally has to move to a skid, separate the top sheet from the stack of sheets, maneuver it to the brake and position it in the tool. After the machine cycle, he removes the piece, carries it and stacks it as neatly as the shape allows. These work elements offer many opportunities for a high degree of variation in times required. The distance to and position of the skid, the degree to which the sheets adhere to each other because of oil, the degree to which the shape and size of the piece affect handling it, the positioning conditions, the distance and position of the stack of finished work, the degree to which the finished pieces can tangle, the strength and dexterity of the operator, all can result in variations of as much as 100 percent. If the machine cycle time is one-half of the total cycle time, a 100 percent increase in operator's time can increase the total cycle time by one-third.

This same kind of variation also is found in other types of manufacturing processes. Good planning requires that the planning data should be based on operator time as well as on equipment cycle time. If a bottleneck arises in this type of situation, both the equipment cycle time and the operator's time should be examined. The avoidance of bottlenecks through proper planning calls for scheduling the utilization of the equipment based on actual experience with use of the equipment.

The cause of low operator performance is often not easily identifiable. There are many factors that can affect it, some directly attributable to the individual operator. The factors include:

— Improperly trained operators.
— Excessive absenteeism of skilled operators, so that operators with less skill must be used.
— Poor quality of work produced, resulting in time spent on rework.
— Improper interpretation of the learning curve.
— Improperly motivated operators.
— Excessive overtime, resulting in operator fatigue.

Other factors can result in poor operator performance, but are not directly attributable to the individual operator. Some of these factors are:

— Materials coming from prior operations that are not maintaining quality specifications.
— Inadequate process specifications.

CASE IN POINT

In a midwestern job shop foundry several examples of bottlenecks were observed arising from inadequate process specifications. The foundry has deservedly earned a reputation for high quality castings; high quality is emphasized, and the employees are impressed with the fact that the success of the foundry depends on quality. As a consequence, because of a lack of process specifications, unnecessary work was sometimes being done. The molders were over-responding; they were spending too much time in manually ramming the molds or in jolting molds on the jolt molding machines. To bring that part of the situation under control, a series of tests were made by the quality control supervisor, working directly on the molding floor with the molders. The results demonstrated that the ramming time and the number of jolts could be substantially reduced without reducing quality. This eliminated one bottleneck and improved operator utilization.

A closely related condition can appear in a somewhat different form.

CASE IN POINT

An eastern glass and plastic manufacturer was experiencing bottlenecks in his plastic operation. It was found that, after lamination, the plastic sheets were passed through a continous washer-dryer, were folded and stored for as long as two weeks. While in storage, the sheets would adhere. When the sheets were delivered to the cutting room, time was lost in separating pieces.

In the cutting room, the cutting machine had not been properly maintained with the result that it was being operated at far below rated speeds.

The cutting machine was renovated and moved adjacent to the washer-dryer. Sheets coming from the washer-dryer were cut before being placed in storage. The time required for the cutting operation was long enough to allow the plastic to dry completely before going into storage, so that the cut pieces did not stick while in storage. Eliminating the separating operation and speeding up the cutting machine brought the capacity back to the planned value, which was about one-third greater.

During the examination, it was observed that one man could be eliminated from the crew of the washer-dryer, if the equipment were changed slightly. It was also found that the setup man for the cutter had less than two hours work each day; he has been furnished with a cutting table, so that he now cuts raw glass when he is not setting up. Moving the cutter near to the washer-dryer eliminated one material handler. The total reduction has been three people, valued at about $200 per day. These savings were achieved as the result of an examination made to break a bottleneck.

LOOK BEYOND THE EQUIPMENT AND THE OPERATOR

The contribution of poor maintenance of equipment to bottlenecks was touched on in the previous case. There is one item of equipment that warrants a separate consideration. That item is the tooling. The first thought that comes to mind is tool maintenance such as the need for sharpening drill bits and other cutting tools. Another early thought is the effect of normal wear of other tools: blanking and forming dies, clamps and other holding devices, drill bushings and other locating devices.

There are other factors beyond tool and tooling maintenance. Changes in raw materials may raise a requirement for changes in tools or tooling. Changes in product design must be met with proper changes in tooling, of course, but sometimes changes in design will, by their nature, cause increases in cycle time. Examples of such changes are: deeper draws that call for slower rates of drawing and increasing the number of holes to be manually drilled in an operation.

A partial listing of bottleneck sources related to tooling includes:

— Improper maintenance of tools.
— Improper use or handling of tools.
— Poor tooling design which results in excessive unscheduled downtime.
— Mismatch between tooling and product.
— Mismatch between tooling and the equipment on which it is being used.
— Improper makeshift tooling.
— Poor design causing excessive changeover time.

CASE IN POINT

A search for causes of bottlenecks in the plant of an eastern bearing manufacturer resulted in a thorough examination of changeover time and of the difficulty of achieving accurate setups. It also brought about a definitive examination of the relationships of the machine-controlled cycle elements and product quality.

Reductions of machine downtime increased available machine time by 11 percent. This was achieved by taking several actions.

The tooling, consisting of dies, was redesigned and rebuilt for the specific purpose of decreasing the time required for changeover and for achieving the needed accuracy. A preparation area was set aside and properly equipped with tool and die parts, so that tooling could be prepared for installation prior to machine shutdown. A changeover procedure was developed and installed to provide advance coordination of production schedules, product specification and tooling availability.

Reductions amounting to 12 percent were made in the machine-controlled elements, with no reduction in quality standards. Part of this reduction is attributable to the revisions of the tooling, the rest to clearer process specifications.

The total increased earnings resulting from these actions has been valued at more than $140,000 annually.

As can be seen from this case, and from the previous case at the foundry, the effect of quality on bottlenecks is not always given proper consideration.

EXAMINE THE EFFECT OF QUALITY CONSIDERATIONS ON BOTTLENECKS

The influence of quality considerations on bottlenecks can begin with incoming materials. If specifications for incoming materials are inadequate or improper, bottlenecks occur because machines that have been set up cannot use the material at all, or only at a reduced speed. Bottlenecks also occur when incoming material has to be returned to the vendor for replacement, or when equipment or personnel has to be diverted to perform rework operations.

Quality considerations can influence available equipment capacity in other ways. If quality requirements are beyond the normal capability of the equipment, rejection rates may be higher than planned, or equipment speed may have to be reduced. Higher rejection rates, of course, not only result in reduced useful production output, they also can cause excessive consumption of raw material so the stocks may be exhausted prematurely. This shifts the bottleneck to the replenishment procedure, but its basic source is a quality consideration.

Quality considerations should be treated in the same way as the utilization or availability of labor and equipment is treated. Planning the utilization of capacity should recognize that there may be differences between standards for product yield and actual yield. Multipliers to be applied to yield standards should be developed in the same way as employee or equipment performance multipliers are developed, by routine comparisons between standard and actual yields.

Some of the quality considerations that may influence bottlenecks are:

— Marginal quality materials.
— Worn or damaged production tooling or inspection gauges.
— Improper or inadequate tooling inspection and control.
— Improper or inadequate operator training or supervision.

CASE IN POINT

A southwestern foundry that was operating as a job shop developed an opportunity to produce a large number of castings of one pattern for an extended period. The contract was to begin with 200 castings per week and was to increase over a period of years. This appeared to be an excellent opportunity to achieve a dramatic reduction in finishing and grinding costs by virtue of establishing a finishing line, with individual operators assigned to carry out specific repetitive operations. Detailed job instructions were prepared for each work station, engineered job standards were developed for each station and a crew was assigned to the stations according to current operator performance data. The finishing line personnel were observed to be actually working at the level reported in the operator performance data, but deliveries were falling behind. More than sufficient quantities of castings were being molded and poured; therefore, the bottleneck had to be in the finishing operation.

A very detailed examination of the situation revealed that individual castings were being reworked in the finishing operations an average of 4 times, with the maximum observed 16 times.

The finishing operations called for grinding of the castings to specific dimensions, with specific tolerances. The tolerances were extremely close for castings. That was the first quality consideration: process capability versus product requirement. To compound the difficulty some of the product specifications and tolerances opposed each other. In other words, if one specification was met for some dimensions, another specification could not be met. Consequently, a casting could be returned to the finishing line for rework and, after the rework had been properly carried out, another cause for rejection and rework would be found.

The effect of this condition can be measured easily. If each casting was processed an average of four times, and if past experience called for 10 percent rework, the relationship the actual work to the standard amount of work was 4 to 1.1, or 26 percent more than it ould have been.

The matter was resolved by **reexamining** the specifications with the customer, mak-ıg appropriate changes to the specifications and, more importantly, revising the yield ,tandard and cost estimate to reflect the true nature of the situation.

CAREFULLY EVALUATE THE COST IMPLICATIONS
OF BREAKING BOTTLENECKS

The previous discussions of bottlenecks have not covered the analyses of evaluations of the known options that preceded the decisions on actions to be taken. In all of the cases, the decisions were based on evaluations of the alternatives. Even though some of the implemented options represented relatively small costs, the evaluations were made. The point is that there may have been several other low cost options, but they did not provide benefits to the extent that the selected actions did.

Very frequently, the least-cost solution to a bottleneck condition is considered to be utilization of the employable reserve. The difference between rated capacity and deployed capacity is capability for producing what is available for emergency use only for short periods of time without harmful overall effect. Continued use of the employable reserve will yield excessive long-run costs. It was established only after a careful analysis of conditions.

An examination of the deployable capacity of any bottleneck should include a similar examination of the process or equipment that operates before and after the bottleneck. Elimination of any bottleneck creates another potential bottleneck; some part of the system has limiting characteristics. It is important to make certain that opening one bottleneck, in fact, does expand the system's capacity. The thorough examination is necessary for determining the total cost of breaking the bottleneck.

A different cost implication is based on the fact that a 1 percent increase in output at a bottleneck actually means a 1 percent increase in output of the entire system. The reduction in costs of the entire system may be directly proportional to the amount of increase in total capacity. Just as it is important to make a thorough examination of the cost of breaking a bottleneck, it is also important to determine the total benefit. The total benefit may reach beyond a reduction in costs. It may have a more significant effect; an important increase of income and profits, the ultimate benefit of breaking bottlenecks.

APPROACH BOTTLENECKS WITH OPTIMISM

Frequently, bottlenecks occur because of practices that have been established for long periods of time. The occurrence of a bottleneck is the opportunity and the justification for a thorough examination of all of the conditions surrounding the bottleneck situation. Experience shows that the result of such an examination is frequently a beneficial change in practices that would not have otherwise been considered. It is important that the examination is unrestricted and is extended to all conditions that have any relationship to the bottleneck.

Chapter 7

Controlling and Measuring Your Equipment Utilization to Avoid Runaway Production Cost

Equipment utilization is a significant, yet frequently overlooked, cost factor in the actual manufacturing cost of a product. The control of equipment utilization requires an understanding of: (1) the conditions that contribute to "good" or "poor" utilization and, (2) the factors that can be controlled to increase equipment throughput. Occasionally the true impact of schedule changes on downtime is overlooked in manufacturing planning and, consequently, customer service suffers. Uncovering the hidden causes of poor equipment utilization can lead to improved relationships between production and sales and customers. The subject matter in this chapter will pursue principal themes:

— Equipment utilization targets are important instruments for controlling production and inventory costs. Targets may differ from company to company.
— The nature of opportunities for improving equipment utilization is frequently misunderstood. Opportunities may vary in the same way that targets may vary.

DEVELOP YOUR OWN DEFINITIONS OF "GOOD" AND "POOR" UTILIZATION

A machine that produces 10,000 units of product per minute may well be thought of as a highly productive piece of equipment. On the other hand, if it only operates for one minute each year, there would be second thoughts about its productivity.

Basically, there are two distinctly identifiable factors to be considered relative to evaluating a machine's productivity or utilization:

— The quantity of units produced per unit of operating time.
— The relationship of the operating time to the available time.

Before continuing, it would be best to give the meanings of a few terms, according to the way they are used in this chapter.

- *Total Scheduled Times* is the sum of the times specified by schedules for:

Operating Time—when the equipment or machine is operating to make products.
Setup Time—when the equipment is being prepared to make products.
Scheduled Maintenance Downtime—when the machine is undergoing preventive or corrective maintenance, *according to an established schedule.*

- *Total Actual Time* is the sum of the actual times spent in performing the work scheduled for:

Operating Time
Setup Time
Scheduled Maintenance Downtime

- *Total Nonscheduled Time* is the sum of:

Nonscheduled Downtime Due To Breakdown—time *lost* because of machine breakdown or material supply breakdown.
Open Time—time when the machine's capacity for making the product is not required.

- *Total Available Times* is the sum of:

Total Scheduled Time
Total Nonscheduled Time

Those meanings can lead to at least three simple formulas for "utilization," putting aside for the moment any difference between scheduled time and actual time:

$$\text{1. \% Machine Utilization} = \frac{\text{Scheduled Operating Time}}{\text{Total Scheduled Time}} \times 100$$

$$\text{2. \% Machine Utilization} = \frac{\text{Scheduled Operating Time}}{\text{Total Available Time}} \times 100$$

$$\text{3. \% Machine Utilization} = \frac{\text{Total Operating Time}}{\text{Total Available Time}} \times 100$$

Any evaluation of utilization using the above formulas will be relative. For example, the value of a machine that is operated infrequently is determined from the value, over the long run, of its output.

CASE IN POINT

To use an extreme case to explore this further, consider a machine that can produce 10,000 units of product per day. If the products from that machine are worth $1,000 per unit, its output is worth $10 million per day. If that machine cost $1 million to bring into existence, and if its operating costs are $1 million per day, it is a valuable piece of equipment. In fact, that machine needs to operate only for one day to be extremely valuable. If it continues to operate only one day per year, regardless of the reasons for the restriction, it is still a valuable machine, even though its utilization might be judged to be "poor" according to the third formula.

Because an evaluation of utilization using simple ratios can be relative, a low numerical value for % Utilization is not necessarily a "poor" value. In some instances it may be justifiable to establish an arbitrary numerical value as the boundary between "good" and "poor." Sometimes that boundary might be 80%; at other times it might be 30%. The use of some specific examples should help gain a fuller insight.

The first two of the formulas will be used for the examples. A differentiation will be made between the two utilizations by giving them expanded identification:

1. $\textbf{\% Operating Utilization} = \dfrac{\textbf{Scheduled Operating Time}}{\textbf{Total Scheduled Time}} \times \textbf{100}$

2. $\textbf{\% Investment Utilization} = \dfrac{\textbf{Scheduled Operating Time}}{\textbf{Total Available Time}} \times \textbf{100}$

The third formula will not be discussed in detail except to say that the factor "Total Scheduled Time" emphasizes that the scheduled maintenance downtime is needed to provide for proper care of the equipment. It was mentioned earlier to stress the point that there are many possible formulas for measuring utilization.

CASE IN POINT

Figure 7-1 contains the data for the examples. That data will be used to demonstrate the ease with which an improper evaluation can be made by considering only the numerical values of the % Utilization. To make a proper judgment as to whether the utilization is "poor" or "good," it is necessary to have a clear understanding of how the numerical values were derived.

Examples 1, 2, and 3 compare the effects of setup hours. Example 2 shows what happens when the hours required to make a setup increase; the increase causes a reduction in % Operating Utilization. Conversely, if the setup hours are reduced, let's say through an application of work simplification methods, the % Operating Utilization increases. But, all three examples show the same % Investment Utilization.

To understand the application of the % Investment Utilization as a measuring tool, it is necessary to examine examples 4, 5 and 6. In examples 4, 5 and 6 the need for production capacity is greater than the first three examples. Under that condition an increase in scheduled setup time causes a drop in % Investment Utilization. And a reduction in scheduled setup time results in a corresponding improvement in % Investment Utilization. The % Operating Utilization varies exactly in the same way as the % Investment Utilization.

The % Operating Utilization, as defined here, varies inversely as costs vary. When increased setup labor is required, the % Operating Utilization decreases. When increased use is made of the equipment, both the % Operating Utilization and the % Investment Utilization increase. However, it should be noted that "use" in these cases refers to hours of use. The effects on the numerical values of the % Utilization when "use" refers to output can be seen by comparing example 7 with example 1.

The increase in hourly output in example 7 yields a reduction in the operating hours

EFFECTS OF VARYING CONDITIONS ON UTILIZATION

Example No	Operating Hours	Setup Hours	Scheduled Hours	Nonscheduled Hours	Available Hours	% Operating Utilization	% Investment Utilization	Output Per Hour	Output Per Week
1	15	5	20	20	40	$\frac{15}{20} \times 100 = 75\%$	$\frac{15}{40} \times 100 = 38\%$	10	150
2	15	9	24	16	40	$\frac{15}{24} \times 100 = 63\%$	$\frac{15}{40} \times 100 = 38\%$	10	150
3	15	1	16	24	40	$\frac{15}{16} \times 100 = 94\%$	$\frac{15}{40} \times 100 = 38\%$	10	150
4	30	10	40	0	40	$\frac{30}{40} \times 100 = 75\%$	$\frac{30}{40} \times 100 = 75\%$	10	300
5	22	18	40	0	40	$\frac{22}{40} \times 100 = 55\%$	$\frac{22}{40} \times 100 = 55\%$	10	220
6	38	2	40	0	40	$\frac{38}{40} \times 100 = 95\%$	$\frac{38}{40} \times 100 = 95\%$	10	380
7	12	5	17	23	40	$\frac{12}{17} \times 100 = 71\%$	$\frac{12}{40} \times 100 = 30\%$	12.5	150
8	22	18	40	0	40	$\frac{22}{40} \times 100 = 55\%$	$\frac{22}{40} \times 100 = 55\%$	12.5	275
9	18	5	23	17	40	$\frac{18}{23} \times 100 = 78\%$	$\frac{18}{40} \times 100 = 45\%$	8.3	150

% Operating Utilization = $\dfrac{\text{Scheduled Operating Time}}{\text{Total Scheduled Time}}$

% Investment Utilization = $\dfrac{\text{Scheduled Operating Time}}{\text{Total Available Time}}$

154

for the same weekly output as is shown in example 1. Example. 7 shows 12 operating hours, compared to 15 operating hours in example 1, for a weekly output of 150 units. Because of the fewer operating hours example 7 shows a decrease in both % Operating Utilization and % Investment Utilization from those in example 1. When the hourly output is decreased the opposite occurs, as shown in example 9.

Example 5 may be compared to example 8 to further emphasize that hours of use is not necessarily a useful factor for evaluating utilization. Example 8, with increased hourly and weekly output, shows the same numerical values for both utilization measurements.

These examples emphasize that:

— A simple numerical value for % Utilization does not necessarily represent a meaningful measurement of the utilization of a machine.
— A change in numerical value is not necessarily indicative of a corresponding change in actual utilization.
— Numerical values of % Utilization will be meaningful only if their derivation is completely understood.
— Proper evaluation of equipment utilization must take into account the hourly outputs and changes in hourly outputs.

It is not the intent of this discussion to imply that the measurement of utilization is an extremely difficult task. On the contrary, the intent is to make clear that simple measurements can be used with confidence when they are interpreted with a little care. To help the interpretation there are some common sense principles that can be applied in evaluating the utilization of equipment. These principles can be used to guide the evaluation and to help understand the meaning of the numerical values resulting from the use of formulas. Common sense says that utilization of equipment improves when:

1. The number of units produced per operating hour is increased.
2. Setup and changeover times are reduced.
3. Nonscheduled time is reduced.

The formulas do not establish firm definitions of "poor" or "good" utilization. They do, however, help determine if the utilization is:

1. Getting worse.
2. Getting better.
3. Good enough to provide the capacity needed to meet demand.

Evaluation of utilization can be given a broader scope and additional meaning. The introduction of the three simple % Machine Utilization formulas was on the basis of, "putting aside for the moment any difference between scheduled and actual time." Bringing that difference back into the picture adds another factor to evaluation of utilization—the factor of performance.

COMPARE SCHEDULED HOURS AND ACTUAL HOURS TO MEASURE PERFORMANCE

The two measurements previously discussed, % Operating Utilization and % Investment Utilization, represent planned utilization targets. Good control of costs requires evaluation of performance against targets. One formula that evaluates performance is:

$$\% \text{ Utilization (Performance)} = \frac{\textbf{Scheduled Hours (Operating and Setup)}}{\textbf{Actual Hours (Operating and Setup)}} \times 100$$

The targets for scheduled hours, both operating and setup, are most frequently calculated from job standards. The most reliable values of job standards are those derived through formal work measurement techniques, although historical data is sometimes used. When the actual hours are less than the scheduled hours, the % Utilization (Performance) will be greater than 100%. When the actual hours are greater than the scheduled hours, the % Utilization (Performance) will be less than 100%.

The use of the % Utilization (Performance) as an evaluation factor is independent of the use of the % Operating Utilization or % Investment Utilization factors. The % Utilization (Performance) evaluates how well plans are met. The other two evaluate the planning effort. In evaluating the planning effort, cognizance should be taken of the fact that it is possible not only to underutilize, but also to overutilize, equipment.

BE ALERT TO POSSIBLE OVERUTILIZATION OF EQUIPMENT

Overutilization of equipment may result from either one or both of two causes. The first cause evolves when the equipment is used to such a great extent that proper preventive or corrective maintenance is not provided. The other condition arises when the need for output calls for the fullest possible use of the equipment and there is a mix of product output so that a competition for equipment time develops. The second condition also results in the neglect of maintenance, but its most insidious effect is a reduction of total output. The competition for equipment time may lead to many setup changes and this reduces operating time.

There are some highly visible signals to warn of overutilization. One such signal is in the inability of inventory to support sales to customers. When the sales department complains that production can't meet customer needs, one of the causes might be found in attempts to overutilize equipment.

Other signals are in the form of increasing overtime. This will show up both for equipment operating labor and for maintenance labor.

Sometimes the maintenance supervision joins in the signaling by complaining of an inability to get machine downtime needed for preventive or corrective maintenance.

The last signal is an increase in machine downtime due to breakdowns. At that time, even concentrated efforts by maintenance personnel seem to be ineffective.

There are some remedies that might be applied early in the situation. These all come under the heading of planning the utilization of the equipment to control the competition for equipment time. At the first sign that production is not keeping up with sales, steps should be taken to:

1. Determine the initial maximum possible output, realistically recognizing existing downtime conditions.

2. Plan the most profitable, or the most desirable on any other basis, utilization of the equipment by planning:

   A. Product mix to gain maximum benefit from operating time.

   B. Setups and changeovers to reduce downtime for those activities and thereby to increase operating time.

3. Plan sales and production efforts to make certain that commitments made to customers can be met.

4. Take maximum advantage of capacity that can be purchased outside of the plant.

5. Plan preventive and corrective maintenance schedules to obtain a balance between need to operate and need to maintain.

6. Change the plans only after consideration of the consequences of changes.

CASE IN POINT

The sales department of a midwestern hardware manufacturing company was complaining that production couldn't meet customer needs. Examination of the situation revealed that the problem was one of overutilization of a number of pieces of equipment. Competition had developed for equipment time resulting in excessive setup changes with a corresponding reduction in operating time. A procedure was designed to cover the first three items on the preceding list of remedies. This action made time available for putting more effort than before into carrying out the fourth item.

An early step taken to correct the situation was the establishment of a fixed, repetitive weekly schedule of throughput for the final operation. The weekly schedule calls for fixed quantities of the several products. It is established jointly by sales and manufacturing. The schedule produces the maximum benefits possible under the conditions to the company in terms of profits and customer relations.

The capacity problem area was in earlier operations, rather than in the final operation. Establishing a firm, final operation schedule simplifies the task of planning the earlier operations. Interruptions in runs are almost eliminated and setups are reduced. This results in an increase of operating hours and therefore in throughput. With the final operation schedule made firm, the sales department is able to make delivery promises to customers that manufacturing could reasonably be expected to meet. With this settled and the scheduling of earlier operations made easier, everyday crises have been significantly reduced. Time and effort are now available for doing a thorough job of taking advantage of outside capacity.

Overutilization occurs most frequently because of a lack of understanding of how to evaluate utilization. One factor that is in special need of clarification is downtime.

PUT DOWNTIME IN ITS PROPER PERSPECTIVE

Machine downtime is that portion of the time available for operating when the machine is down, not operating. Thinking of downtime in that way might lead to thinking of downtime as the time when the machine should be operating, but is not. Extension of that train of thought might lead to the judgment that all downtime is bad and should be eliminated. When that judgment carries strong convictions, and those convictions cannot be implemented, it is found that downtime becomes ignored as a distinct condition of production planning. Perhaps the hope is that thinking it won't exist can make downtime disappear.

The opposite extreme is also found. Downtime is accepted readily and its cause is not examined. It is considered as being an all-inclusive percentage of operating time that just disappears into the equipment capacity values. The possibility of reducing it is forgotten. In any case, downtime is again ignored as a distinct condition of the production plan.

There can be no justification for ignoring downtime. Downtime does and always will exist. Any discussion of machine utilization must take downtime into account. Ignoring the existence of downtime as a distinct condition leads to improper decisions and confusion.

Recognizing and working with downtime might be made more comfortable if it is understood that downtime may consist of:

1. *Open Time.* This is the time when there is no need for the available capacity.
2. *Scheduled Maintenance Downtime.* In some rare situations, the economics of equipment replacement favor operating the equipment without maintenance until complete breakdown. For those special cases, it is more beneficial to replace the equipment than to maintain it. In most situations, however, preventive and corrective maintenance must be scheduled to reduce lost time due to breakdowns.
3. *Scheduled Downtime for Setups and Changeovers.* This covers the changing of equipment for different products and sizes.
4. *Unscheduled Downtime.* This consists of lost time due to breakdowns of equipment or material supply.

RECOGNIZE AND FORECAST DOWNTIME

The need for capacity can be predicted from sales forecasts. The lack of need, therefore, can likewise be predicted.

Scheduled maintenance can be measured for each occurrence. Any downtime required can be predicted whether it is to be performed periodically or according to the number of operating hours or both.

Setups and changeovers can be measured for each occurrence. The downtime required for these activities can be predicted according to the production plans.

There is one thing certain about breakdowns. It is certain that breakdowns will occur. The uncertainties are the frequency of occurrence and the length of time per occurrence. One method in general use for predicting downtime due to breakdowns is based on history of the equipment. The history is examined to determine the relationship between the downtime due to breakdowns and the operating time. From the history, the expected downtime due to breakdowns is established as a percentage of the operating time.

If the condition of the equipment is known to be deteriorating, the prediction of future expected downtime due to breakdowns should be a larger percentage than was experienced in the past. If the condition of the equipment has been improved through corrective action or if material supply procedures have been improved, the prediction should be a lower percentage than that of past history. If there is no known reason for revising the historical percentage, that value should be continued in use.

The purpose of predicting the four causes for downtime is to control downtime to the greatest extent possible. Maximum utilization of equipment can be achieved only through the control of the use of the equipment.

To make the best possible effort to reduce downtime, it is necessary to know the expected amount of and the schedule for the downtime. This information will provide important guidance to the effort that should be exerted to reduce the downtime. Without that information the effort will proceed blindly and perhaps in the wrong direction.

Preventive and corrective maintenance must be scheduled. Careful scheduling of maintenance downtime can provide proper care of the equipment at a minimum loss of operating time.

Setups and changes must be planned to achieve proper size runs of economical order quantities. Unless the values of setup and changeover costs are known, economical order quantities cannot be determined. There are frequently opportunities to plan the sequence of setups and changeovers to reduce the time required for that downtime. Some of those opportunities contain possible reductions of important magnitude.

CASE IN POINT

A well-known example of sequence planning is in the steel industry. Rolling mill schedules are established so that changes in thickness are always in one direction, downward.

Unless the magnitude of nonscheduled downtime is known and appreciated, very little effort will be directed toward its reduction. Although it is not possible to control breakdown downtime, recognition of its existence will permit the development of realistic production schedules. Ignoring its existence leads to theoretical schedules and overutilization, together with the accompanying problems and aggravations.

When downtime is ignored and, as a result, is allowed to remain uncontrolled, two important cost elements are neglected.

DON'T NEGLECT ANY SIGNIFICANT COST ELEMENTS

Of all of the cost elements related to the utilization of equipment, most attention is generally given to operating and maintenance labor and closely related costs. Two other costs are frequently treated like the weather; they are targets for complaints but not for action. These two costs are:

1. Setup and changeover labor.
2. Downtime, due to
   Setup and changeovers (Scheduled Downtime)
   Breakdown (Nonscheduled Downtime)

Setup and changeover time can be measured. The work can be analyzed for opportunities for reduction. The measurement, perhaps, cannot be precise. Even establishing a range of times for making a setup provides better control than no time value at all.

People who perform unmeasured setups might well be working next to people who perform measured operating work. The result is inconsistent treatment of people working together. The person working under a measured condition is more closely scrutinized than the person who is not measured.

Second, without measurement there can be no control. Control of the time spent requires targets for the time.

Because the activities are not measured, opportunities for improvement might well remain unidentified and unrealized.

CASE IN POINT

Experience in many industries and companies shows that there are important opportunities for improvement by as much as 50% of setup and changeover times to be derived from:
1. Instructing and training of personnel.
2. Providing proper tools and gauges.
3. Reducing the number of types of fasteners.
4. Providing easier access to the equipment.
5. Systematically storing and maintaining the equipment parts being set up or changed.
6. Redesigning the equipment and its parts.

In order to determine the value of the potential improvements, it is necessary to know the value of the reduction in time. That requires work observations and measurements. Measurements are also needed for determining the reduction in changeover time resulting from the improvements made.

Nonscheduled downtime is generally neglected as a separate extra cost because it is not identified completely and separately in the cost accounting system. Actually it is composed of two cost elements.

One of the elements results from the enforced idleness of the operators, plus the extra cost of the mechanic that is incurred while the breakdown is being corrected. The enforced idleness of the operators very often will be lost in the numerical value of the % Utilization (Performance). This is improper because the excess time may not be caused by poor operating performance. Sometimes, when the downtime exceeds a preestablished limit, the operators are instructed to charge their time into a special "lost time" account. But, when the downtime is less than the limit, there is no special identification. It is also a general practice in the case of equipment breakdown that the mechanic's time is generally considered as an indirect labor cost and becomes charged to and lost in a burden account. In the case of material supply breakdown, the extra costs for materials handling, clerical work, as well as other efforts, are also lost in burden accounts.

The second cost element has to do with the loss of operating time. As will be shown later in this chapter, the second cost element may well be more important than the first, and examination of it may provide stronger motivation for corrective action than examination of operator idleness. Although the second cost element is a loss, rather than a cost, it results in a reduction of profit, just as a cost does. On that basis, the loss of output and the resulting loss of profit should be given the attention it merits.

Because visible targets provide stronger motivation than invisible targets, some companies report loss of income due to downtime much in the same way as they report other costs. It should be noted, however, that there is no loss of income if there is no need for the output lost because of downtime.

CASE IN POINT

In a company making complex turret lathe products, loss of profit is emphasized.

If a machine yields 10 product units per hour and if the plant works one shift per week, with a two week vacation each year, the maximum possible output is:

10 units/hour x 40 hours/week x 50 weeks/year = 20,000 units per year

If setups and changeovers average 15% of the time, and if downtime due to breakdowns averages 5% of the time, the expected total downtime is 20% of the operating time.

The maximum expected output would then become:

(100% - 20%) = 80%; 80% of 20,000 = 16,000 units per year

If the customers will buy only 8,000 units per year, doubling the expected total downtime to 40% results in no loss of income; supply still exceeds the demand:

(100% - 40%) = 60%; 60% of 20,000 = 12,000 units per year

On the other hand, if customers are willing to buy 18,000 units per year, there is a loss of profit from 2,000 units that results from the present expected total downtime. The 2,000 units will require 2,000 ÷ 10 units per hour, or 200 hours to produce. Any one hour reduction in downtime, up to 200 hours, is worth the profit from each additional 10 units.

This line of reasoning, however, is valid only to the extent that the sales forecast is valid.

An approach more frequently used assumes that any increase or decrease in operating time results in a corresponding increase or decrease in income (rather than profit) equal to the current value of the operating time.

The values in the example above can be used to illustrate the approach, assuming that all output can be sold. Reducing output from 16,000 units per year to 12,000 units represents a loss of 4,000 units. Multiplying 4,000 by the sales value per unit will show the yearly income loss.

This approach simplifies the accounting analysis of the situation, and eliminates the argumentative subject of determination of profit. This particular approach is very useful because it:

1. Appears to be consistent, assigning the same value to increasing or decreasing operating time.
2. Operates within a comparatively small range of time.
3. Is arithmetically straightforward and easy to follow.
4. Provides motivation in the proper direction. It calls attention to the otherwise neglected cost element: nonscheduled downtime.

If nonscheduled downtime is found to be an important cost or loss factor it can be reduced, if it is attacked systematically. The causes for downtime should be identified and ranked in order of importance. The corrective action can then be scheduled according to value and ease of implementation.

CASE IN POINT

The following causes for downtime and successful remedial actions have been observed in a number of industries and companies over a period of many years. The list does not reflect frequency or magnitude, those both being highly variable.

Cause: operating beyond the capability of the equipment. Remedy: recognition that desired objectives are not being met.

Cause: improper machine setup. Remedy: simplification of setup procedure, improved training of setup operator, including tool preparation.

Cause: improper quality or type of material being supplied to equipment. Remedy: review of material specifications vs. nature of equipment; installation or improvement of inspection procedures for materials being supplied to the equipment.

Cause: improper use of equipment. Remedy: simplification of use procedures; improved training of operator.

Cause: absence or inadequacy of preventive maintenance procedures. Remedy: installation of proper preventive maintenance procedures accompanied by the use of checklist to guide and verify work done.

Cause: shortage of material supply. Remedy: make certain that material is available before scheduling and setting up equipment.

Downtime is not only an important consideration in the utilization of existing equipment, it also should be considered in evaluations for replacing equipment.

CONSIDER ALL THE ALTERNATIVES BEFORE REPLACING EQUIPMENT

There are several reasons for replacing equipment. One obvious one is that a much-needed machine can no longer be repaired. Also obvious is the case where repair of a much-needed machine costs more than replacing it. There are other situations that are not obvious and that require more thought.

If the need is for additional capacity and versatility, it should be recognized that they can be obtained by adding equipment as well as by replacing it. The decision of whether to add or replace should be based on an evaluation of the advantages and disadvantages of both alternatives. The evaluation should consider various cost aspects, availability of space, availability of utilities and maintenance requirements, among other factors.

If the need is for reduced operating costs, an evaluation of those costs for both the existing equipment and the candidates for replacement should include:

— Operating labor
— Setup and changeover labor
— Scheduled downtime for setup and changeover
— Scheduled downtime for maintenance, preventive and corrective
— Nonscheduled downtime due to breakdowns.

In some industries there is a wide variety of options available in the selection of equipment. A tendency has been observed in those who select equipment to overemphasize the benefits of high rate of output and to underemphasize other factors of cost.

CASE IN POINT

A typical situation is the selection of packaging equipment in food, confections, cosmetic and pharmaceutical industries. The variety of packaging operations can range from completely manual to high-speed, completely automatic with many possible intermediate steps. It is not the intent here to discuss return-on-investment considerations, except to summarize a few aspects of costs that are sometimes overlooked or misunderstood. Some of these aspects are tabulated in Figure 7-2.

The data in Figure 7-2 represents three hypothetical equipment situations similar to those frequently encountered in the food, confections, pharmaceutical and cosmetic industries. The operating labor costs and the setup labor costs in Figure 7-2 have been used to construct the chart in Figure 7-3. In Figure 7-3, the total of those two labor costs have been plotted against the number of units produced for those labor costs for the three equipment situations. Two equi-value points are shown. The equi-value points are the points where, for the quantity of material produced, the total operating and setup labor costs are the same for the two equipment situations involved.

The equation for equi-value points is easy to establish. It is the point where the total operating and setup labor costs equal each other for the two equipment situations involved. For the 100 per hour machine, Figure 7-3 shows the operating labor cost per unit is $.05, and the setup labor cost per setup is $4.00 for some unknown quantity of units, which will be called "Q":

The total cost = $.05Q + $4.00

In the same way for the 500 per hour machine:

The total cost = $.03Q + $48.00

Putting the two total costs equal to each other (because the lines cross each other at point "X"):

EQUIPMENT EVALUATION: PRODUCT UNIT COST COMPARISONS

Factors of Comparison	Equipment Options		
	Slow Speed	Intermediate Speed	High Speed
1. Production rate, units per hour	100	500	2000
2. Equipment hours per unit	.01	.002	.0005
3. Operating labor			
A. Number of operators	1	3	6
B. Hours per unit	.01	.006	.003
C. Cost per unit, @ $5.00 per hour	$.05	$.03	$.015
4. Equipment hours per setup	.5	3	6
5. Setup labor			
A. Number of setup operators	1	2	4
B. Hours per setup	.5	6	24
C. Cost per setup, @ $8.00 per hour	$4.00	$48.00	$192.00
6. Equi-value point: 100/hour vs. 500/hour			
A. Quantity	2,200	2,200	
B. Operating labor cost per unit	$.05	$.03	
C. Setup labor cost per setup ÷ quantity	$.0018	$.0218	
D. Operating and setup labor cost per unit	$.0518	$.0518	
7. Equi-value point: 500/hour vs. 2000/hour			
A. Quantity		9,600	9,600
B. Operating labor cost per unit		$.03	$.015
C. Setup labor cost per setup ÷ quantity		$.005	$.020
D. Operating and setup labor cost per unit		$.035	$.035
8. Unscheduled Downtime			
A. Operating labor per equipment downtime hour			
1. Hours	1	3	6
2. Costs, @ $5.00 per hour	$5.00	$15.00	$30.00

FIGURE 7-2

EQUIPMENT EVALUATION: PRODUCT UNIT COST COMPARISONS			
	Equipment Options		
Factors of Comparison	Slow Speed	Intermediate Speed	High Speed
B. Maintenance labor per equipment downtime hour			
1. Hours	1	1	1
2. Costs, @ $8.00 per hour	$ 8.00	$ 8.00	$ 8.00
C. Operating and maintenance labor costs per equipment downtime hour	$13.00	$23.00	$38.00
D. If downtime is 5% of operating time			
1. Operating and Maintenance labor for downtime per equipment operating hour	$ .65	$ 1.15	$ 1.90
2. Operating and Maintenance labor cost per unit	$.0065	$.0023	$.00095
E. If downtime is 10% of operating time, Operating and Maintenance labor cost per unit	$.0130	$.0046	$.00190
F. If downtime is 20% of operating time, Operating and Maintenance labor cost per unit	$.0260	$.0092	$.00380
9. At Equi-value point: 100/hour vs. 500/hour, Operating and Setup and Downtime labor cost per unit			
A. 5% downtime	$.0583	$.0541	
B. 10% downtime	$.0648	$.0564	
C. 20% downtime	$.0778	$.0610	
10. At Equi-value point: 500/hour vs. 2,000/hour, Operating and Setup and Downtime labor cost per unit			
A. 5% downtime		$.0373	$. 0360
B. 10% downtime		$.0396	$. 0369
C. 20% downtime		$.0442	$. 0388
11. No. of units not produced			
A. 5% downtime	5	25	100
B. 10% downtime	10	50	200
C. 20% downtime	20	100	400

FIGURE 7-2 (Continued)

165

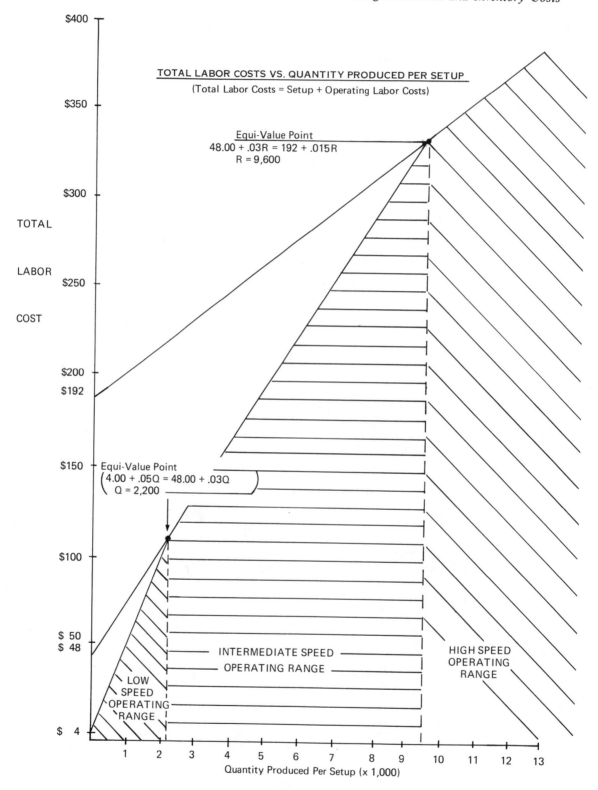

TOTAL LABOR COSTS VS. QUANTITY PRODUCED PER SETUP
(Total Labor Costs = Setup + Operating Labor Costs)

Equi-Value Point
48.00 + .03R = 192 + .015R
R = 9,600

Equi-Value Point
$\left(\begin{array}{l} 4.00 + .05Q = 48.00 + .03Q \\ Q = 2,200 \end{array}\right.$

TOTAL LABOR COST

INTERMEDIATE SPEED OPERATING RANGE

HIGH SPEED OPERATING RANGE

LOW SPEED OPERATING RANGE

Quantity Produced Per Setup (x 1,000)

FIGURE 7-3

$$\$.05Q + \$4.00 = \$.03Q + \$48.00$$
$$Q(\$.05 - \$.03) = \$44.00$$
$$\$.02Q = \$44.00$$
$$Q = \frac{\$44.00}{\$.02} = 2{,}200 \text{ units}$$

$$\$.03R + \$48.00 = \$.015R + \$192.00$$
$$\$.03R - \$.015R = \$192.00 - \$48.00$$
$$R(\$.030 - \$.015) = \$144.00$$
$$\$.015R = \$144.00$$
$$R = \frac{\$144.00}{\$.015} = 9{,}600 \text{ units}$$

The two equi-value points set the boundaries for the three operating ranges. With those points determined, the data for Figure 7-4 can be readily developed. Figure 7-4 shows a maximum of 13,000 units, but that is an arbitrary value established solely for convenience.

It is important to note in Figure 7-4 that the unit costs decrease rapidly at first, and that the rate of decrease becomes less as the quantities decrease. In other words, the cost reductions are quite dramatic at first and they are more difficult to achieve as the quantities increase. The unit costs tend to level off as the quantities become larger. It is quite possible that cost reduction can become a minor reason for the purchase of high speed equipment, unless a reduction in downtime is expected. Increased capacity might well be the major reason for selecting high speed equipment.

Returning to Figure 7-2, it can be seen from the data there that additional labor cost results from unscheduled downtime due to breakdown. But not only is there an additional labor cost, there is also a loss of income. Whether considered as an extra cost or as a loss, the effect of downtime on income must be considered in an evaluation of equipment.

Figure 7-5 shows a sample calculation of the effects of unscheduled downtime. The example uses the intermediate-speed equipment described in Figure 7-2. It assumes an average downtime of 10%. It also assumes that most of the runs will lie in the middle of the operating range for that equipment. In the example, recognition is given to the practice normally encountered of extending run time to produce the number of units required to fill the production order. The extension of run time results in a reduction in the number of runs each year.

The calculation in Figure 7-5 shows that the enforced idleness of the equipment operators during downtime, plus the cost of the mechanic needed to correct the situation, increases the unit labor cost to $.0432 from $.0381. The extra labor cost is over 13% and amounts to $3,590 per year.

On the other hand, the loss of 61,360 units for the year probably is more important. The profit per unit might reasonably be expected to lie in the $.10 to $1.00 range. At $.10 per unit the loss would be $6,136. At $1.00 per unit the loss would be $61,360.

Overemphasis of the benefits of high-rate equipment has led to unfortunate consequences in some instances. One of the typical outcomes is that the sought-for cost reductions are not realized. Another result is that, with the high-speed capability being available, and with setup costs being increased, there is apparent justification for increasing production order quantities. Increased order size, of course, leads to increase in average inventory levels. These consequences are unfortunate because they had not been anticipated. The evaluations used for deciding to purchase the replacement equipment had overlooked these considerations.

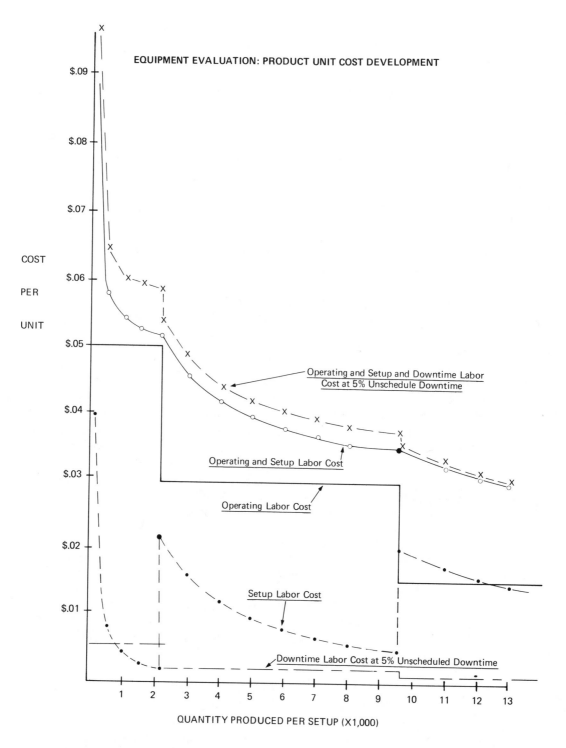

EQUIPMENT EVALUATION: PRODUCT UNIT COST DEVELOPMENT

COST

PER

UNIT

Operating and Setup and Downtime Labor Cost at 5% Unschedule Downtime

Operating and Setup Labor Cost

Operating Labor Cost

Setup Labor Cost

Downtime Labor Cost at 5% Unscheduled Downtime

QUANTITY PRODUCED PER SETUP (X1,000)

FIGURE 7-4

SAMPLE CALCULATION: LOSSES RESULTING FROM DOWNTIME

BASIC CONDITIONS

Start with	52 weeks per year	
Less: 2 weeks vacation shutdown	- 2	
Less: 10 holidays	- 2	
Leaves	48 weeks per year	

For one shift, with 40 hours per week, 40 x 48 = 1,920 hours available per year

For example, the intermediate equipment has
lower end of operating range = 2,200 units per run
upper end of operating range = 9,600 units per run
(2200 + 9600) ÷ 2, gives an average
$$\begin{rcases} \text{Average} \\ \text{Operating} \\ \text{Time} \end{rcases}$$
= 5,900 units per run

$$\frac{5,900 \text{ units per average run}}{500 \text{ units per operating hour}} =$$
= 11.8 operating hours per run

Operating hours per run = 11.8
Setup hours per setup = 3.0

Total scheduled hours = 14.8 per run

$$\frac{1,920 \text{ hours available per year}}{14.8 \text{ hours per run}}$$ = 129.7 runs per year

129.7 runs per year x 5,900 units per run = 765,230 units per year

129.7 runs x 11.8 operating hours per run = 1,530 operating hours
1,530 hours x $15.00 per hour, cost of operating = $22,950
129.7 runs x 3 setup hours per run = 389 setup hours
389 setup hours x $16.00 per hour, cost of setup = $6,224
$22,950 operating labor + $6,224 setup labor = $29,174 total labor cost

$$\text{Expected Cost} = \frac{\$29,174 \text{ labor cost}}{765,230 \text{ units}}$$ = $.0381 per unit

EFFECT OF UNSCHEDULED DOWNTIME

With 10% downtime, to get hours needed to produce
5,900 units: 11.8 operating hours ÷ 90% = 13.1 hours used per run

Hours used per run = 13.1	
Setup hours per setup = 3.0	
16.1 per run	

$$\frac{1,920 \text{ hours available per year}}{16.1 \text{ hours per run}}$$ = 119.3 runs per year

119.3 runs per year x 5,900 units per run = 703,870 units per year

119.3 runs x 13.1 operating hours per run = 1,563 operating hours
1,563 operating hours x $15.00 per hour, cost of operating = $23,445
119.3 runs x 3 setup hours per run = 358 setup hours
358 setup hours x $16.00 per hour, cost of setup = $5,728
Downtime per run = 13.1 - 11.8 = 1.3 hours per run
119.3 runs x 1.3 downtime hours per run = 155 downtime hours
155 downtime hours x $8.00 for mechanic cost = $1,240
$23,445 operating labor + $5,728 setup labor + $1,240 mechanic labor

= $30,413 total labor cost

With 10% downtime, actual costs = $$\frac{\$30,413 \text{ labor cost}}{703,870 \text{ units}}$$ = $.0432 per unit

Total loss from 10% downtime:
Loss from excess labor cost = 703,870 units ($.0432 - $.0381)
per unit = $30,413 total labor cost

PLUS

Lost revenue = (765,230 - 703,870) units x unit profit = 61,360 x unit profit

FIGURE 7-5

169

AVOID HASTY JUDGMENTS IN EVALUATING
EQUIPMENT UTILIZATION

There are no pat answers to the questions, "What is good utilization?" and, "What is poor utilization?" Those questions must be answered specifically for each individual situation. There are many possible definitions for the term % Utilization. Four of them have been examined and discussed here. It has been demonstrated, quantitatively, that a thoughtful analysis is needed to achieve a clear understanding of how % Utilization values change and why they change.

There are common sense principles that can be helpful in examining utilization to determine if it is getting better or worse, and if it is good enough to provide needed capacity.

Lack of understanding regarding evaluating equipment utilization can lead to overutilization. There are some clear signals that warn when equipment is headed for overutilization. There are some simple steps to be taken to correct that condition.

The difficulties of understanding how to interpret % Utilization values are more apparent than real. The simple application of common sense can help examine utilization to determine if it is getting better or worse and to determine if the utilization is good enough to provide needed capacity.

The practical value of understanding how to evaluate utilization goes beyond the direct control of labor costs. Part of the additional value comes from understanding how to avoid the misjudgments that can lead to overutilization, and how to respond to the signals that warn of the approach of that condition. Various instances have been observed of hasty decisions, based on lack of understanding, that have aggravated rather than alleviated overutilization conditions.

Hasty decisions have also been seen to increase downtime, both scheduled downtime for changeovers and nonscheduled downtime for breakdowns. Of all of the factors that can adversely affect equipment utilization, downtime apparently is the one that is least understood and therefore not given proper attention. Granted that an analysis of downtime requires painstaking examination of many illusive, indistinct details, the potential rewards are many and meaningful. Among the possible rewards are:

— Reduced product costs.
— Increased capacity.
— Increased income and profits.
— Improved evaluation of equipment replacement analyses.

To sum up, understanding how to interpret utilization evaluation can be a key factor in controlling production and inventory costs.

Chapter 8

Selecting the Right Crew Sizes
and Controlling Overtime Costs

One of the most fundamental management functions concerns manpower planning and control. This control is exercised through decisions regarding overtime, hiring and firing. The basis for these decisions often includes considerations of inventory levels, pricing policies, capital expenditures (new equipment), and labor contracts. This chapter will deal with manpower control and how to evaluate in quantitative terms various manpower policies and alternatives.

It would simplify matters to talk about manpower control alone and assume that minimization of labor costs is an end in itself. Manpower control, however, is a tool that is used interactively with other management tools in an effort to maximize profits. For example, the easiest way to lower manpower costs may be to change the finished goods inventory level. In such a case, the cost of maintaining a higher inventory should be compared to the savings in labor cost to determine whether the increase in inventory is justified. First, we must determine the cost of changing output directly as sales change. This must then be compared to maintaining a constant output and allowing the finished goods inventory to cover the peaks and valleys of the sales demand. This leads us to the basic question: "What are the various alternatives for changing output and what is the cost associated with each alternative?"

Some of management's options for meeting increased production levels would include:

1. Add an additional shift(s) to an operating production line. This would normally entail hiring a crew for that shift.
2. Add a partial shift to a line. This is usually accomplished by working an existing crew overtime—i.e., a nine or ten-hour day.
3. Start up an idle production line. Hiring additional manpower would probably be the means for manning the line.
4. Build a new line. This is usually considered a long-term decision. However, it

cannot be ignored since a policy of varying production requires more productive equipment than a constant output policy.

5. Operate six days a week. This almost certainly will result in overtime premium paid to the Saturday crew.

6. Operate seven days a week. Most short-term seven-day operations are manned using overtime. However, a four crew rotating swing schedule can be used to eliminate the overtime.

7. Contract work out. Contracting work is generally quite expensive since you pay for the contractor's overhead and profit. However, it can be effective in covering the extreme peaks in production.

USES OF OVERTIME

Some firms adhere to a no overtime policy while others routinely incur 30% overtime. Why such dramatically different policies? To answer that question, we should look into the reasons for overtime.

Firms have many reasons for working overtime which include the following:

1. To supplement a work force where there is a general shortage of available men with the required skills. This is a very common reason given for overtime for specialized or highly skilled jobs. Many companies feel that after investing years of training in a skilled worker, their return will be enhanced by his working overtime rather than by training a new man.

2. To cover peak production loads. Another common use of overtime is to man a plant to handle seasonal or other short-term production peaks. Firms use overtime in this instance where there is no supply of short-term labor or the training and fringe benefit costs of new employees is greater than the overtime premium for the existing work force.

3. To supplement total capacity. In a capital intensive industry, one of the keys to profitability is to fully utilize machines and equipment. This means operating Saturday and even Sunday. Short of a rotating[1] or other scheduling schemes, overtime is normally the only means for manning this weekend work. Thus, many companies routinely work Saturday overtime throughout the year.

4. To maintain a continuous process. Many industries *must* operate certain types of production facilities continuously because of the very nature of the process. This would include public utilities, steel blast furnaces, and aluminum smelting. These industries have typically used the rotating schedule. However, recent labor contracts are requiring premium pay for those working rotating shifts. The alternative is a straight schedule with weekend overtime or a four-crew, twelve-hour day which under most contracts requires overtime pay.

5. To cover for absenteeism. Overtime is a commonly applied means for filling in crews. The other alternatives for handling absenteeism are simply to run short

---

[1]Four production crews, staggered over the weekend, and rotating shifts each week.

or to maintain a standby labor pool to fill in vacant jobs. The labor pool concept saves overtime, but often can be quite expensive, since labor pool personnel spend much of their time on nonproductive work.

6. To reduce process flow time to meet special customer needs. Almost all plants have "hot jobs" where customers need shipment faster than the normal process time would allow. Sometimes a plant can comply with such a demand by rearranging production schedules. However, overtime is often used to compress the production flow time.

7. To cover up operating mistakes. Jobs often become "hot" because of production problems such as high scrap. Overtime is often the means for manning-up to remake the job to meet the delivery date.

8. To perform maintenance work on equipment that operates 15 shifts per week or more. This is a common reason for the overtime of maintenance personnel and is often a sizeable segment of a plant's overtime.

Overtime—A Tool Or A Crutch?

By looking at the list of reasons for overtime, it becomes apparent that overtime can be used or misused. High overtime can be a symptom of a mismanaged plant or it can be the result of a carefully analyzed, rational policy.

How can high overtime be good? Managers are often confronted with a typical situation where the alternate solutions are:

1. To hire and train new people and lay them off when product demand falls,
2. To increase the average finished goods stock to cover for business peaks, or
3. To work overtime to cover the peaks.

By properly analyzing all the economic and societal factors, it is often the proper conclusion that working overtime is the best solution. This is how overtime can be used as an effective tool in planning and cost control.

However, overtime can often be the result of poor planning and operating practices. Many plants accept or are forced to accept sales orders without having given full consideration as to whether they can produce the item (along with all their other production commitments) in time to meet all promised delivery dates. Too often, it is well after the order has been placed (and often started in production) that it is realized that overtime is required to get the job out on time. Overtime is also used to speed up the finishing of a job because the job was not given proper scheduling priority in its initial phases of manufacture. These are some cases of how the overtime crutch is used.

An overall overtime percentage by itself is not a good measure of management's effectiveness. It is the reasons for, and uses of, the overtime that can often be an indication of whether it is being used as a tool or a crutch.

COSTS TO CONSIDER

The basis for proper manpower planning and control is to first determine the explicit economic impact of each alternative solution (overtime, hiring, training, layoffs, and subcontracting) for the types of production problems that arise. The economic factors can then be weighed against the social factors and implicit risks of each alternative to arrive at a final decision in each circumstance.

The kinds of costs normally considered in manpower planning include the following:

1. *The Costs of Maintaining an Individual on the Payroll.*

These are the continuing costs associated with current employees and for any newly hired workers.

a) First are the obvious hourly costs such as base labor rate, cost of living allowances, incentive pay, and shift premium. These are a function of hours worked and can be expressed in dollars per man-hour.

b) The second type of expenses are annual costs per employees that do not vary with hours worked. These so-called "fringes" can often include FICA, contributions to the pension fund, workmen's compensation, vacation pay, holiday pay, sick pay, bereavement pay, hospitalization, major medical insurance, life insurance, and a portion of unemployment insurance. These costs can normally be expressed in dollars per year per employee. In some cases, the cost of fringe benefits can be as high as 50% of an employee's base rate over a year's period of time. In such cases, the manager may conclude that since overtime can have little or no fringe benefit cost, it (at time and a half) is no more expensive than straight time with fringes. While this may be true, such logic is dangerous if used as an excuse to work overtime. It can result in the loss of control. The uncontrolled use of overtime can lead to the typical slowdown during the week to guarantee Saturday work.

2. *The Costs of Hiring a New Employee.*

These are normally one-time costs and include recruiting, medical exam, clerical processing, orientation, formal job training, poor initial productivity (with associated lost capacity and/or time) and high scrap. These can be shown as costs per newly hired employees.

There is an implicit cost of the probability of incurring a future layoff cost (see Item 4).

3. *The Cost of Recalling a Laid-Off Employee.*

This would be a minimal clerical processing cost but with the implicit potential extension of the supplemental unemployment benefits (S.U.B.) obligation in case of a re-layoff. The clerical costs can be shown as dollars per recall.

4. *The Cost of a Layoff.*

a) First are the clerical processing costs, severance pay, and the lost productivity or premium pay related to the "bumping" which often results from the layoff. These one-time costs are incurred at the time of the layoff.

b) The second category are the costs that relate to the duration of the layoff. These potentially include increased unemployment premiums, S.U.B. payments, continued hospitalization, major medical, and life insurance premiums. Another consideration in a layoff must be the risk of permanently losing the employees and having to train a new man when the need arises for a recall.

5. *The Costs of Adding Additional Shifts.*

In addition to the hourly shift premium, the cost of a paid lunch can be incurred when a third shift is added. Making a process continuous through the addition of a third shift can have a favorable or unfavorable effect on process costs. Extra shifts often result in a dilution of supervisory talent and do not receive the same level of staff support as the day shift.

THE BASIC MODEL

Now that the costs associated with manpower decisions have been defined, we can formulate the basic model. The key to developing an accurate model is to include the incremental cash flow associated with each alternative solution or strategy. This means looking at costs in considerably more detail than is normally shown on typical accounting reports. Most accounting systems, for good reasons, are based on averaging costs and distributing them to products and/or departments. We must look at the detailed elements that go into the average costs. For example, accounting systems typically add up all fringe benefit costs and distribute them "per labor hour" or "as a percent of base labor rate." But as we have already found, all fringe costs do not vary directly with hours worked but are often a step function. In addition, temporary employee fringes are much lower than benefits for permanent workers because temporary workers generally get no vacation, pension or S.U.B.

Let's now look at an example of a typical situation:

A machine shop has 5 automatic screw machines utilized fully on a five-day work week. Forecasts show a 20% increase in sales over the next five years. Should the firm buy a new machine or work the five existing ones six days a week?

To simplify our discussion, we will initially assume:

1. The current work force would be willing to work six days per week,
2. There is no seasonality of demand,
3. The new machine would be identical to the old ones, and
4. Direct labor costs are the only costs to consider.

Data

Current work force works 2,000 hours/man/year
Base labor rate = $5.00/hour
Fringe benefits = $3,000/man/year

Total Current Direct Labor Costs

Base Labor Cost = 5 machines ×
3 men/machine ×
2,000 hours × $5   = $150,000

5 machines X
3 men/machine X $3,000/year   = +   45,000
                                               $195,000

Same Work Force Working Six Day Wk. $195,000
    15 men X 50 Saturdays year X
    8 hours/Saturday X 1.5 X $5/hour   = +   45,000
                                               $240,000

Buy New Machine and Hire 3 People $195,000
    3 men X 2,000 hours/year X $5/hours   = +   30,000
    3 men X $3,000/year   = +   9,000
                                               $234,000

This analysis shows that purchasing a new machine and hiring new people would save $6,000 per year in labor costs over working overtime. Without getting into a discussion of justification of capital expenditures, it would appear unlikely that $6,000 per year would justify an automatic screw machine.

However, let's look again at the assumptions we made in light of a more practical situation:

1. It is extremely naive to think that every worker will work every Saturday—particularly the Saturday evening shift. You, therefore, must consider that some of the overtime work must be done on Sundays at double time.

2. Most products have some ups and downs in demand. A new machine with more workers will give you more capacity to handle higher peaks. However, when business is low, a layoff (with its associated costs) could result. With the five machine, six day schedule, the business valley can be handled simply by cutting overtime.

3. Rarely is a newly purchased machine identical to the old machines. New machines generally incorporate advanced features and are more efficient and productive than older, existing machines. Therefore, the increased productivity of the new machine must be considered.

4. Many items other than direct labor costs must be considered. These include indirect labor, material handling, supervision, staff support, maintenance, operating supplies, utilities, and employee morale.

When To Add Another Shift/Another Line

A typical situation that arises when business is increasing concerns whether to work weekends, add an extra shift, or start up another production line. The analysis of this situation is quite complex but can be followed most logically with an example.

CASE IN POINT

A sheet metal fabrication plant operates several continuous roll form, shear-to-length, paint lines. Two lines are in operation, two shifts per day, five days a week. A third less efficient line has been "mothballed." A large order has just been received which will increase the total shop workload to 30% over its current operating capacity for three months. How should the company operate to fill the order?

Data

	Direct Labor Crew	Tons/Hr.	Current Output
Line 1	5 men	10	2 shifts-800 Tons/Wk.
Line 2	5 men	10	2 shifts-800 Tons/Wk.
Line 3	4 men	5	0

1. Four indirect people required each operating shift regardless of number of lines operating.
2. Addition of a third shift will only add 6.4 productive hours because of a forced paid lunch resulting on all three shifts.
3. Base labor rate is $5 per hour and fixed fringes for permanent employees are $4,000 per year.
4. Hiring cost for new employees is $500 per man.
5. Fringes for a temporary employee are estimated to be $100 per man per month.
6. Layoff cost for employees with less than six months' service is $300 per employee.
7. Start-up costs for Line 3 are $1,000.
8. Additional output required = 30% × 1,600 tons per week
   = 480 tons per week for 13 weeks.

The instinctive way to solve the problem is to itemize all the alternative solutions, calculate the cost of each, and select the cheapest. A partial list of the alternatives is shown in Figure 8-1.

Theoretically, the final solution to a problem of this type could be one of, or any combination of, these or other alternatives. Since there are millions of such combinations, it becomes obvious that it is impractical to analyze every combination. We must, therefore, use a procedure assigning priorities to the alternatives. A good procedure for doing this is by first calculating the additional output and incremental cost of each alternative. These calculations are shown in Figure 8-2.

Several assumptions were made in the unit cost calculations. For example, it was assumed that for any particular shift, Line 1 would have first priority; therefore, all of the indirect labor costs were assigned to Line 1. This means that in prioritizing the alternatives, Line 1 must be selected before the other lines even if the other lines have apparently lower unit costs. Similarly, for the unit costs to be valid, Line 3 must operate Monday through Friday on the first shift (Alternative 3) before other Line 3 alternatives are selected. This is because the $1,000 start-up cost was assigned to Alternative 3 (Monday through Friday on 1st shift).

Once the unit costs are calculated, each alternative can be ranked by cost—the lowest unit cost getting the highest rank. The output, unit cost, and ranking for each alternative are shown in Figure 8-3. To find the low cost solution to the original problem, we select the alternatives in economic rank sequence until the 480 tons per

ALTERNATIVES

1. a) Add 3rd shift to Line 1, 5 days/week.
      Hire new employees for direct and indirect labor.
   b) Same as 1a but work existing employees overtime.
2. a) Add 3rd shift to Line 2, 5 days/week.
      Hire new employees for direct labor.
   b) Same as 2a but work existing employees overtime.
3. Start up Line 3, 1 Shift, 5 days/week.
   Hire new employees for direct labor.
4. Add 2nd shift to Line 3, 5 days/week.
   Hire new employees for direct labor.
5. a) Add 3rd shift to Line 3, 5 days/week.
      Hire new employees for direct labor.
   b) Same as 5a but work existing employees overtime.
6. Work Line 1, 1st Shift on Saturday.
7. Work Line 1, 2nd Shift on Saturday.
8. Work Line 1, 3rd Shift on Saturday.
9. Work Line 2, 1st Shift on Saturday.
10. Work Line 2, 2nd Shift on Saturday.
11. Work Line 2, 3rd Shift on Saturday.
12. Work Line 3, 1st Shift on Saturday.
13. Work Line 3, 2nd Shift on Saturday.
14. Work Line 3, 3rd Shift on Saturday.
15. Work Line 1, 1st Shift on Sunday.
16. Work Line 1, 2nd Shift on Sunday.
17. Work Line 1, 3rd Shift on Sunday.
18. Work Line 2, 1st Shift on Sunday.
19. Work Line 2, 2nd Shift on Sunday.
20. Work Line 2, 3rd Shift on Sunday.
21. Work Line 3, 1st Shift on Sunday.
22. Work Line 3, 2nd Shift on Sunday.
23. Work Line 3, 3rd Shift on Sunday.

FIGURE 8-1

month output level is reached. Therefore, the solution is to pick Alternatives 3, 4, and 6.

This solution to our problem (Alternatives 3, 4 and 6) says that we should start up Line 3 for a two-shift, five-day operation and run Line 1 for one shift on Saturday. This is the lowest cost means for meeting the given conditions of the problem.

This procedure for economically evaluating alternatives is reasonably straight-forward. However, it becomes extremely cumbersome when difficult product classes are considered. The only practical way to solve a problem with multiple line and multiple products is by a linear program. The framework for how to set up a L.P. solution is shown in the Appendix to this chapter.

ADDITIONAL OUTPUT CAPACITY AND
LABOR COST/TON FOR ALTERNATIVES

1a. Output = 6.4 hours/day x 5 days/week x 10 tons/hour $\qquad$ = 320 tons/week

$(5 \text{ direct} + 4 \text{ indirect}) \times \$5/\text{hour} \times \dfrac{8 \text{ hours}}{10 \text{ tons/hour} \times 6.4 \text{ hours}} + 9 \text{ people} \times$

($500 hiring + $300 fringes + $300 layoff)/(13 weeks x 320 tons/week)

$\qquad$ = $8.00/ton

1b. Output = 320 tons/week

$(5 \text{ direct} + 4 \text{ indirect}) \times 1.5 \times \$5/\text{hour} \times \dfrac{8 \text{ hours}}{10 \text{ tons/hour} \times 6.4}$ $\quad$ = $8.44/ton

2a. Output = 6.4 hours/day x 5 days/week x 10 tons/hour $\qquad$ = 320 tons/week

$5 \text{ direct} \times \$5/\text{hour} \times \dfrac{8 \text{ hours}}{10 \text{ tons/hour} \times 6.4 \text{ hours}} +$

5 direct x ($500 + $300 + $300)/(13 weeks x 320 tons/week) $\quad$ = $4.45/ton

2b. Output = 320 tons/week

$5 \text{ direct} \times 1.5 \times \$5/\text{hour} \times \dfrac{8 \text{ hours}}{10 \text{ tons/hour} \times 6.4}$ $\qquad$ = $4.69/ton

3. Output = 8 hours/day x 5 days/week x 5 tons/hour $\qquad$ = 200 tons/week

$4 \text{ direct} \times \$5/\text{hour} \times \dfrac{1}{5 \text{ tons/hour}} + \$1,000/(13 \text{ weeks} \times 200 \text{ tons/week})$

+ 4 direct x ($500 + $300 + $300)/(13 weeks x 200 tons/week)

$\qquad$ = $6.08/ton

4. Output = 200 tons/week

$4 \text{ direct} \times \$5/\text{hour} \times \dfrac{1}{5 \text{ tons/hour}}$

+ 4 direct x ($500 + $300 + $300)/(13 weeks x 200 tons/week) $\quad$ = $5.69/ton

5a. Output = 6.4 hours/day x 5 days/week x 5 tons/hour $\qquad$ = 160 tons/week

$4 \text{ direct} \times \$5/\text{hour} \times \dfrac{8 \text{ hours}}{5 \text{ tons/hour} \times 6.4 \text{ hours}} + \$1,000/(13 \text{ weeks} \times$

160 tons/week) + 4 direct x ($500 + $300 + $300)/(13 weeks x 160 tons/week)

$\qquad$ = $7.60/ton

5b. Output = 160 tons/week

$4 \text{ direct} \times 1.5 \times \$5 \text{ hour} \times \dfrac{8 \text{ hours}}{5 \text{ tons/hour} \times 6.4 \text{ hours}} + \$1,000/(13 \text{ weeks} \times 160 \text{ tons/week})$

$\qquad$ = $7.98/ton

6. Output = 8 hours x 10 tons/hour = $\underline{\underline{80 \text{ tons}}}$

$(5 \text{ direct} + 4 \text{ indirect}) \times 1.5 \times \$5 \times \dfrac{1}{10 \text{ tons/hour}}$ $\qquad$ = $6.75/ton

7. Same as 6.

8. Output = 6.4 hours x 10 tons/hour = $\underline{\underline{64 \text{ tons}}}$

$(5 \text{ direct} + 4 \text{ indirect}) \times 1.5 \times \$5 \times \dfrac{8 \text{ hours}}{10 \text{ tons/hour} \times 6.4 \text{ hours}}$ $\quad$ = $8.44/ton

FIGURE 8-2

9. Output = 8 hours x 10 tons/hour = $\underline{\underline{80 \text{ tons}}}$

   5 direct x 1.5 x \$5 x $\dfrac{1}{10 \text{ tons/hour}}$ = $\underline{\underline{\$3.75/\text{ton}}}$

10. Same as 9.

11. Output = 6.4 hours x 10 tons/hour = $\underline{\underline{64 \text{ tons}}}$

    5 direct x 1.5 x \$5/hour x $\dfrac{8 \text{ hours}}{10 \text{ tons/hour} \times 6.4 \text{ hours}}$ = $\underline{\underline{\$4.69/\text{ton}}}$

12. Output = 8 hours x 5 tons/hour = $\underline{\underline{40 \text{ tons}}}$

    4 direct x \$5/hour x 1.5 x $\dfrac{1}{5 \text{ tons/hour}}$ = $\underline{\underline{\$6.00/\text{ton}}}$

13. Same as 12.

14. Output = 6.4 hours x 5 tons/hour = $\underline{\underline{32 \text{ tons}}}$

    4 direct x \$5/hour x 1.5 x $\dfrac{8 \text{ hours}}{5 \text{ tons/hour} \times 6.4 \text{ hours}}$ = $\underline{\underline{\$7.50/\text{ton}}}$

15. Output = 8 hours x 10 tons/hour = $\underline{\underline{80 \text{ tons}}}$

    (5 direct + 4 indirect) x 2.0 x \$5/hour x $\dfrac{1}{10 \text{ tons/hour}}$ = $\underline{\underline{\$9/\text{ton}}}$

16. Same as 15.

17. Output = 6.4 hours x 10 tons/hour = $\underline{\underline{64 \text{ tons}}}$

    (5 direct + 4 indirect) x 2.0 x \$5/hour x $\dfrac{8 \text{ hours}}{10 \text{ tons/hour} \times 6.4 \text{ hours}}$ = $\underline{\underline{\$11.25/\text{ton}}}$

18. Output = 8 hours x 10 tons/hour = $\underline{\underline{80 \text{ tons}}}$

    5 direct x 2.0 x \$5/hour x $\dfrac{1}{10 \text{ tons/hour}}$ = $\underline{\underline{\$5.00/\text{ton}}}$

19. Same as 18.

20. Output = 6.4 hours x 10 tons/hour = $\underline{\underline{64 \text{ tons}}}$

    5 direct x 2.0 x \$5/hour x $\dfrac{8 \text{ hours}}{10 \text{ tons/hour} \times 6.4 \text{ hours}}$ = $\underline{\underline{\$6.25/\text{ton}}}$

21. Output = 8 hours x 5 tons/hour = $\underline{\underline{40 \text{ tons}}}$

    4 direct x 2.0 x \$5/hour x $\dfrac{1}{5 \text{ tons/hour}}$ = $\underline{\underline{\$8/\text{ton}}}$

22. Same as 21.

23. Output = 6.4 hours x 5 tons/hour = $\underline{\underline{32 \text{ tons}}}$

    4 direct x 2.0 x \$5/hour x $\dfrac{8 \text{ hours}}{5 \text{ tons/hour} \times 6.4 \text{ hours}}$ = $\underline{\underline{\$10/\text{ton}}}$

FIGURE 8-2 (Cont.)

Alternative	Selection Must Follow Alt. Number	Output Capacity (Tons/Week)	Cost ($/Ton)	Economic Rank
1a	-	320	8.00	9
1b	-	320	8.44	-
2a	1a or 1b*	320	4.45	10
2b	1a or 1b*	320	4.69	-
3	-	200	6.08	1
4	3**	200	5.69	2
5a	1a or 1b + 3	160	7.60	11
5b	1a or 1b + 3	160	7.98	-
6	-	80	6.75	3
7	-	80	6.75	5
8	-	64	8.44	12
9	6***	80	3.75	4
10	7	80	3.75	6
11	8	64	4.69	13
12	6***	40	6.00	7
13	7	40	6.00	8
14	8	32	7.50	14
15	-	80	9.00	15
16	-	80	9.00	18
17	-	64	11.25	21
18	15	80	5.00	16
19	16	80	5.00	19
20	17	64	6.25	22
21	15	40	8.00	17
22	16	40	8.00	20
23	17	32	10.00	23

*   2a or 2b must follow selection of alternative 1a or 1b because 1a and 2b include the indirect labor cost for 2a, 2b, 5a, and 5b.

** 4 must follow 3 because 3 includes the start-up costs for line 3.

*** 9 and 12 must follow 6 because 6 includes the indirect labor for 9 and 12.

FIGURE 8-3

The example shown has been based on given conditions. The fact is, however, that in real life the conditions are rarely given. Such things as anticipated sales volumes, training costs, and start-up costs are often difficult to predict. Each parameter really is a distribution of expected values and any one expected value can be different from the actual value. Since the cost of some alternatives are more vulnerable to errors in input than other alternatives, it is essential to measure the effect to each alternative of input errors or variations. This is called *risk analysis*. This type of analysis can be accomplished by calculating the cost of each alternative based on various expected values of input. Then we can zero in on break points such as the "start-up cost of Line 3 over which it would be cheaper to work Line 1 Saturday" or "the training cost of new workers over which it would be cheaper to work existing employees overtime." It is this kind of information that managers need in order to make the critical decisions regarding manpower planning.

APPENDIX

Linear Program Solution To Scheduling Model

Linear programming can be used to determine the minimum cost production schedule for a multiple line, multiple product plant. It can tell you which products to run on which line, how many shifts to operate each line and whether to work any line overtime.

A Sample Problem

A plant has two products and two production lines. Let's first define the L.P. variables. Each variable represents units (quantity) of a particular product produced on a particular line on a particular shift on a particular day type (weekday, Saturday, or Sunday). The variables for this problem would be:

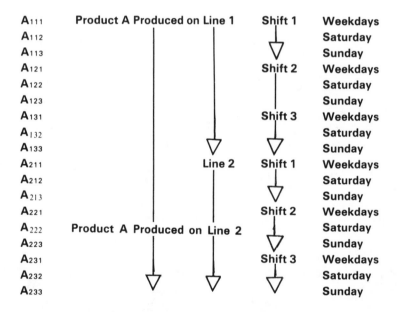

A similar group of variables exist for Product B. The number of variables in any problem are: The number of products times the number of production lines times the number of shifts times the number of day types. Therefore, in this example:

$$
\begin{array}{r}
2 \text{ Products} \\
\times\ 2 \text{ Production Lines} \\
\times\ 3 \text{ Shifts} \\
\times\ 3 \text{ Day Types} \\
\hline
36 \text{ Variables}
\end{array}
$$

The objective of the L.P. solution is to determine what values of the stated variables result in the minimum total production cost. To quantify this, we calculate the unit production cost for each variable. These values are called the cost coefficients and are represented in the total cost equation:

$$K_{A111} A_{111} + K_{A112} A_{112} + \ldots + K_{B232} B_{232} + K_{B233} B_{233} = \text{Total Cost}$$

This is called the objective function because it is our objective to minimize it.

The values that these variables can take are subject to constraints that we will now quantify. The first type of constraint is sales demand. We simply state how many units of each product are to be produced:

$$A_{111} + A_{112} + \ldots + A_{232} + A_{233} = S_A (\text{Sales demand of product A})$$
$$B_{111} + B_{112} + \ldots + B_{232} + B_{233} = S_B (\text{Sales demand of product B})$$

The next constraints are production capacity limitations. Since these are usually expressed in hours (per week), we must convert the variables (in output units) to hours by multiplying each variable by its appropriate production hours per unit (N). There is, therefore a constraint equation for each line for each shift for each day type, i.e.:

Line 1   Shift 1 Monday →Friday
$$N_{A111} A_{111} + N_{B111} B_{111} \leq 40 \text{ hours}$$
Line 1   Shift 2 Saturday
$$N_{A112} A_{112} + N_{B112} B_{112} \leq 8 \text{ hours}$$
$$\ldots$$
Line 2   Shift 3 Sunday
$$N_{A233} A_{233} + N_{B233} B_{233} \leq 8 \text{ hours}$$

The total number of constraint equations is the number of products plus the number of lines times the number of shifts times the number of day types. In this example, there are: $2 + (2 \times 3 \times 3) = 20$ constraints.

The solution to the L.P. will tell you the value of each variable that will minimize the objective function while meeting each constraint.

In a hypothetical example, the solution for a specific set of coefficients (parameters) takes the following form:

$$A_{111} = 20 \text{ units}$$
$$A_{112} = 4 \text{ units}$$
$$B_{211} = 60 \text{ units}$$
$$B_{221} = 60 \text{ units}$$

Based on $N_{A111} = 2$, $N_{A112} = 2$, $N_{B211} = .67$, $N_{B221} = .67$,

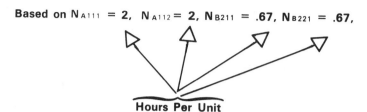

Hours Per Unit

The L.P. indicates that to minimize total costs the following schedule should be followed:

1. Produce 20 units of A on Line 1, Shift 1, Monday-Friday (20 × 2 = 40 hrs./wk.)
2. Produce 4 units of A on Line 1, Shift 1, Saturday (4 × 2 = 8 hrs./wk.)
3. Produce 60 units of B on Line 2, Shift 1, Monday-Friday (60 × .67 = 40 hrs./wk.)
4. Produce 60 units of B on Line 2, Shift 2, Monday-Friday (60 × .67 = 40 hrs./wk.)

While such a solution can theoretically be solved manually, the only practical way to solve the equations is by computer.

Fortunately, L.P. packages are readily available for most any in-house or time-sharing computer. If the number of variables and constraints becomes large, the L.P. will rapidly tax the capacity of a small computer. This can be handled by renting time on a larger, more powerful computer. Otherwise, the number of products or constraints must be reduced. This can be accomplished by grouping, but care must be taken. Improper grouping can render the solution of little value.

Chapter 9

Determine the Proper Balance For
Machine Manning

OVERVIEW OF MACHINE LOADING CONSIDERATIONS

The most effective man and/or machine loading plan is determined by the end result being sought. Establish the relative importance of the following:
— Maximize output to reduce sales or production backlog.
— Maximize output to replenish inventory or build stock.
— Maximize machine or process running time to minimize preparation, start-up and shut-down cost or delays.
— Maximize machine or process running time to achieve consistent quality or better utilization of high capital investment equipment.
— Optimize manpower resources, machine utilization, and materials consumption to achieve minimum costs.
— Minimize manpower and materials costs to insure minimum variable costs per unit.
— Closely coordinate and synchronize output with preceding or following operations to achieve the most effective combined performance.
— Meet agreed schedules on a less stringent daily, weekly or monthly basis to provide flexibility for processing a variety of products or operations and balance manpower or machine use.
— Achieve level manpower utilization over long time periods in order to provide a secure, stable and efficient work force.

FACTORS TO CONSIDER IN DETERMINING HOW MANY
MACHINES PER PERSON

Analysis of Machine Capacity
Analyze operations to establish the extent of operator control over the rate of machine speed or production, the variety and consistency of materials processed and

the relative effects of the machine, operator and materials on the quality of finished work.

Scrutinize the machine design and controls to determine the limits to speed variability. Clearly define the speed range within which normal operations are expected to occur. For some mechanisms or processes, the rate of production may be fixed or limited to a small range, and the output variable only according to the feed rate of materials or the removal of completed work. A basic familiarity with the electro-mechanical components, which establish or limit the physical capacity of the machine, is essential in attempting to design the most efficient loading and scheduling program.

If the machine is of a fixed speed type, determine the components that effectively establish the speed in order to evaluate the possibilities for minor modifications for improved rates. For instance, a change in sheave or sprocket sizes may be all that is required to accommodate an improved output or synchronized scheduling with other units.

When operator control is the paramount influence on output, the extent to which the machine speed can be varied should be established to define the upper limits of output when additional operators or automation are employed.

An operator's influence on fixed speed equipment is usually limited to set-up, preparatory and unloading work, but the extent to which the output can be affected must be established and measured to effectively plan machine loading.

By virtue of these preliminary steps the factors that control or limit outputs can be identified. In addition to operator skill and effort, nearly all controlling or limiting factors are within one of the following categories:

1. Mechanisms
2. Materials
3. Tools
4. Quality Measures

Mechanisms can be measured through direct calculation. Motor R.P.M., sheave sizes, sprockets and the number of gear teeth are examples of common, observable mechanisms that can be measured through direct calculations. In addition, the actual outputs achieved under varying load conditions should be timed using appropriate techniques and direct observation.

Historical output data may suffice for loading in some situations, but is not usually satisfactory for effective machine loading or in identifying the limiting factors. However, comparisons of the historical output data with the calculated data or formal time studies can prove useful in evaluating the opportunities for improved loading efficiency and identifying major delays.

To be most useful in loading, the measurement of the limiting factors must be translated into the units used for loading and scheduling. Normally the finished product or the equivalent should be the ultimate unit of measure.

Analysis of External Work

The measurement of capacity will require a measurement of the operator's work as well as the machine capacity. All of the work performed outside of the machine operating time is called external work—in other words, work external to the machine time. Operator time spent in setting up the machine, getting necessary tools or removing finished work from the machine is called external work. Operator time spent in controlling the machine during the normal machine operating cycle is called internal work. It is work performed by the operator internal to the machine or process time.

The operation of multiple machine or processing units can be accomplished when external work required on one machine is performed during the machine time of one or more other machines or processes. In loading multiple machine or processing units to achieve optimum man and machine utilization there must be accurate and reliable measurement of several factors.

These factors are:

- Work—Operator   W
- External Work—Operator   EW
- Internal Work—Operator   IW
- Machine or Process Time   MT
- Interference—(Allowance for Operator) IT
- Enforced Attention Time—Operator   EAT
- Enforced Idle Time—Operator   EIT
- Net Production Cycle—Machine and
    Operator   NC

These factors are illustrated in the following way:

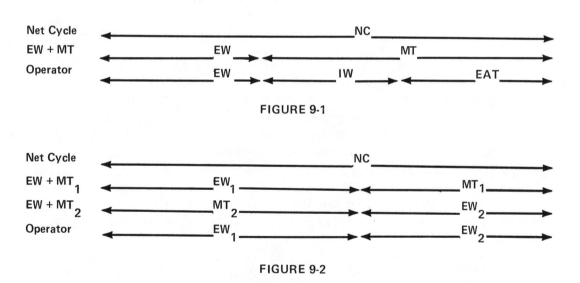

FIGURE 9-1

FIGURE 9-2

The net production cycle for one operator and one machine is illustrated in Figure 9-1. The cycle is the sum of the machine time with the external work. Within the machine time the operator performs internal work. The internal work required is less than the machine time and enforced attention time is required to complete the balance of the production cycle. The bottom line of Figure 9-1 illustrates the operator's required time for external, internal and enforced attention time.

In Figure 9-2 two machine or process steps are required to complete the production cycle. In this illustration the external work and the machine time required are balanced between the two machines to equal the net production cycle. The bottom line of Figure 9-2 illustrates the operator's required time which is the sum of the external work required to operate two machines.

External work (EW) may include the time necessary to acquire materials, tools and receive production orders as well as the machine set-up or other preparatory operations. The initial production cycle at the beginning of a shift or new production run will usually require special attention and time allowances for added operations.

Internal work (IW) can be complicated by variable conditions of operator control, machine reliability, material and tool conditions and outside service factors. Accurate measurement using time study techniques should be utilized when necessary. Norms can be established for low volume or infrequently occurring operations. Effective loading of multiple machine or process units requires a higher degree of machine reliability and longer machine or process cycles to minimize the interference that occurs when the chances of several machines needing operator attention at one time are high.

Special note of the necessity for operators to monitor, observe or otherwise give attention to machines or processes is separated from the manual operations that may be required during the machine or process time. This portion of the operator cycle is described as enforced attention time (EAT).

In some cases the operator is not occupied with either manual work or attention to the machine or process during the machine time. If it is not possible to arrange for other activity this portion of the cycle is designated as enforced idle time (EIT). It indicates an opportunity to improve the loading, particularly when it becomes a large part of the net cycle.

An additional variable must be measured when multiple machines or processes are being considered. As the number of machines to be attended is increased, interference or the chances of simultaneous completion of the machine time of two or more machines increases as well. It can be shown that the tendency for interference to occur during multiple machine assignments increases according to the number of machines to be attended and the percent of the production cycle devoted to the operator's work.

Interference occurs in multi-machine assignments when a machine is non-productive because the operator is tending another machine. When one operator tends two or more machines that operate independently of one another and have irregular and unpredictable stops, the running time cannot be coordinated and therefore interference results.

Instances of such conditions are numerous in industry. For example one automatic screw machine may be down longer than necessary because of having run out of stock while the operator is already occupied rodding or adjusting tools on another machine. Rodding occurrences are more or less predictable but tool adjustments are not, and the operation of two or more machines cannot be synchronized to prevent loss of machine time.

The same is true for operations such as weaving and braiding, involving breakage of threads or wires and respooling at irregular intervals, all of which usually cause the machines to stop through some control devices. If the operator is not already otherwise occupied he can give the machine immediate attention and put it back in operation, but a prior stoppage may be already under treatment by the operator, thereby preventing him from giving immediate attention to the new stoppage and causing a loss of machine time and production, or machine interference.

The mathematical laws of probability provide a measure of interference on such multi-machine assignments when man and machine time cannot be summarized to conform to a repetitive pattern.

These laws are as follows:

1. If any event is given the opportunity to occur or not to occur, the sum of the probabilities of the possible occurrences must be unity. In other words, the sum of the probabilities of occurrence and failure of occurrence of downtime for a given machine is equal to unity when machines act independently of each other.
2. If any event is given the opportunity to occur or not to occur, the probabilities of the possible occurrences will be distributed according to the terms of a binomial expansion.

The following pages include the results of machine interference studies and also the development of a method for computing operator enforced idle time.

DERIVATION OF AVERAGE INTERFERENCE CURVES

For purposes of discussion, the following symbols will be used:

W = Total Work per Unit in Standard Minutes = $W_e + W_i$
W_e = External Work per Unit (performed while machine is stopped)
W_i = Internal Work per Unit (performed with machine running)
MT = Machine Running Time per Unit in Minutes
NC = Net Cycle Time per Unit = $W_e + MT$
I = Machine Interference in Minutes

In any multi-machine assignment that *does not* contain internal work, the total cycle per unit becomes:

$$TC = W_e + MT + I$$

Since interference can cause interference, for example, two or more machines may stop while an operator is working on another machine, the part of the total cycle that tends to cause downtime or interference is $W_e + I$ and the part of the total cycle that tends to resist downtime or interference is the machine time.

However, when internal work is introduced, the internal work becomes an additional factor which tends to cause interference. Therefore, the total cycle per unit becomes:

$$TC = (W_e + W_i) + (MT - W_i) + I$$

The part that tends to cause downtime or interference is $W_e + W_i + I$, or $W + I$, while the part of the total cycle that tends to resist downtime or interference is $MT - W_i$.

Since the interference (I) and total cycle (TC) are unknown, it becomes necessary to develop a measure or index for interference in terms of net cycle (NC) which is known or can be measured. It will be noticed that the percent work per net cycle evaluates all of the factors that tend to cause interference except interference itself:

$$\%W/NC = \frac{W_e + W_i}{W_e + MT} = \frac{W}{W_e + MT}$$

In order to change the % W/NC to percent of total cycle

$$\%W/TC = \%W/NC\ (1 - \%I) = \%W/NC \left(1 - \frac{I}{TC}\right)$$

Now, let d = % of total cycle that tends to cause interference or downtime
        r = % of total cycle that tends to resist interference or downtime.
Then, according to the laws of probabilities, the sum of the two is equal to unity.

$$d + r = 1$$

Then, $d = \%W/NC\ (1 - \%I) + \%I$ and $r = 1 - d$, thus it is possible to determine by the binomial expansion of $(d + r)^n$, the average percent of interference per machine when % W/NC is the average value for n machines.

It will be noticed that the method of successive approximations must be employed since it is necessary to assume the %I to find the %I.

As an example of the calculation for one point on the Average Interference Chart (Figure 9-3), let us assume that from accurate measurement a multi-machine assignment of six machines results in an average % W/NC of 19% and let us assume that this assignment will result in an average percent interference per machine of 19% of TC (the 19's are pure coincidence).

$$d = .19\ (1 - .19) + .19 = .1539 + .19 = .3439$$
$$r = 1 - .3439 = .6561$$
$$(d + r)^6 = d^6 + 6d^5r + 15d^4r^2 + 20\ d^3r^3 + 15d^2r^4 + 6dr^5 + r^6$$

Inspection and study of this equation will show that each part of the expansion will indicate the probable percentage of work time and interference for the number of machines indicated by the exponent. Thus the expansion may be expressed:

AVERAGE INTERFERENCE CHART

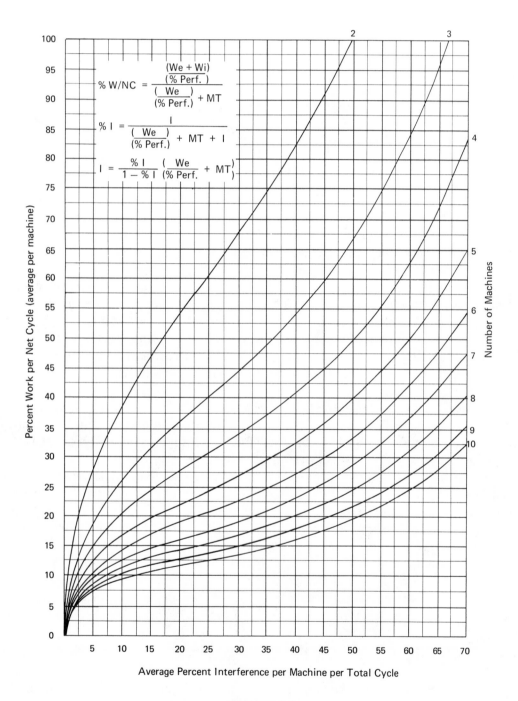

Average Percent Interference per Machine per Total Cycle

FIGURE 9-3

No. of Machines Down Together	Coefficient Sums		(d)	(r)	Waits	Interference
6	1	X	$(.3439)^6$		X 5 =	.00825
5	6	X	$(.3439)^5$	$(.6561)^1$	X 4 =	.07574
4	15	X	$(.3439)^4$	$(.6561)^2$	X 3 =	.27100
3	20	X	$(.3439)^3$	$(.6561)^3$	X 2 =	.45946
2	15	X	$(.3439)^2$	$(.6561)^4$	X 1 =	.32874
1	6	X	$(.3439)^1$	$(.6561)^5$	X 0 =	0
0	1	X		$(.6561)^6$	X 0 =	0
			Total Interference		=	1.14319
			% Interference per machine		=	.19053

Thus, the assumed 19% of the total cycle is the correct average interference per machine for this assignment. It will be noticed that the number of waits indicated above is always one less than the number of machines that are down or being worked on, since it is assumed that the operator will always perform work on one machine whenever this work is available.

Many similar calculations for possible %W/NC from 1 to 100% and for assignments of 2 to 10 machines resulted in the average interference chart. While the shape of the curves on this chart was somewhat unexpected, it is understandable when it is recognized that as interference increases it becomes a greater and greater percentage of the total cycle and the work becomes a lesser part. Therefore, additional work past a critical point does not increase the interference as fast as additional work below that critical point.

Practical application of the interference calculations in man machine loading requires that there be sufficient volume and an accurate analysis of cycle times, developed through professional time study techniques. Both external and internal work required to operate the machines or processes and the average non-repetitive work resulting from intermittent troubles or machine fixtures and material deficiencies that are an inherent part of the work, but not controllable by the operator, must be included. Nevertheless, a knowledge of the average interference for a particular loading arrangement is invaluable in estimating the total cycle time in order to make an accurate estimate of the maximum production or operators needed under the conditions created by a multi-machine assignment.

The interference chart can be used for estimating purposes, but it should be remembered that the percent interference derived from the chart is a percent of the total cycle rather than the net cycle.

Percent Interference from Chart is Percent of Total Cycle

From the derivation of the various points on the interference chart it should be recognized that %I is actually a percentage of the total cycle that includes I.

$$\% \text{ I (Chart)} = \frac{\text{I}}{W_e + W_i + (MT - W_i) + \text{I}} = \frac{\text{I}}{W_e + MT + \text{I}}$$

$$\text{Then I (Time)} = \frac{\% \text{ I}}{1 - \% \text{ I}} \times (W_e + MT) = \frac{\% \text{ I}}{1 - \% \text{ I}} \times \text{Net Cycle}$$

For example, where the average interference for a five machine assignment under the conditions described is 22.7%, and the average interference time will be:

$$\text{I} = \frac{\% \text{ I}}{1 - \% \text{ I}} \times \begin{matrix}\text{(Average Net}\\\text{Cycle Time)}\end{matrix} = \frac{.227}{1 - .227} \times 11.45 = .294 \times 11.45 = 3.36 \text{ min.}$$

or 22.7% of total cycle actually represents 29.4% of average net cycle time.

Thus, a knowledge of the average interference for a particular assignment is essential if it is desirable to find the total cycle time or to make an accurate estimate of the maximum production possible under the conditions created by a multi-machine assignment.

SCHEDULING MULTI-MAN, MULTI-MACHINE OPERATIONS

Scheduling multi-man, multi-machine operations is designed to accomplish the following:

—Minimize delays and costs.
—Maximize output.
—Meet agreed delivery dates.
—Balance available work and manpower.
—Fully utilize equipment and facilities resources.
—Assure quality.

Utilizing the information on machine capacity and operator work requirements, a variety of practical tools are available to determine the most effective combinations of machines or processes and manpower. Among the most frequently employed are:

—Multiple activity charts.
—Gantt charts.

A multiple activity chart (Figure 9-4) is particularly useful in analyzing the process and manpower requirements for long cycle operations and complex sequences of operations. The following is an explanation of the component parts of the chart.

The chart is designed to clearly show the activity of the machine, process or product in the right column and the activity of the operators in the left column. An analysis of several men working as a crew is similarly accomplished using this chart. The chart is particularly valuable in multi-machine or manpower operations because it

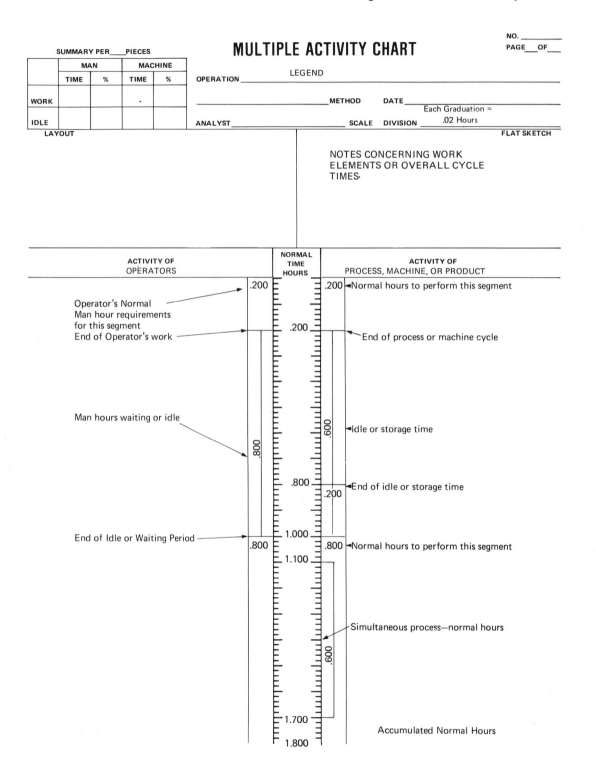

FIGURE 9-4

conveniently shows delays, short-term attention requirements and can be useful in improving methods as well as establishing precise schedules.

Utilizing the data obtained from the multiple activity charts, a series of Gantt charts can be conveniently constructed to provide an overview of the cycle time and simultaneous activity for several processes or operations and the interrelationships of each process. The limiting operations are shown on the top and the operations with slack time, or available time, are shown below. The operations are generally following the sequence of the production steps as well, going from top to bottom. The "blocked" areas indicate non-operating time, due to the requirement for preceding or following operations to be completed.

Summarizing the information revealed from the multiple activity chart analysis and the Gantt chart overview provides a recommended crew composition and a utilization index for the proposed schedule.

Chapter 10

Eliminating Excess Inventory and Adjusting Production When the Demand Is Seasonal

Production and inventory planning is receiving considerable attention because of its role in cost improvement programs. Better inventory control through improved production control can enable a company to reduce its aggregate inventory levels without disturbing customer service policies.

This chapter will present a technique that will eliminate excess inventory and stabilize production even when sales are seasonal. This technique will be identified throughout the chapter as *horizon planning*. This name was selected since it describes the basis of the technique—a focal point in time is selected for the inventory target level and production is planned toward that point in time. Progress toward that goal can be regularly monitored and corrective action can be taken if necessary.

Horizon planning is an arithmetical technique that requires a minimum of three inputs. They are:

— Monthly sales (forecast and actual)
— Monthly production (forecast and actual)
— Month end inventory targets

The system is modular. Results can be obtained by considering the three factors of production, sales and inventory levels. Additional sensitivity can be incorporated by considering:

— Inventory carrying costs
— Overtime premium costs
— Out-of-stock costs
— Hiring costs
— Layoff costs

The explanation of horizon planning will be primarily devoted to the consideration of the three basic variables and then the additional variables will be explained.

The methodology employed is similar to a computer simulation. The arithmetical model is:

Beginning Inventory + Production − Sales = Ending Inventory.

The manual calculations are based on intuitive judgments relative to production inputs. In the working of the model, past experience has shown that the most effective method is to use good judgment for the initial series of calculations and then to adjust as necessary. The goal is not to attain an optimum solution but to "sub-optimize" realistically and practically.

All production, sales and inventory data should be expressed in common units. The common units can be tons, machine shifts, line shifts, 1000 cases, or 1000 gallons. The importance of common units is related to the need to add and subtract production and sales forecasts in the development of an inventory level.

The horizon planning approach is systematic and conducted as follows:

— The sales forecast is converted into common units. The degree of detail provided in the forecast is used as the reference for horizon planning. If the sales forecast is by line item then conversion factors for each line item must be developed. After the base sales forecast is converted to common units the common units are grouped together in logical production-oriented subgroups. Three to five subgroupings are recommended. The subgroupings are then combined into a total.

— A planning time interval is selected. This time interval is usually equal to the time periods presented in the sales forecast. One month is typical. If the sales forecast is weekly, the forecasts can be summed to provide a monthly base. If the sales forecast is presented in quarterly intervals, the planning interval should be quarterly. The beginning inventory is expressed in common units for each line item and summed for subgroupings. The subgroupings are then totaled.

— Production capacities are defined in terms of common units and maximum limits are defined. It is advisable to prepare a production availability table by time period. Equipment availability, new equipment start-up, holidays, vacations, and forecasted downtime for repairs should be considered in preparing this table. Since subgroupings often have equipment constraints, it is recommended that subgrouping production availabilities be determined first and the total second. One example is:

MAXIMUM PRODUCTION AVAILABILITY TABLE

Normal work days		22 Jan.	20 Feb.	22 Mar.	20 Apr.	22 May	21 Jun.	11 Jul.	23 Aug.	19 Sept.	23 Oct.	20 Nov.	19 Dec.
Subgroup A	40	880	800	880	800	880	840	440	920	760	920	800	760
Subgroup B	10	220	200	220	200	220	210	110	150	190	230	200	190
Subgroup C	5	110	100	110	100	110	105	55	75	95	115	100	95
TOTAL		1210	1100	1210	1100	1210	1155	605	1145	1045	1265	1100	1045

— Prepare a worksheet. The worksheet will require columns for the time periods and rows for three identifications. The three identifications are production, sales and inventory. Post the beginning inventory and sales forecasts on the worksheet. (Refer to Figure 10-1 which illustrates a worksheet composed of a total and three subgroupings.)

— Post the desired ending inventory for the horizon point or points. The horizon point can be the year-end inventory or the inventory after a sales peak.

CASE IN POINT

A confection manufacturer in the Midwest employed two horizon points. One horizon point was the year-end inventory because of tax concern and the second inventory horizon point was after Halloween sales. The purpose of the second horizon point was to ensure sufficient supplies for the sales peak and to avoid excess inventories for the ensuing low sales period.

— Subjectively allocate production to each time interval and calculate time interval ending inventories. Perform this calculation for the "total" only. The calculation is: Beginning Inventory + Production — Sales = Ending Inventory. (The ending inventory for any time interval is the beginning inventory for the next time interval.)

— Review the result and circle inventories that appear unacceptable. Revise production plans per time interval preceding the unacceptable inventories. During this revision, as well as when the first plan was developed, do not exceed the defined production capacities.

Refer to the production availability table for each time interval. Change the inventory level that is unacceptable and, working backwards in time (Example: June, May April), revise production plans and inventory levels until you reach an inventory time period that is the same as your revised calculation.

An example of this technique is as follows:

FIRST PLAN

		Jan.	Feb.	Mar.	Apr.	May	June	July	Aug.
Production		660	600	660	1000	1100	1050	440	
Sales		600	650	700	1050	950	1050	800	800
Inventory	600	660	610	(570)	(520)	(670)	670	310	

REVISED PLAN

		Jan.	Feb.	Mar.	Apr.	May	June	July	Aug.
Production		660	700	1100	1000	1100	1050	440	
Sales		600	650	700	1050	950	1050	800	800
Inventory	600	660	710	1110	1060	1210	1210	850	

Note: Underlined production indicates change in plans.

DAYS		Jan.	Feb.	Mar.	Apr.	May.	June.	July.	Aug.	Sept.	Oct.	Nov.	Dec.
	(LINES)	22	20	22	20	22	21	11	23	19	23	20	19
TOTAL	PROD.												
	SALES												
	INV.												
SUB-GROUP A	(LINES)												
	PROD.												
	SALES												
	INV.												
SUB-GROUP B	(LINES)												
	PROD.												
	SALES												
	INV.												
SUB-GROUP C	(LINES)												
	PROD.												
	SALES												
	INV.												

FIGURE 10-1

	Jan.	Feb.	Mar.	Apr.	May	June	July	Aug.	Sept.	Oct.	Nov.	Dec.
DAYS	22	20	22	20	22	21	11	23	19	23	20	19
TOTAL (LINES)	30	35	50	50	50	50	40	30	30	30	30	30
PROD.	660	700	1100	1000	1100	1050	440	690	570	690	600	570
SALES	600	650	700	1050	950	1050	800	800	750	600	600	600
INV. 600	660	710	1110	1060	1210	1210	850	740	560	650	650	620
SUB-GROUP A (LINES)	15	20	35	38	38	38	25	20	20	20	20	20
PROD.	330	400	770	760	836	798	275	460	380	460	400	380
SALES	400	450	450	600	600	900	600	500	500	450	400	400
INV. 400	300	280	600	760	996	894	569	529	409	419	419	399
SUB-GROUP B (LINES)	10	10	10	7	7	7	10	5	5	7	7	7
PROD.	220	200	220	140	154	147	110	115	95	161	140	133
SALES	150	150	150	300	150	100	150	200	100	100	150	150
INV. 150	220	270	340	180	184	231	191	106	101	162	152	135
SUB-GROUP C (LINES)	5	5	5	5	5	5	5	5	5	3	3	3
PROD.	110	100	110	100	110	105	55	115	95	69	60	57
SALES	50	50	100	150	200	50	50	100	150	50	50	50
INV. 50	110	160	170	120	30	85	90	105	50	69	79	86

FIGURE 10-2

The revision consisted of increasing the production manning at an earlier date. The revision is one of many possible production plans that would satisfy the inventory requirement.

CASE IN POINT

Figure 10-2 illustrates a production plan developed for an East Coast food processor. The sales, inventory and production figures were created for this example, but the concepts and methodology would be the same for almost any company. The common production unit that was selected was a "line shift." A line shift is equal to the output of one processing line working an eight hour shift. Because of processing constraints the maximum capacity per day was 40 line shifts for subgroup A, 10 line shifts for subgroup B and 5 line shifts for subgroup C. The methodology employed in developing the completed production plan was:

1. The sales forecast, expressed in common units, was posted on the worksheet.
2. The beginning inventory for the year, expressed in common units, was posted on the worksheet.
3. The available production days per month were determined. Saturdays, Sundays, holidays and plant shutdowns were not included in the available days forecast.
4. Inventory target levels for the horizon points were determined. The horizon and target levels were:
   — 4 weeks of inventory after the July shutdown.
   — 4 weeks of inventory at year end.
5. The sales demand from January to July was totaled and added to the expected change in inventory requirements for the end of July. (July inventory—beginning inventory.)
6. This total was divided by the available work days from January through July. The answer is a guide to determining if capacity will be strained. The guide also allows for predetermining the amount of build-up that will be required.
7. A tentative production plan was developed by forecasting the line shift per day required by month and multiplying the line shift by the number of days. The answers were posted in the production row of the "total" category. Inventories were calculated for each month. "Beginning Inventory + Production − Sales = Ending Inventory" was the formula used.
8. The first production plan normally has to be revised because of inventory levels or too many manning changes.
9. After the total forecast has been developed, the subgroup forecast is prepared. The first subgroup calculated is the subgroup with the least amount of flexibility in capacity. In the example, subgroup C was selected. Because of limited capacity and a lack of beginning inventory, periodic short supplies were predicted. Saturday work or overtime would be required to overcome this situation.
10. The next subgroup selected was B, also because of capacity constraints. The developed plan indicated no inventory problems.
11. Subgroup A, the last group, is an arithmetical calculation. The total minus the two subgroups yields the production plan for this grouping.

The basic planning model is designed to supply sufficient inventory at predetermined levels without violating production capacity constraints. Occasionally the basic model has to be modified to accommodate unique circumstances. The reason for modification may be inventory carrying costs, labor availability, or the desire of management to limit changes in manning levels to once per year.

In these situations the recommended approach is to develop a production plan using the base model and then alter the plan to fit the constraints. This allows management an opportunity to factually review the cost considerations of the imposed constraints.

One method to review the cost impact of a series of production plans is to evaluate each production plan using the following formula:

Plan # = C + O + H + L where:

C is the sum of each month's ending inventory multiplied by the weighted average inventory carrying cost.

O is the planned overtime expressed in production units multiplied by the overtime rate.

H is the hiring cost multiplied by the number of times the manning level was increased.

L is the layoff cost multiplied by the number of times the manning level was decreased.

(C) Carrying Costs

This cost should be calculated as a dollar per month by common unit. The common unit is the same as used in the development of the production plan. For example, in a plant with five manufacturing lines and operating two shifts, a variety of items are produced. However, the production planner knows how many cases of product can be produced in a work shift on one line. In this situation the inventory carrying cost would be expressed in dollars per line shift month. This can be developed as follows:

  a. Determine from accounting data the annual inventory carrying cost per case or per pound considering insurance, taxes, interest rates, storage costs, and any other additional handling costs.
  b. Using established standards such as cases or pounds per line shift, convert the unit carrying cost to a cost per line shift.
  c. Convert the annual cost per line shift to a monthly cost per line shift.

     In an eastern food processing plant, the carrying cost for a case of product was $1.25 per year. One line shift produced 800 cases. The annual carrying cost per line shift was: 800 × $1.25 = $1,000. The monthly carrying cost was $1,000 ÷ 12 months (1 year) = $83.33 per month.

     If carrying cost information is not available use 25% of manufactured cost for the calculations.
  d. Add the month ending inventories from the total row of the production plan or plans.
  e. Multiply the sum of the inventories by the monthly inventory carrying cost.

(O) Overtime Premium

The cost of overtime is expressed in dollars per common unit. If line shifts are the common units, the cost should be expressed in dollars per line shift. This cost is obtained by summing the individual premium for each employee on the line. For example: There are 20 employees on a line, 10 who earn $2.00/hr. and 10 who earn $3.00/hr. Company policy is to pay time and a half for all overtime. The overtime premium cost in this example is: 10 employees $\times$ $1.00/hr. premium $\times$ 8 hrs. + 10 employees $\times$ $1.50/hr. premium $\times$ 8 hrs. or $80 + $120 = $200 *per line shift*.

The base rate for the employees is not included in this calculation since labor cost is not included in the evaluation equation. It's the premium "penalty" cost that is of interest in evaluating the production plan.

When manning varies by product line, a weighted average can be used.

(H) Hiring Cost

The hiring cost is expressed in dollars per common unit. Calculate a hiring cost per employee and multiply this cost by the average number of employees needed to produce a "common unit."

In the previous example for overtime premium, there were 20 employees on a line and the common unit was a line shift. In this situation the hiring cost is 20 employees multiplied by the hiring cost per employee. Examples of costs to be considered in calculating a cost per employee:

1. Recruiting costs
2. Medical examination
3. Clerical processing of paper work
4. Training and company orientation
5. Productivity losses while an individual is learning the job.

The personnel/industrial relations department is a good source for information regarding hiring costs. If no information is available the following guidelines can be used:

— Recruiting costs are approximated by dividing the salary of the interviewers by the number of company employees hired during a year. If this is not a full-time job, factor the salaries by the estimated percentage of time devoted to recruiting.
— Medical examination usually costs $50.
— Clerical processing of paperwork usually requires 3 hours of clerical work.
— Training and orientation is approximately equal to three days' wages for the employees.
— Productivity losses vary considerably by industry. Personal experience is a good guide. Material waste and labor hours should be considered and a range from 2 weeks' wages to 9 months' wages has been observed.

(L) Layoff Costs

The layoff cost is expressed in dollars per common unit. The methodology is similar to the calculation of hiring costs. Calculate a layoff cost per employee and multiply this cost by the average number of employees needed to produce a "common unit." In the previous example there were 20 employees on a line and the common unit was a line shift. The layoff cost in this situation would be 20 employees multiplied by the layoff cost per employee. Layoff costs are subjective and require top management assessment. The costs to be considered are:

1. Increases in unemployment compensation premiums.
2. Severance pay.
3. Wage protection for remaining employees. This cost is occasionally incurred when personnel are moved to lower paying jobs and their pay rates are "frozen" at the higher level job for a period of time.
4. Clerical processing costs.
5. Reputation and morale.

The reputation and morale cost can vary from zero to a significantly large cost. This cost is management's opportunity to evaluate its attitude toward changing manning levels. This cost is also normally expotentially graduated. The first manning decrease per year is usually the least costly but each additional manning decrease is "costed" at a higher rate. These increased costs reflect the value that management places on stability. Some of management's considerations are: the availability of labor, community goodwill, and the effect on company personnel.

Each developed production plan can be evaluated using this formula and the impact of management decisions can be assessed objectively.

The formula for evaluating production plan impact presented in this chapter is based on an aggregate cost analysis using averages. Whichever evaluation method is selected the most important "ingredient" is human judgment. A practical production plan should be based on a high attention to common sense and the realization that the two-dimensional world of paper and pencil planning has to be translated to the world of production, sales and inventory.

Chapter 11

Selecting the Right Scheduling System

for Your Plant

RESULTS FROM THE RIGHT SCHEDULING SYSTEM

The right scheduling system for a production operation is expected to accomplish two things:

- Deliver the goods at the time promised.
- Optimize the cost of production.

Delivery of the goods on time is an obvious objective; but the role of scheduling to utilize labor, plant and inventories has a significant impact on production costs.

The delivery promise is the most sensitive matter in the scheduling process. The manager faced with a delivery date that is too soon must decide either to miss it, or to delay other jobs, or to spend money to buy capacity; and he may do all three. The manager still has some problems if the promise dates are too distant. The sales manager will probably complain, but also he may have to scramble to find work for his plant. Ideally, the delivery promise should be an output of the scheduling process to achieve the best results from the system.

SCHEDULING STARTS WITH PLANNING

The right scheduling system requires an adequate planning system. The planning system determines what product to make and when it is required. The scheduling system determines how to assign the work to the plant to accomplish the plan. The scheduler who has more work to assign than he has capacity to produce is in trouble. The planning scheme must be sensitive to the capacity requirements or it will not be compatible with even the most sophisticated scheduling system.

PLANNING SYSTEM PLUSES AND MINUSES

There are some planning systems used commonly in industry that create part of the scheduling problem. A brief review of planning systems identifies their relative acceptability for scheduling. Planning systems can be sorted into three basic categories: order point systems, forecast systems, demand systems.

Order Point Systems

Order point systems are extremely common. An item is reordered when its inventory level declines to the order point. The first difficulty is establishing the order point. It depends on the rate of use of the item and the time interval required to replenish the stock. Use rates are often unpredictable over a short term, and time to replenish becomes unpredictable as soon as there is a backlog to be produced. A safety stock is established to cushion the errors in the estimates of use rate and replenishment time. The order point, including safety stock, often represents considerable inventory. Despite this, there likely will be stockouts, making a safe order point difficult to establish.

The second difficulty is the reorder quantity. Typically an economic order quantity (EOQ) is calculated to trade off setup costs and inventory carrying charges at the minimum level. The use rate is an input to this calculation also. Setup time reduces capacity if the use rate is significantly underestimated. The scheduling problem introduced by this error is that capacity is reduced when the demand is increased.

There is another problem with order point systems aside from the difficulties with establishing the operating parameters. The demand on the production plant from an order point system is inherently unstable. It varies radically even if the product demand is steady.

Table 11-1, Classic Order Point System, illustrates a classic concept. Inventories are nicely balanced, their total is constant, parts used and parts ordered are equal, and the system reflects demand nicely. The real world does not allow matters to remain so neat, however. Inventories get out of balance for many reasons: a production overrun on a lot; a quality problem causes partial rejection of a lot; a tool failure causes an aborted run; or an order quantity is revised to reflect a change in demand.

Table 11-2, Real World Order Point System, illustrates what happens. Sales are steady for five months and yet parts demand varies from zero to two times usage. It is not too comforting to note that over the fall period parts used and parts ordered are equal. The problem is compounded if sales are not stable as illustrated by months 6, 7, and 8.

An order point system is a simple planning scheme; but it is incompatible with any orderly scheduling process, particularly if the fabrication of components is required. It is possible for an item assembled entirely from purchased components to be planned by order point. The materials manager who counts on his suppliers to meet the peaks of demand is likely to be disappointed. Common items like nuts, bolts, and washers, that are available from a variety of suppliers on a commodity basis, are probably the only ones that are manageable by the order point planning concept.

CLASSIC ORDER POINT SYSTEM

ASSUMPTION: 10 parts, 1 each per unit sold, and for each part. Reorder Point 1,000. Reorder Quantity 5,000.

PERIOD AND STATUS	SALES	PARTS USED	PARTS ORDERED	INVENTORY OF PARTS										TOTAL INVENTORY
				1	2	3	4	5	6	7	8	9	10	
Starting Inventory				1,000	2,000	3,000	4,000	5,000	1,000	2,000	3,000	4,000	5,000	30,000
Month 1	1,000	10,000	10,000	5,000	1,000	2,000	3,000	4,000	5,000	1,000	2,000	3,000	4,000	30,000
2	2,000	20,000	20,000	3,000	4,000	5,000	1,000	2,000	3,000	4,000	5,000	1,000	2,000	30,000
3	3,000	30,000	30,000	5,000	1,000	2,000	3,000	4,000	5,000	1,000	2,000	3,000	4,000	30,000
4	4,000	40,000	40,000	1,000	2,000	3,000	4,000	5,000	1,000	2,000	3,000	4,000	5,000	30,000

TABLE 11-1

REAL WORLD ORDER POINT SYSTEM

ASSUMPTION: 10 parts, 1 each per unit sold, and for each part. Reorder Point 1,000. Reorder Quantity 5,000.

PERIOD AND STATUS	SALES	PARTS USED	PARTS ORDERED	INVENTORY OF PARTS										TOTAL INVENTORY
				1	2	3	4	5	6	7	8	9	10	
Starting Inventory				3,000	3,000	3,000	4,000	5,000	5,000	5,000	4,000	4,000	4,000	40,000
Month 1	1,000	10,000	-0-	2,000	2,000	2,000	3,000	4,000	4,000	4,000	3,000	3,000	3,000	30,000
2	1,000	10,000	-0-	1,000	1,000	1,000	2,000	3,000	3,000	3,000	2,000	2,000	2,000	20,000
3	1,000	10,000	15,000	5,000	5,000	5,000	1,000	2,000	2,000	2,000	1,000	1,000	1,000	25,000
4	1,000	10,000	20,000	4,000	4,000	4,000	5,000	1,000	1,000	1,000	5,000	5,000	5,000	35,000
5	1,000	10,000	15,000	3,000	3,000	3,000	4,000	5,000	5,000	5,000	4,000	4,000	4,000	40,000
Subtotal		50,000	50,000											
6	2,000	20,000	-0-	1,000	1,000	1,000	2,000	3,000	3,000	3,000	2,000	2,000	2,000	20,000
7	3,000	30,000	100,000	3,000	3,000	3,000	4,000	5,000	5,000	5,000	4,000	4,000	4,000	40,000
8	1,000	10,000	-0-											

TABLE 11-2

Therefore an order point type of planning system is not always a satisfactory companion for a scheduling system that is expected to result in on-time delivery and good control of costs.

Forecast Systems

Forecast systems of planning attempt to project future demand. The concept is excellent for scheduling purposes because capacity requirements are defined when the demand is forecasted. A good system accomplishes the plant loading aspects of scheduling in the process of releasing orders for production.

The principal difficulty with forecast systems is with the accuracy of the forecast. A necessary feature of any forecast system is a procedure for adjusting it to correspond with reality. The adjustment feature can give some early warning on capacity problems if changes in demand are predictable.

The advantages of forecasting relative to scheduling generally outweigh the difficulties of accuracy. However, there are products with demand histories that defy modeling. Gross errors in forecasting cannot normally be corrected by the best of scheduling systems; and, similarly, a scheduling system that does not adjust to changes in demand will make the best forecast look bad.

Demand Systems

Demand systems are the simplest of all planning systems because nothing is planned until the demand is real. A job shop operation is the classic demand system. This is the most satisfactory system for items with an unpredictable demand.

The key to successful scheduling with a demand system is in making the delivery promise after the job is scheduled. A demand system is quite compatible for scheduling as long as the capacity is not overcommitted.

Multiple product operations can reasonably expect to use a variety of planning systems: forecasts for major volume items, demand for special order items, and order points for purchased parts and supplies. A scheduling difficulty occurs when forecast and demand items are produced through the same plant facilities. The most manageable arrangement is to give priority to the forecast items, and fit the demand items into the available capacity. A scheduling system giving priority to demand items gets in trouble unless the capacity and total short-term requirements tend to stay equal, but that is not typical of demand business. The desire to give priority to demand items is usually a marketing consideration. Facilities dedicated for the demand items may be the best option if the market requires rapid response.

Material Requirements Planning (MRP)

The material requirements planning concept that has gained such broad acceptance for planning systems requires some special comment. The key idea in MRP is the management of requirements rather than management of inventories. Finished goods demands are exploded into requirements for components. Orders are issued to fulfill the requirements and any resulting inventory is dedicated to finished goods on order. The finished goods demand may be either forecast, actual, or a combination. The principal impact of MRP is inventory cost reduction; and its impact on scheduling compares with other planning systems that are either forecast, demand, or a combination of them.

MRP in its simplest form is an asset to scheduling. A case study illustrates this:

CASE IN POINT

A manufacturer of steel floor grill for use in home heating systems was operating with an order point system and an informal scheduling system. The finished goods inventory was on order point, and each of the components (about ten) was carried on inventory with an order point system. Product demand was strongly seasonal. The peak season brought stockouts, three-shift schedules, and parts everywhere. Deliveries were late and costs were out of control.

A system of forecasting and material requirements planning was introduced as the initial step. The forecast planned a leveling of plant demand and a deliberate build-up of finished goods inventory in the slow seasons. Finished goods orders were placed on the plant by the forecast system, parts explosions were made to determine requirements to make the finished goods ordered, and shop orders were released for quantities of parts to match the assembly orders.

The first dramatic result of this initial step was the elimination of parts inventory records! A short time later there was no inventory of parts other than work-in-process. This is typical of MRP systems. This simple program was all performed manually too.

Later, a scheduling system was established. It was a simple manual equivalent of a critical path with a resource allocation system. This type of system results in the release of orders into the shop and all the parts orders for a given finished goods order tend to be completed at the same time. Prior to this step, there was some movement of completed parts into storage. After this step, work-in-process was in the assembly area and not in storage.

Material requirements planning systems are not always this simple. The concept came of age with the advent of computer systems that could handle the data involved in multiple product applications with parts common to several products. Scheduling is facilitated with these systems when the demand data is forecasted. The scheduling task becomes more complicated when the demand data is actual orders or where it is a combination of forecast and actual.

WHAT A SCHEDULING SYSTEM SHOULD DO

The role of the scheduling function is to assign work. It can be simple or complicated depending upon the character of the operation. The elements of information required to be able to assign work include the following:

- Availability of materials required in the production process.
- Routing of the product through the production process including alternates.
- Preparation and processing time for each step along the route.
- Status of all orders in process.
- Relative priority of all orders in process and in backlog.
- Backlog and potential capacity of each work station.

The details of communication, paper work, and records may be unique for each operation, but they should convey the required information.

The scheduling system should determine the what, when, where, who and how for each order:

- What operation to perform.
- When to start the operation.
- Where the operation is to be done; which work station.
- Who is to do the work, i.e., what is the work assignment of employees.
- How the capacity is to be obtained if the production process is falling behind.

A scheduling function could do all the things described thus far and still not achieve the objectives of on-time delivery and optimum costs. The total system should include analytical and feedback elements that accomplish the following:

- Use all available labor hours.
- Optimize the amount of work-in-process.
- Detect late orders when they become late rather than at the end of the process.
- Determine completion dates on orders.
- Determine the need for overtime, additional crew, or outside contracting to provide required capacity.

There is one other essential requirement of a scheduling system. It must have credibility with production management people. Rapid response to identified problems is often necessary to avoid additional problems. Production managers will not respond well to information they cannot believe. The system must produce consistently good results or it will not be credible.

THE CRITICAL PATH CONCEPT

The development of the critical path method of scheduling for one-of-a-kind products is recognized as a landmark in project management. Most manufacturing processes have such simple precedence relationships among their elements that the CPM analysis seems unnecessary. Actually, the diagramming is unnecessary, but the decision logic of the concept meets the needs for scheduling. The essential elements of the CPM method will be described as they relate to production scheduling.

The precedence diagram is the first step in CPM (Figure 11-1). The diagram describes graphically the sequence in which activities must be done to complete a product. Some activities go on concurrently while others cannot proceed until certain prior activities are completed. The time required to accomplish each activity on the

PUMP AND TURBINE OVERHAUL, PLANNING BY USE OF CRITICAL PATH

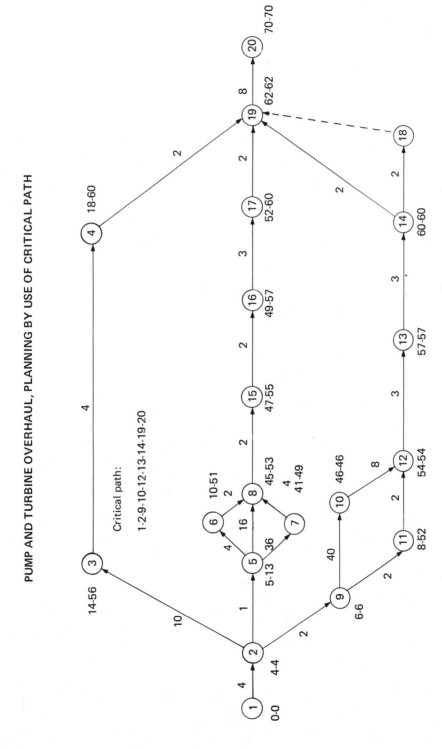

Critical path:
1-2-9-10-12-13-14-19-20

FIGURE 11-1

diagram is estimated. The network of precedence relationships is then analyzed to determine which path through the network requires the longest time. The longest is the critical path. Shorter paths are said to have float relative to the critical path. The more float, the less critical an activity is. Work must proceed without delay on the critical path sequence of activities to accomplish the job in the minimum time.

The completion date on a project can be given quite reliably once the critical path is known. Data on earliest and latest starts and finishes are also known for all activities in the whole network. This is essential information for scheduling and for control.

This same array of information would be useful for scheduling the manufacture of one-of-a-kind items on facilities that were used for only that one item. That is a situation comparable to construction. Unfortunately, production operations seldom have dedicated facilities, and the scheduler is apt to find that a single machine is needed for two or more activities that must be scheduled at the same time. This is a problem in resource allocation and it fits neatly into the CPM logic. The allocation mode of CPM identifies the resource required for each activity. A resource may be a machine, an assembly line, a storage area or a skilled worker. The resource is allocated first to the activity with the least amount of float when more than one activity converges on a single resource. This addition to the decision logic allows completion dates and other control dates to be developed in a context that is more compatible with production scheduling requirements. (Table 11-3.)

It is nice to be able to have complex systems work manually before committing to a computer application of the system. How do you do something so complicated without a computer? Here is an actual case.

CASE IN POINT

A manufacturer of sheet metal products has an array of about 2,000 standard parts that constitute about 80 percent of the piece volume. The balance of the volume is special order items. Production lots are small on most items and moves are frequent. The typical part requires four or five operations, for example:

- Shear, notch, pierce, form.
- Shear, draw, trim, notch, form.
- Cut off, pierce, form, form.

There are about 75 machines in the shop. They include shears, brakes, and presses ranging from 2 tons to 500 tons.

The shop order consists of a set of orders for each operation. The information on the form identifies the part, the quantity, a priority code, the machine for the operation, and the machine for the next operation. Two copies of the set are sent to the shop when the order for the operation is released and the original remains in the control center. The order is assigned to an operator by a foreman.

When the operation is completed, one copy goes with the goods to identify the next location and the other is returned to the control office as a notice of completion.

The priority code is a two-number set. The first number indicates a planning week. All orders planned for a given week constitute a priority group. The second number in the set is the sum of the setup times and the running times required on all of the operations needed to produce the item. The latter number defines the length of the path for the item. The larger this number, the more critical it is in the priority group and the higher its priority.

The planning function originates the orders and delivers them to scheduling. The order sets are separated and sorted by machine. There is a set of three boxes for each machine labeled *scheduled, ready* and *not ready.* The new order sets are placed in the *not ready* box for the respective machines in order number sequence. The normal sequence of events after that is:

1. The material planner confirms the availability of sheet or coil stock for orders on initial operations like shear, cut off, roll, and form, and then places those order sets in the *ready* box in priority sequence.
2. The orders in the *ready* boxes are released in priority order to be run on the indicated machines. This is done as orders previously released are reported complete. The original of the order set is placed in the *scheduled* box.
3. The operation is performed in the shop and the operation complete ticket is returned.
4. The original is removed from the *scheduled* box and the set for the next operation is moved from its *not ready* box to the *ready* box and filed in priority order, and the sequence is repeated until the order is complete.

Periodically the schedule board is inventoried to determine the backlog of work by machine and the amount due in each priority period. This process provides information for planning crew size, hours of work, and running time requirements by machine.

A critical path schedule with resource allocation is accomplished manually by this routine. The decision process is simple and yet the total operation is complex. This routine is successful with this type of operation because there are no complicated precedence relationships. The critical path network for all of the items in a priority group looks like Figure 11-2, so the item with the longest time requirement is critical. Occasionally there is a need for parts for subassembly prior to final assembly, and then there is a precedence requirement. This situation is accommodated by placing the subassembly parts in an earlier priority group. The net result is the accomplishment of a fairly sophisticated scheduling process by a simple manual routine.

There are some negative aspects of the manual system just described:

- The clerical effort required is tedious and subject to error; however, it is not an expensive process.
- The volume of paper to be handled is large in proportion to the work being tracked.
- The periodic work load inventory is a large clerical task.
- It is not practical to predict actual completion dates for individual orders if they require more than one or two operations. There is too much data to assimilate manually.

It is anticipated that a computer application would be made on this operation eventually. It would eliminate the negatives described above. The same basic system is in use in less complicated situations, and the replacement of the manual system is clearly not justified.

CRITICAL PATH NETWORK FOR A
VARIETY OF SHEET METAL PARTS

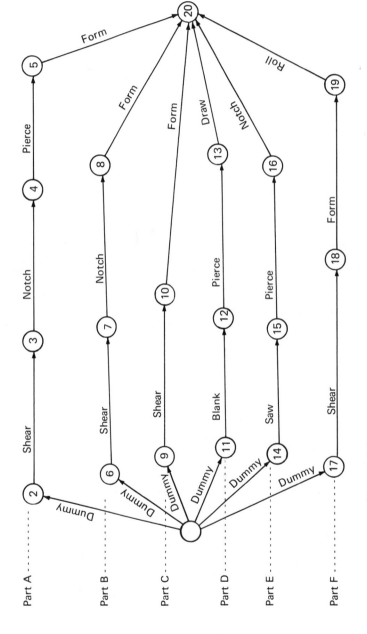

Characteristics:

- Each path is independent—no precedence requirements.
- Path length is determined by the number of units, the total fabrication time per unit, and the duration of the set-ups.
- The critical path is that of the order requiring the longest time.

FIGURE 11-2

The key idea developed relative to scheduling is that the logical principles of the critical path method have almost universal applicability to scheduling situations. Some situations are so simple that it is only an academic consideration, but the more complicated the situation, the more likely CPM is to succeed.

PRACTICAL SCHEDULING APPLICATIONS

There are a variety of scheduling situations. It is not possible to describe all of them but it is possible to define typical ones.

There are two broad classes of manufacturing for purposes of this analysis: continuous operations and incremental operations. There is a fuzzy boundary between the two, but there are some characteristics that differentiate them.

Continuous Operations

Some products that are typically produced in a continuous operation are flour, beer, laundry detergents, paper, corn starch, oil and sulphuric acid. Most of these more obviously continuous process products are ultimately packaged. This may seem a little contrary since packages are such discrete units of output. The classification refers more to how a production lot is identified and controlled. A great many more packaged products are included in this class for that reason. For example: cake mixes, toilet articles, meat products, and cereals. These are all essentially process products.

Quite frequently, this type of product is produced on dedicated facilities. The mill, dryer, still, or line can only be used for the single product in such cases. The scheduling problem is confined to when to run the facility and for how long. The resources that have to be allocated are labor and storage space. The situation is complicated if the facility is used for more than one product or if two or more dedicated facilities are run intermittently with a single crew.

The device for describing and communicating the production program for this type of operation is most commonly a simple chronological schedule. The scheduler has defined what hours, shifts, and days the unit is to run and on what product. Some situations may not even require a formal schedule. Verbal communication of hours of work may be sufficient. Other situations may warrant graphic displays and more formal communications.

Planning and scheduling should be a single function for this type of operation. The planning function really allocates the time of the production facilities and probably also the storage facilities. Labor is the only resource remaining to be scheduled in such cases. Some problems and peculiarities of particular operations in this class are:
- **One Product on a Dedicated Unit**
  Typical Operation: — Spray drying detergent
                                — Milling starch

The schedule is determined by the quantity required and when it is due in most cases. There are exceptions, like a hog kill and cut operation, where the capacity is variable with crew size. Most operations of this type require at least some forecasting or production for stock to be able to optimize costs.

- **Multiple Products in Parallel Facilities**

  Typical Operation: — Toilet article making and packaging

  — Welded steel tube mills

  — Cake mix mixing and packaging

This is another case of dedicated facilities. It is complicated by the possibility of sharing the labor among the processing units. The range of options is illustrated by the three typical product groups listed.

— A toilet article manufacturer might reasonably forecast the demand of slow movers, produce them for inventory, and use the crew the balance of the time on high volume products and stay closer to demand.

— Welded steel tubes are fairly bulky to store so this manufacturer would probably operate a demand system.

— A cake mix manufacturer has a much more perishable product than a toilet article, so he may prefer to produce low volume items on demand and forecast the high volume requirements.

- **Multiple Products in Single Continuous Processing Unit**

  Typical Operation: — Flour milling

  — Baking mix blend and package

This is not a difficult scheduling situation in that the options are limited to choosing the length of run and choosing the sequence of products. The baking mix situation is an interesting case from a sequence standpoint. The changeover is shorter if the sequence is from lighter to darker mixes. Faster changeovers have a significant impact on capacity. A large food packager made a study to define design specifications for an ultrahigh speed mixing and packaging facility. The capacity of such a facility is a function of line speed and changeover time. The conclusion of the study was to concentrate on reducing changeover time rather than on achieving high speeds.

Incremental Operations

Some products that are typical of an incremental operation are screw machine products, fabricated sheet metal products, windows and doors, castings, appliances, valves, switches and fasteners.

Assembled items are quite often assembled on dedicated facilities. Some component items are also produced on dedicated facilities. The scheduling of this type of facility is very similar to that for dedicated facilities on continuous operations.

A great many component items produced incrementally require more than one operation and involve sharing facilities for those operations. These are the classic critical path types of scheduling situations.

The control system for this type of product typically involves shop tickets to identify each lot or order. The number of such lots in process at a given time can be quite large. Prepared schedules of work assignments are often neither possible nor effective. More often, the schedule execution is accomplished through rules for issue and assignment of work. The scheduling function in this environment requires feedback and dynamic response to accomplish its objectives.

Planning is often only a related function in these operations. Its function is to order quantities of goods. There usually are problems if the planning function also determines delivery dates. Scheduling results are so sensitive to delivery requirements that the scheduling function should specify dates or at least work with the planning function in a framework of very open communication.

Some problems and peculiarities of particular operations in this class are:

- **Fabricating Small Standard Components**

    Typical Products: — Screw machine parts

    — Nails

These tend to be one operation products and hence are similar to continuous operations items. The principal difference is the paper work required.

- **Fabricating Large Standard Components Requiring Multiple Operations**

    Typical Products: —Exhaust pipes

    —Drawn or spun sheet metal items

This level of complexity involves allocation of resources because several machines are used, setups are required, storage space may be a limited resource, and a variety of products are run on demand. The critical path approach will apply in these situations. The key requirements are to know the capacity and the setups. Sequences that reduce setup stretch the capacity in these plants.

- **Fabricating Nonstandard Components on Demand**

    Typical Products: — Fasteners

    — Containers

The difficulty with scheduling this type of production is that setup and production rates may not be known, so the capacity is uncertain. Multiple operations are also probably involved. The critical path method will apply in these situations, but it will probably be important to predict the completion date with the system and to be able to revise it quickly when the capacity differs from expectation.

- **Fabrication and Assembly of Standard Items**

    Typical Products: — Light fixtures

    — Door locks

    — Grills and registers

    — Appliances

These operations entail the difficulties of parts manufacture, but also probably involve precedence considerations related to subassemblies. The critical path method will apply, but it will be necessary to determine where to program subassembly parts. The situation is somewhat simpler if the items are forecast rather than ordered on demand.

- **Fabrication and Assembly of Nonstandard Items**

This is a classic job shop operation. The ability to estimate completion dates is essential to this operation. The CPM will apply.

- **Combination of Standard and Nonstandard Fabrication and Assembly**

The combining of standard and nonstandard work in a single operation is often the most difficult situation for successful scheduling. Nonstandard implies customer

PUMP AND TURBINE OVERHAUL, PLANNING BY USE OF CRITICAL PATH

Work Segment Number	Work Description	Est. Job Time	Earliest Starting Time	Latest Starting Time	Earliest Finishing Time	Latest Finishing Time	Float	Critical Work
1-2	Check standby electric pump	4	0	0	4	4	0	4
2-3	Rebuild and calibrate all gauges	10	4	4	14	14	0	
2-5	Dismantle pump cover	1	4	4	5	5	0	
2-9	Dismantle turbine cover and remove rotor	2	4	4	6	6	0	2
3-4	Clean out all gauge and control lines	4	14	56	18	60	42	
4-9	Replace gauges	2	18	60	20	62	42	
5-6	Rehabilitate lubrication system	4	5	13	9	17	8	
5-7	Rebuild impeller	36	5	13	41	49	7	
5-8	Clean pump casing	4	5	13	9	17	8	
6-8	Fit pump bearings—lower	2	9	51	11	53	42	
7-8	Balance impeller	4	41	49	45	53	4	
8-15	Reinstall impeller	2	45	53	47	55	8	
9-10	Rebuild turbine rotor	40	6	6	46	46	0	40
9-11	Dress turbine bearings	2	6	6	8	8	0	
10-12	Balance turbine rotor	8	46	46	54	54	0	8
11-12	Fit turbine bearings	2	8	52	10	54	44	
12-13	Reinstall turbine rotor	3	54	54	57	57	0	3
13-14	Reinstall turbine cover	3	57	57	60	60	0	3
14-18	Test components	2	60	60	62	62	0	
14-19	Check clearances	2	60	60	62	62	0	
15-16	Fit pump bearings—upper	2	47	55	49	57	8	
16-17	Reinstall pump cover	3	49	57	52	60	8	
17-19	Install shaft packing	2	52	60	54	62	8	
19-20	Final tests	8	62	62	70	70	0	8

TABLE 11-3

order, and standard implies stock. Management outside of the plant operation is more concerned with delivery of customer orders. The difficulty is that a late order to a customer may affect the one customer, but a late order to stock may affect several customers.

It is very important to define the rules for priorities and to enforce them in the scheduling of the shop. It is also important that the system be capable of predicting completion dates.

POINTS TO REMEMBER

The basic objective of a scheduling system is to assign work to the production operation in a sequence that will control the delivery time. A good system will accomplish the basic objective while also making use of labor, plant, and inventories in the most economical way. The planning system and the scheduling system must be complementary if total success is to be achieved. The critical issue in achieving total success is the delivery promise date. It should be achievable by available options for capacity first of all; but, further, it should be achievable by the least cost option if maximum profits are to be obtained.

Every planning and scheduling situation has unique characteristics. Elements of difference arise from several sources:

— The marketing and distribution conditions.
— The product itself in terms of its perishability, storage characteristics and value.
— Manufacturing methods in continuous or incremental processes.
— Dedicated or shared facilities.
— Labor intensive or capital intensive methods.

The possible combinations are many. Yet, there are some common principles that are useful in guiding the development of any system:

• Forecast demand if possible, plan actual demand if forecasting is erratic, and avoid order point systems in manufacturing situations.
• Plan requirements rather than inventories.
• Generate delivery promise options in the scheduling system.
• Employ the Critical Path Method concept in any scheduling and the more complicated it is, the better.

Chapter 12

Getting the Right Material
at the Right Time

PROCUREMENT

The procurement function encompasses two broad areas. These are: 1) the acquisition or the purchasing of material and 2) the possession or the storage of material until used. Acquisition includes searching and maintaining relationships, ordering, controlling and tracking of orders and material. Possession includes such activities as reorder, usage rates and control systems. An overview will be presented in both subject areas with emphasis on analysis of systems for better control of costs.

ACQUISITION

The purchasing department should be the primary activity center in the acquisition function and, as such, becomes a buyer for all company users of this service. This results in a somewhat unique position for the purchasing department as a major linking pin for material control.

Requisitioning Material: A Request For Purchase

The system generally installed to request that the purchasing department start the acquisition procedure is for all requesting users to submit purchase requisitions to the purchasing department for consideration, screening and initiation of the action of acquiring material. Instead of being required to act individually on each issue, to reduce procurement costs most purchasing departments are given the authority to reorder (for example, on blanket orders) certain commodities that are replenished on a regular cycle.

The purchasing department, after receipt of the purchase requisition, fulfills the activities of examination, comparison, analysis and ordering of the material specified on the requisition.

Acquisition Function: A Search for Material Sources

The first step upon receipt of a purchase requisition is to examine it. This examination is basic and detects gross inconsistencies, adherence to company and purchasing policy, proper sources, amounts, accounts and a multitude of other administrative considerations.

The comparison phase considers what was contained on previous orders, sources of supply, current vs. past prices, discounts and terms.

Analysis includes the activities of contacting suppliers for information in regard to impending strikes, price increases, new sources, government règulations and discounts offered on special orders.

After all of these steps are completed for an individual purchase requisition, the ordering phase takes place and the requisition is then translated into a purchase order. An order placed with the supplier is performed as the final step.

In addition to handling the purchase requisition as described above, the purchasing department must perform other tasks related internally to the purchasing department. These are identified as vendor selection, supplier relationship maintenance, and procurement research.

Vendor Selection: Who Gets the Order?

With whom should the order be placed?

A record of acceptable vendors (Figure 12-1) should be maintained and the function of measuring, evaluating, recruiting, reviewing and selecting vendors must be an ongoing concern.

Multiple sources of vendors or suppliers should be cultivated and maintained for proper cost control. Some sources of potential vendor names would include Sweet's catalog, telephone directories, Thomas' Register, MacCrea's Blue Book, salesman interviews and various other outside contacts.

The selection process should consider the answers to such questions as:
- How many suppliers do I need?
- What are price level considerations including discounts, freight charges, and special sales offers?
- What is the dependability of the supplier in terms of delivery, accuracy of billing and following instructions?
- What quality of product will I expect and receive?
- What technical assistance is available?
- What is the supplier's credit policy?
- What is his overall reputation with other customers, financial institutions?

Supplier Relations

Building solid relationships with suppliers can lead to significant cost reductions not only in the procurement area, but also in areas of production and process. Sugges-

VENDOR RECORD

Material Supplied: _____

Name Bledsoe Steel
Address 1234 Main Street
Contact Mr. Bledsoe, Manager
Telephone 618-123-4567

PURCHASE DATE	NAME OF VENDOR	INVOICE OR REQUISITION NUMBER	UNIT PRICE	RECEIVED		ITEM NAME	BALANCE ON HAND	
				QUANTITY	VALUE		QUANTITY	VALUE
Nov. 1	Balance		11				962	105.82
Nov. 1		76					834	91.74
Nov. 3		249					609	66.99
Nov. 4	Bledsoe Steel	110215	11	1250	137.50		1859	204.49
Nov. 7		458					1513	166.43
Nov. 10		588					1428	157.08
Nov. 12		689					1168	128.48
Nov. 15		842					685	75.35
Nov. 16	Bledsoe Steel	110928	11	1250	137.50		1935	212.85
Nov. 18		1016					1613	177.43
Nov. 21		1214					1495	164.45

FIGURE 12-1

tions from vendors, packaging alternatives and alternative sources of supply leading to competitive pricing can be obtained from suppliers and vendors simply by spending some time establishing and maintaining these relationships and listening to their suggestions. These can be extremely valuable because of the large number of different situations observed by these people in the normal course of their day.

Their relationships can be developed through technical assistance, financing, and a possible increased share of the purchase requirements.

Procurement Research

One important source of information for purchasing is the salesman contact. Information on competitor's activities, supplier company activities, industry updates and various reactions to competitive situations by each of these factors are all important parts of procurement research.

In addition to salesmen contacts, the analysis of the cost of purchase or potentially purchasable items must be undertaken. Value analysis techniques are extremely important and such considerations as make or buy, redesign of item, substitution of a similar product, buying techique modifications, quality control or modifications and specification changes all may contribute to specific cost reduction.

The investigation of seasonal trends as they relate to the procurement function is another possible source of cost reduction. Possible purchased part standardization can be explored in conjunction with product design, manufacturing and process engineering.

Control techniques that serve as reference for procurement research are records such as purchase order files, vendor files, quote files, stock records and price records.

Techniques of Analysis for Cost Reduction

A listing of all purchased items should be generated and would include yearly volumes purchased of each item and the yearly amount of money spent for these items. This list, in many cases, can be generated as output from a computer program assuming, of course, the availability of proper input and equipment. If electronic data processing equipment is not available to obtain this listing, a tabulation by hand would not be too difficult. In either case, the proper paper work system to collect this should be in effect to order material. Methods of utilizing this data will vary depending upon the form in which the basic data is presented.

After this is done, the ABC analysis technique can be used to segregate those purchased items representing the greatest yearly expenditure. For example, approximately 30% of the purchased items normally represent around 70% of the total yearly expenditure.

The ABC technique simply categorizes the expenditures into an "A" group containing those items consisting of 70% of the total annual cost. Next the "B" group consists of the block of items making up 20% of the total annual cost. Whatever is left then goes into the "C" group which obviously will be a total of 10% of the total annual cost.

This technique should reveal which items are accounting for the greatest amount of money. Attention can be focused upon corrective action to reduce these costs.

Examination in detail of each of these items in the 70% range or "A" group for multiple suppliers, product substitution, redesign price considerations, volume discount and the various other cost reduction analytical techniques can lead to substantial cost reduction. Experience has shown that a 10%-20% overall cost reduction can be expected with normal effort over a period of time by working within this "A" group category.

Considerations in Purchased Materials

Materials that are purchased as a part of a production system normally relate to components used to complete a part, assembly or new product. Included would be such items as screws and fasteners, special manufactured subassemblies, castings, raw materials or any number of other standard, stock or unique items. Obviously, prime consideration must be given when procuring this type of material so that it is not only on hand when it is required by production, but also that a sufficient quantity is available to satisfy the production run requirements.

Because of this availability requirement, most production systems require an inventory of parts and material. How to control this inventory then becomes a major cost consideration.

POSSESSION

The possession of material primarily involves:

— The storage and warehousing function.
— Control of quantities of material purchased, received or issued.
— The control and valuation of material.
— Inventory classification for record-keeping, allocation, and identification of rate of utilization.
— Economical location and handling of stored materials.
— Control process for locating.
— Techniques for record-keeping to determine the physical flow rate.

Thus, the costs that can be controlled through this function include: inventory costs; certain aspects of production costs; costs associated with production rates, lead times, delays, reorder times and quantities, sales predictability, steadiness, seasonality, rates and quantities.

Inventory Classification

The most common methods of classification are:

— Raw materials
— Finished goods

— Work-in-process
— Parts
— Supplies
— Tools
— Miscellaneous material

For ease of identification, code numbers are assigned to each group or classification and then each item within this group is given sub-code numbers for individual identification. In addition, work-in-process, finished goods, parts or miscellaneous materials can contain other subgroups such as purchased parts, manufactured parts or subassemblies.

For example, the following system may be used:

Raw Materials Code 01 -

    Sub-Code such as purchased materials 100 -

        Sub-Sub or Individual Code such as: Soda Ash 01

                                    Dolomite 02

                                    Coal   03

                                    Rouge   04

The resulting individual product code for Dolomite might then be represented by the overall identification and classification code number of:

01 - 100 - 02

A system such as this will allow cost tracking, cost accumulation, cost analysis and possible cost reduction by individual product. In addition, ordering costs and receiving and paper work costs could conceivably be reduced.

Be sure to allow room for expansion of products or categories when designing the numbering system.

Storage and Warehousing

The location of storage facilities is either centralized or decentralized depending upon manufacturing locations, transportation costs and personnel costs.

Space must be provided for receiving material and checking it in, actual storage, access aisles, and possible expansion of material storage requirements at a future date.

Efficient storage improves not only handling and transportation costs, personnel costs and storage costs but in addition, exposes obsolete or inactive stock, reduces the risk of stolen material and improves low turnover identification. Locating material within the storage area for effective cost control must include the following:

— Turnover of material dictates the location for convenience for obtaining material; high turnover items must be located most conveniently.
— Bulky items must be located for access by material handling equipment such as cranes and/or fork-lift trucks. They should also be located to minimize handling and transportation costs.
— Segregation of inflammable or special storage items such as those requiring refrigerated storage.

Ordering/Delivery Cycle

Even though material may be removed from inventory in batches for production use, its actual depletion or usage rate will normally be a gradual process.

The following chart illustrates this gradual usage and replenishment cycle.

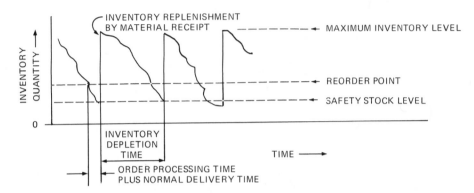

FIGURE 12-2

Inventory depletion time or usage rate must be closely monitored, not only for the most recent period, but also for at least two previous periods in order that unusual production demands do not distort the average usage rate.

Ordering time must take into account: 1) order processing time of the purchaser, 2) order processing of the suppliers and, 3) normal supplier delivery time. Normal supplier delivery time is best gauged on actual delivery schedules rather than promised delivery schedules and should include dock time and time to place into inventory. A time example is:

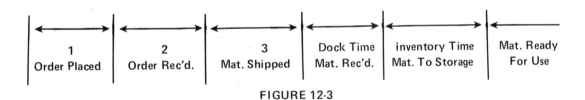

FIGURE 12-3

A partial section of a typical inventory control card illustrates a method of tracking information for the ordering/delivery cycle. (Figure 12-4, page 230.)

To this point, only existing products with known usage rates have been considered. In the case of a new product, never before produced, the use of projected production start times, product forecasts and supplier furnished delivery promises must be used.

On complex products or production schedules requiring close control and coordination, the use of PERT and/or CPM scheduling methods may be required.

```
                                                    USAGE RATE

            ORDER          E.O.Q.          PERIOD NO. 1
            POINT
                                           NO. UNITS  _____
            _____         _____

            ORDER AMOUNT                   PERIOD NO. 2
                                           NO. UNITS  _____
            _____

NORMAL DELIVERY TIME    ADJUSTED ORDER AMOUNT    PERIOD NO. 3
                        BASED ON LAST 3 PERIODS
   _____           USAGE RATE  _____   NO. UNITS  _____

   _____
```

FIGURE 12-4

Purchase Amounts and Order Points

Several factors influence the decision on how many units to purchase to replenish the inventory of a part in stock. Primary among these factors is the purchase of material to minimize total cost to the company.

Some firms make decisions on purchase amounts and order points based on sales forecasts, either formal or informal, lead time required to replenish the stock from a supplier and the amount of physical storage space available for inventory holding.

All of these factors are valid considerations; however, they neglect to reconcile these factors relative to minimizing costs and so should also consider holding costs and ordering cost.

Holding Material in Inventory

In addition to calculating economic order quantities, the inventory control system must also take into account the future production plans. The effect of seasonal sales, for example, may require either a build-up of inventory over a period of time or a shift to peak production prior to seasonal requirements. In cases such as these, it may be found by incremental cost analysis which considers both inventory and production costs for alternate plans, that the use of basic economic order quantity formulas alone do not yield the desired results of producing the lowest *total* cost. In other words, an inventory control system which relies only on E.O.Q. and order point calculations may be faced with a situation whereby the inventory levels cause production to incur extra costs for overtime, layoffs or labor turnover, particularly in situations of fluctuating demand.

For this reason, procurement systems must also be designed to determine the total effect of forecasted seasonal changes in production levels.

This is not as critical a problem for ordering economic quantities as one might expect. Due to the flatness of the total cost curve, considerable order quantity variance can be permitted and the total cost will still approximate that value which theoretically is the optimum. Figure 12-5 illustrates this point:

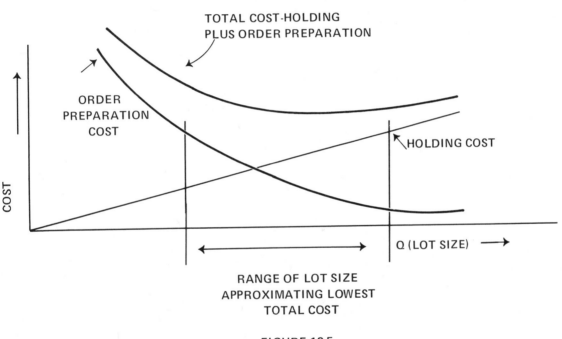

FIGURE 12-5

Storage Records

Probably the simplest method of controlling storage inventory amounts is a simple bin tag arrangement coupled with a stores record.

An example of a type of bin tag used for this purpose is as shown in Figure 12-6.

This tag is simply fixed to the opening of the particular bin containing the material, for example a bin of washers. The description, date of receipt of material or issuance of material and the quantities involved for each change is posted for each transaction.

Each time material is added to or removed from storage, an entry is recorded on the bin tag. Running balances of receipts, withdrawals and material balances on hand are then kept as a perpetual inventory. This is then translated periodically to a stores record as illustrated in Figure 12-7 to allow overall control of all stores material.

BIN TAG

PART NO.	LOCATION	
DESCRIPTION		
ORDER NO.		DATE
RECEIVED		UNIT

DATE	QUANTITY & BALANCE	ORDER NO.

FIGURE 12-6

STORES RECORD   CODE

Stack No.   Max. Quantity _____   Location
Name   Min. Quantity _____

Date	Vendor	Invoice No.	Unit Price	Received		Issued		Balance	
				No.	Value	No.	Value	No.	Value

FIGURE 12-7

DESCRIPTION	BIN NO.
	MAX.
	MIN.

VENDOR	TERMS
1.	
2.	
3.	
4.	
5.	

REMARKS

DATE	VEN-DOR	VIA	DATE NEEDED	QUANTITY	PRICE	UNIT	DELIVER TO	DEPT. CHG.	ON HAND	ON ORDER	REQ. BY	APPD. BY	PUR. BY	RECEIPTS	
									QUANTITY	WEEKS				DATE	QUANTITY

STOREKEEPER FILL IN

TRAVELING REQUISITION

FIGURE 12-8

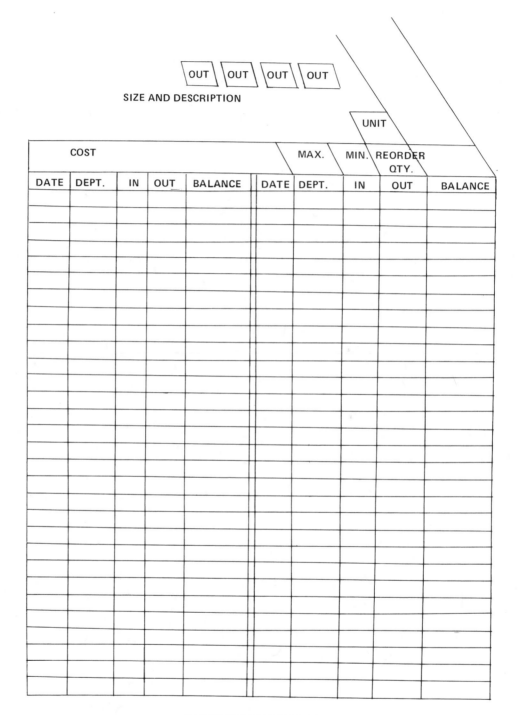

SIZE AND DESCRIPTION

MATERIAL LOCATION CARD
AND STOCK RECORD

FIGURE 12-9

234

Physical inventory should be taken at least once a year to correlate amounts on the bin tags, stores record and actual amounts in the bin. Extra costs such as theft, over-supply and usage rate variances can be detected at those times.

Kardex System

Many card control systems can be utilized. These systems include a bin to contain the traveling requisition card for reordering each item and a locating card.

Examples of each of these are shown in Figures 12-8 and 12-9.

A materials requisition form is required to remove stock from storage. Figure 12-10 is a sample of this type of requisition.

Only properly authorized and documented orders must be released from the stores' containment areas.

MATERIAL REQUISITION			
ORDER NO. _____		CHARGE TO DEPT. _____	
	DEPT. _____	DELIVER TO _____	
ACCOUNT OR CHARGE NO. _____	REQUESTOR _____	DATE DELIVERED _____	
	AUTH. BY _____	DATE REQD. _____	
QUANTITY	DESCRIPTION AND NUMBER	UNIT PRICE	TOTAL PRICE

FIGURE 12-10

Control of the functions of acquisition and possession of material will help reduce inventory, production transportation and handling and personnel costs.

Diligent effort, as well as proper control, is required to manage these functions for reduced procurement costs.

Procurement then should be considered as a dual function: one of acquisition and one of control of material in one's possession until use. Upon use or consumption, the cycle then repeats.

Acquisition cost reduction possibilities exist in the broad areas of:

— Research and vendor selection
— Proper order placement
— Analysis of past purchases for quantity, prices, alternative vendors, usage rate, substitution materials, redesign of material, packaging and delivery method.

Cost reduction in controlling material on hand includes:

— Economic order quantities determination.
— Physical location of storage facilities and material location within these facilities.
— Control of material in storage by means of card systems, including the detection of irregularities in the flow of material into and out of the storage system such as an overstocked position.

Chapter 13

Determine When It Is Time To Go "Outside" for a Helping Hand

HOW SUBCONTRACTING FITS INTO THE PICTURE

Subcontracting is the practice of contracting for a part of a product or service, or for the entire product or service.

The use of subcontracting can add to the effective capacity of a business, and thereby increase its profits, if used astutely. Or it can have an adverse effect on the business, reducing profits, and perhaps adversely affect public relations should product quality be subnormal.

In the housing industry, the normal practice is to subcontract the craft trades work such as plumbing, electrical, foundation, grading, brickwork and roofing. It is the rare builder who performs all of his own craft work. Indeed, it is a more common practice for a builder to subcontract most or all of the craft work, relegating his own activities to monitoring the performance of the "subs".

In manufacturing, those businesses not having complete facilities commonly subcontract a portion of the work such as electroplating, when they have no need for a full-time plating shop.

Part fabrication may be subcontracted where facilities are not balanced, and the work load exceeds the capacity of a section of the plant.

For example, a contract manufacturer producing coin-operated vending machines required a bronze segment gear which actuated the mechanism. He did not have a machine shop equipped to economically produce the part. It was subcontracted at a lower price and higher quality than it could have been produced in-plant.

Engineering or detailing may be subcontracted when the load exceeds capacity. Valid guidelines must be specified in order for the subcontractor to be appraised of the requirements.

Some manufacturing firms conduct their entire businesses largely with subcontractors. An international firm supplying material handling equipment does the engineering and most of the detailing with its own people, but subcontracts the actual fabrication of the equipment.

Another use of subcontracting is to augment facilities, where the capacities or skills are lacking within the business. As an example a large manufacturer of aluminum sheets wanted to expand its product sale in the residential area and needed sheets punched with .050 holes on ¼-inch centers for the production of soffit materials. This required special "gang" punching equipment which the firm did not have. Since the equipment was expensive, and the volume of the product not assured at the time, the company subcontracted the task to another firm.

Tooling is another type of product that is frequently subcontracted. While companies may have some tool-making ability, overloads frequently occur, and orders are placed with an outside firm.

Cost Factors in Make-or-Buy Decisions

Often subcontracting is entered into strictly on the basis of cost. For example, many firms have elected to shut down their captive foundry operations due to the availability of castings from external sources at a lower cost. In fact so many foundries have been closed in this manner that a shortage developed in the foundry industry, creating a seller's market.

Some of the cost factors to consider are:

1. *Material Availability*

    It is possible that an external supplier may have a source of material that is less expensive, or of higher quality, or more available than the prime contractor.

    For instance, if there is excessive offal in a stamped part, it may be more economical to have a producer near a source of material, or the source itself, produce the part and thus reduce the cost of shipping.

    An example of this practice was in the production of automobile grills when most of them were made from stamped aluminum. One of the aluminum suppliers fabricated the grills at the same plant that rolled the metal from ingots. The grills were stacked, and shipped to the automobile manufacturer on pallets.

2. *Better Tooling and Equipment*

    In some cases, external sources of work may be more efficient and thus more competitive due to modernization and specialization of equipment.

    In the case of foundries, those better equipped have overhead sand handling systems, controlled batching and blending of sand, shell core facilities, automatic molding equipment, automatic shake-out equipment and advanced cleaning facilities, which tend to make the older manual facilities noncompetitive. These modern facilities can often supply castings costing less than an older captive facility.

    An example of this was the experience of a Southern steel fabricator. An order for a stacker-recleaner was taken which required the support truck to be made of two-inch steel plate formed and welded. While the truck could have been made in the company's shop, it was decided to seek subcontract bids. One of these bids was obtained from a reputable source which was $25,000 under the estimated cost of making the truck in the firm's own facilities. The reason for the lower cost of a subcontractor was that his equipment was better suited to handle the thicker plate.

Another example is machine shop facilities. Some machine shops have made substantial investments in "NC" equipment which, in many cases, reduces the machine time per piece. A modern machine shop, NC equipped, may well be able to produce and sell parts, especially more complex parts, cheaper than the prime contractor would be able to make them.

3. *Higher Skills*

External sources may have higher skills in their labor forces, along specialized lines, than are present within a given company seeking to increase its volume in some segment of the business. This is particularly true if the captive segment of a prime contractor is a newer phase of the business.

In the case of lack of capacity, it may be cheaper to go to a supplier of the needed item than to expand a captive phase of the business because of skills available in his labor market.

An example of this is the computer industry. The manufacturers of computers do not make all of the peripheral equipment, especially in the area of memory devices. While the largest firm makes a complete line, smaller firms in the computer business are content to buy disc drives from either the largest firm, or one of the smaller companies specializing in them. This is due to the skill level required to make the precision equipment.

Basic Considerations

Some basic questions to be considered in the subcontracting of part or all of a product or service are:

- Has the subcontracted cost been considered in the selling price?
- Is the price reasonable?
- Is the quality sufficient?
- Is the delivery promise valid?
- Are controls over the subcontrctor necessary?
- If special tooling is needed, who will own it after the completion of the current order?
- How should the product be shipped?
- Should the internal facilities be expanded to abrogate the need for subcontracting?

The following will address each of the above factors.

Costing of Subcontracted Work

Obviously, the cost charged by a subcontractor should be included in the cost of sales allowed in the selling price of the product. Normally, this should appear as at least the billed cost of the subcontractor plus a nominal material burden charge. When subcontracting has been anticipated in the sale of the product, it is rather simple to include subcontracting costs.

When this cost has not been anticipated in the selling price and cannot be placed within the included cost of the item, then an analysis must be made to determine the effect of subcontracting on the item's profitability. Some reduction in profit may be necessary to make the delivery of the items. Care must be exercised that the increased cost of subcontracting does not exceed the profit margin of the item, creating a loss situation.

In some cases, it may be possible to actually improve the profit margin by external procurement, provided the item may be obtained at less than the fixed and variable costs assigned to the work subcontracted. It must be borne in mind, however, that the fixed cost of running the business must be absorbed by the remaining inside work.

A large manufacturer of camera equipment planned to introduce a low-priced, special purpose camera, formed largely of plastic components. Here the company found it was cheaper to have a subcontractor produce the entire camera, than it would have been if the camera was made in the firm's own facilities.

Establishing a Reasonable Price

The most common approach used in determining whether or not the price quoted by a subcontractor is reasonable is that of obtaining multiple quotes and comparing the prices and selecting the lowest price as being the most desirable. This time-tested practice may not always be reliable however.

The best way to determine if the price is realistic is to make your own cost estimate of the item being subcontracted. This requires a general knowlege of the subcontractor's labor rates, overheads, and material costs, but these may be closely approximated with a little research. The resulting cost, plus profit markup, should be informative when considering the subcontractor's bid.

In recent years, a magazine called the automotive "Blue Book" has been published for people purchasing a car. Dealer costs are shown for domestic cars plus the cost of the accessories. An astute buyer can determine the dealer cost of the car, equipped as he wants, add the freight and preparation costs plus a reasonable profit, and make an offer on that basis. If the dealer accepts the bid, the purchaser knows the price paid was a "good deal," since he constructed it.

So it is in pricing subcontracted work. Know what the subcontractor's cost is, add a reasonable profit, and his charge can be considered as to its fairness.

Quality

The best price in the world is valueless if the quality of the product procured isn't sufficient. Supplied defective material (in lieu of a quality product) will not meet the need, no matter how inexpensive.

The best way to assure that delivered quality will be adequate is the use of specifications setting the quality demands as a part of the contract for the subcontracted work.

These specifications should clearly cover:

- *Material specifications.*
  State clearly what each material must be, with limits on tolerances to specifications where appropriate.
- *Manufacturing dimensions and tolerances.*
  A common practice is to footnote tolerance, stating that all dimensions are within a stated tolerance unless otherwise indicated.
- *Finishing specifications.*
  Thickness and adhesiveness of paint, thickness and microfinish of plating, should be clearly spelled out.
- *Packaging specifications.*
  Packaging protects the product. Specify how the product should be protected during shipment to you, or your customer if the subcontractor is to drop ship.

  Perhaps Henry Ford provided one of the best examples of planned packaging. Some of his suppliers were under agreement to ship their products in wooden containers, the wood being precut for use as floorboards on the Model "T" automobiles. Perhaps current competition would preclude such practice, but it is something to consider. How can the package from the subcontractor be "recycled"?
- *Performance specifications.*
  How should your product perform? This is especially important where an entire product is being produced by a subcontractor. Your contract should state functional performance criteria.

Once the product is received, a valid incoming inspection should be performed to ascertain that the quality requirements have been met. Should any variance be found, these should be the reason for either price reduction, rework allowance, or return of the item to the supplier for rework or replacement.

Delivery

Some firms make delivery promises just to obtain the order, knowing full well they can't possibly deliver on time. After the order is on the books, and the promised delivery date approaches, the excuses start.

The best assurance of the delivery date being met is to include in the contract a penalty clause for failure to deliver as promised. These penalties should be at a stated rate for each day of failure to deliver an *acceptable* item. This is added inducement not only to deliver on time, but to deliver good quality.

Another reasonable test of the veracity of delivery promises is to make a market survey of customers served by the prospective subcontractor. Inquiries as to the reliability of the supplier can be made as to delivery promises being kept. Firms having a reputation for keeping delivery promises generally maintain a favorable reputation.

Controls

The subject of controls required for subcontractors to assure performance covers a broad spectrum. At one end of this spectrum, no controls are necessary due to the nature of the supplier and the item being purchased.

At the other end, there are subcontractors who supply products of such importance and rigid quality requirements that a full-time resident representative in the plants of the supplier is necessitated.

There is no known "formula" that would reveal the degree of controls necessary. As a general rule, the greater the portion of goods supplied by a subcontractor in comparison with total shipments of the prime contractor, the greater the need for controls. These controls may be simply a matter of a periodic set of reports from the supplier as to his performance against specifications and deliveries.

In more complicated instances, it may be necessary to have a part-time, or even full-time resident inspector who monitors the performance of the subcontractor.

Special Tooling

Many times the subcontractor must supply special tooling to produce a given item. There are two general practices with respect to costing the tooling.

1. Price it as a separate item.
2. Expense it in the unit price of the items supplied.

If the first approach is used, the considerations are the fairness of the price and the custody of the tooling after the order is complete. The concepts applicable to product pricing are equally applicable to tooling prices and should be used.

Custody of tooling is another matter. Here it may be advisable to visit the plant of the supplier and look at his storage facilities. These may either be adequate or unacceptable.

One foundry has over 10,000 customer patterns on hand, stored in a jumbled manner in four separate wooden buildings. In addition to handling damage, there is the possibility of loss due to fire, or simply being unable to locate the patterns when needed.

While optimum security may require the return of tooling after each release to the prime contractor, this may not be acceptable due to shipment costs and delays. A better solution would be to find a supplier who can take adequate care of the tools.

Another matter to consider is the maintenance of tool quality. After excessive use, tools must be either replaced or repaired and assurances of such care must be a matter of agreement between the prime and the sub, and should be a part of the contract.

Shipment

How the product or item should be shipped by the subcontractor should be indicated in the contract and specifications.

One computer manufacturer found it cheapest to ship his product unpacked in household moving vans. Each piece was wrapped with protective pads, as though it were furniture.

Shipment cost must be considered to determine that the best way has been selected. This considers the package, the route, and the mode, as well as the product.

Such costs will be passed along, and it behooves the prime to assure itself that the sub has made proper selections.

Captive Facilities

Whenever subcontracting is employed, the volume of such work must be constantly monitored. Sometimes this volume starts out at a low level, but slowly expands over months or years to become an important factor.

If subcontracting is used to any extent, regular "make-or-buy" studies should be made into the economics of either calling back the work, or of sending additional items out so that in the end, profits are maximized. The astute user of subcontractors makes such analyses on a regular basis.

Need a Bigger Plant: Subcontract!

Capital expansions are expensive in inflationary times. Borrowing money at high interest rates adds to the cost of a plant expansion. Material costs are high, as in construction labor. Land apparently has no ceiling to its price.

If inadequate facilities are present, it may be well to consider the accepted practice of subcontracting part or all of a product or series of products.

One plant actually closed its manufacturing facilities and went entirely to subcontracting because the plant was too small, plagued with labor problems and obsolete equipment. Rather than re-equip, they closed. The result was higher profits and fewer problems.

Is subcontracting for you? Perhaps. Ask yourself these questions:

1. Is there a production bottleneck limiting throughput that is difficult to overcome?
2. Can a portion of the product, or all of it, be subcontracted?
3. Is space to expand a problem? Need more acreage that is not available adjacent to the plant?
4. Is capital to expand unavailable or prohibitively expensive?
5. Could you *sell* more, if you could *make* more?
6. Are there comprehensive part or product specifications?
7. Are there other firms capable of making your parts or products to your satisfaction?
8. Can parts or products be subcontracted at equal or lower costs?
9. Would distribution be affected beneficially by subcontracting?
10. Do you have a short-term need?

If the answers to a majority of the above questions are in the affirmative—consider subcontracting! It may well add to your company's profitability.

Chapter 14

Setting the Right Inventory Level
at the Right Time

Inventories can be regarded as tools to be used for maximizing profits. These tools include all classes of inventories: purchased materials, work-in-process, parts, subassemblies, semifinished products and finished products. The best use of inventories, as for all tools, is made when their use is controlled by planning. One inventory planning technique, Economic Order Quantity (EOQ) calculations, is very widely used. There are other planning techniques and practices available for advantageous use. Some of the other procedures may be used in conjunction with, or in support of, EOQ calculations. Some are independent of EOQ's. Many of the other techniques and practices are very simple and provide inexpensive means of controlling inventories. All have been designed to provide a practical approach toward inventory control.

The discussion in this chapter will emphasize two concepts:

— Planning
— Simplification

One single principle will be found to be common to all good inventory control procedures: Good inventory control is achieved by planning. The greatest benefits will be derived from the application of inventory control procedures when they:

— Are used as integral parts of a defined plan of action.
— Provide flexibility to meet changes in the plan of action.

During the development of the defined plan of action every effort should be exerted to replace complex procedures with simpler ones. With the simplest possible procedures being used, changes in plans can be easily accommodated and the planning is flexible. The flexibility is established by ridding the control system of the encumbrances of complex procedures that yield little or no real benefit. The simplest procedure appropriate to the control of a material in inventory can be determined from an examination of the nature of the material.

SCALE YOUR PROCEDURES TO YOUR INVENTORIES' VALUES

Proper planning does not require the same degree of control over all of the items that are in inventory. The application of a single procedure to all items can result in complicated practices being used where simple practices will suffice and in excessive administrative costs. The first step is considering the total inventory of a manufacturing company as being composed of several separate inventories, each of which may have different characteristics.

For example, the total inventory may be considered as consisting of three major divisions:

— Purchased materials
— Work-in-process
— Finished products

Each of the three major groups may be subdivided further according to two factors:

— Relative significance of each subdivision
— Percent of the total group represented by each subdivision

CASE IN POINT

When one midwestern manufacturer of machine components examined his purchased materials, it became clear that the directly associated cost (purchase price plus delivery costs) of a material was not a true measurement of its real value. For instance, the directly associated cost of an ignition key does not measure the value of the key to the driver of the car when he does not have the key. The relative significance of the purchased materials was determined to be based on:

— Their monetary value
— Their relative importance to continued operations
— The optimum extent of control required
— Their functional application

The result of the determination of direct materials, those used directly in products, is shown in Table 14-1.

Direct Material Purchased

Typical Designation	Percent of Annual Cost	Percent of Items Purchased
A	80	15
B	15	35
C	5	50
	100	100

TABLE 14-1

The three groups are defined as follows:

    Class A — Critical direct materials. Fundamental to products.
            — Aggregating to 80% of assembled material costs.
            — May be consumed in one, or more than one, product type.
            — Delivery lead time is usually one month or longer.
            — Authority to purchase is based on forecast, and disbursement is controlled
              via issuing bills of materials. Scheduled consumption is allocated to inventory
              records.
              Subclass 1—Quality standards must be strictly enforced.
              Subclass 2—Quality standards are less strict.
    Class B — Direct materials not fundamental to the product. Substitutions may be
              allowed, although the item code is shown on the master bills of materials.
            — Delivery lead time is usually less than one month.
            — Authority to purchase is based on historical or forecasted consumption rate.
              Disbursement is made by supervisor's requisition.
            — Quality standards are not strict.
    Class C — Material is of staple variety, consumed in process centers, common to a large
              variety of products. They are not directly expensed to products and are not
              listed on master bills of materials.
            — Delivery lead time is not an important consideration; the materials are usual-
              ly readily available from suppliers.
            — Authority to purchase is based on historical or consumption rates. Disburse-
              ment is made by supervisor's requisition.

(The above definitions can be applied to work-in-process materials if the word *purchase* is replaced by the word *produce,* and the word *delivery* by *production.*)

The definition of the Class A materials led to the conclusion that they were worthy of procedures to provide good control for:

    — Purchasing
    — Receiving
    — Incoming inspection
    — Allocation of materials in anticipation of production plans
    — Specific usage

Class B materials warranted the use of procedures that would adequately provide control for:

    — Purchasing
    — Receiving
    — Periodic review of usage of each individual item

Class C materials needed only to be covered by procedures that adequately provide for:

    — Purchasing
    — Receiving
    — Periodic review of usage of groups of items

(As noted earlier with regard to the definitions, the above considerations for procedures can be applied to work-in-process materials. All that is required is to replace the word *purchasing* with the word *producing* and to replace the word *receiving* with the words *enter into inventory records.*)

Finished goods inventories may also be separated into A, B and C classes, using an-nual sales, either in dollars or quantities, as the basis for separation. This breakdown nearly always shows that for finished goods, there are options as to inventory control procedures. Some of the possible options for finished goods are:

Class A products
— Use EOQ calculations for reorder quantities
— Establish inventories of semifinished products to be used to supply short-cycle finishing operations, or to be used to level work force requirements.

Class B products
— Use EOQ calculations
— Produce when back orders reach a prescribed level

Class C products
— Produce annual requirements once a year
— Examine for possible elimination from product line

The examples demonstrate, in summary, how the nature of the materials comprising the inventory may provide guidance for the procedures to be used to accomplish the control. Costly procedures should be restricted to items of high value. Inexpensive procedures should be used for items of low value. But, for either high or low value items, planning means preparing to fulfill an objective.

BEGIN PLANNING WITH A FORECAST

In the case of inventory control, the objective of the planning is to meet an anticipated sales demand with the least possible cost. Maximum effectiveness of inventory control is realized when the control is directed toward a specific level of anticipated sales. For maximum effectiveness of inventory control, it is essential to have a sales forecast.

In the absence of a forecast, planning of inventories is carried out blindly, because there is no proper guidance. The cost of this lack of guidance can sometimes be very high. The case of an East Coast chemical manufacturer provides an appropriate example for demonstrating the point.

CASE IN POINT

The marketing strategy of the company called for a very rapid response to customers' orders for specialty chemicals. The sales forecast published by marketing was expressed in terms of annual sales dollars. No details were furnished to describe product mix or periods of peak activity. The marketing people attempted to justify their broad forecast by stating that their customers could not supply any details of anticipated usage. Marketing suggested that variations in sales demand should be met by increasing the safety stocks of purchased materials. The cost of implementing that suggestion can be seen from an examination of two of the materials involved.

According to the suggestion, the inventory of one raw material would be increased to a 20-day level from a 14-day level. The value of that inventory would become $221,200 instead of $157,000, an increase of $64,000. The suggestion continued by calling for an increase, in the case of a second material, to a 20-day level from a 10-day level. The value of the inventory of this second material would become $204,500 instead of $102,250, an increase of $102,250. With an inventory carrying cost of 20% the cost of maintaining the increased inventory of the two materials would be 20% of the total of $64,000 + $102,250, that is, 20% of $166,250. The increased carrying cost at 20% would be about $33,400.

There is yet another factor to be taken into consideration. Storage facilities were inadequate. Rail cars would be needed to supply the necessary storage space. This would necessitate increased demurrage charges amounting to about $13,500 per year.

The total cost in this particular instance of using increased inventory levels of the two materials, instead of working to develop proper forecasts, would have been $33,400 + $13,500 or about $46,900 per year. The production staff were determined to avoid that extra cost. They believed that past records would follow a definite pattern of usage.

USE SIMPLE EXTRAPOLATION AS A STOPGAP FOR AN ABSENT DETAILED FORECAST

Because marketing people have the best available knowledge of expected sales to be made, the basic responsibility for preparing the forecast lies with them. If marketing doesn't supply a forecast, other steps should be taken to establish a base for planning and controlling the inventory. Without marketing's best available knowledge of the market, attempting to prepare a detailed forecast may prove to be very disheartening. Preparing a practical substitute, a forecast constructed by extrapolation of historical data is much easier. That is how the production staff of the chemical company solved their problem.

Establishment of ABC classifications showed that the A class consisted of only fifteen items. These fifteen items were the only ones that required close planning. All of the other purchased materials could be controlled with much less effort, through simpler procedures.

A procedure was established for each of the fifteen items to record the history of usage of each item. The record was expressed in terms of a moving monthly average (MMA). The record was started by determining the average pounds per month used for the previous twelve months. As each month passed, the amount used was averaged with the previous MMA to give a new value. An example is shown in Table 14-2.

The effect of averaging each month's value with the MMA is that the influence of the most recent monthly usage is greater than the usage of any single previous month. The employment of previous usage helps smooth the data, reducing the effect of fluctuations in monthly values. The smoothing facilitates the determination of trends. Plotting the data from Table 14-2 shows that the trend of usage for the example is upward, as illustrated in Figure 14-1. Use of the moving monthly average, plotted on a monthly basis, enables the production staff to exercise good control over raw material inventories even though a sales forecast is lacking.

The establishment of control over the inventories of the fifteen A materials

Period of Time Covered	Monthly Usage (Pounds)	Calculation	Moving Monthly Average (Pounds Used)
Average for 12 Months Prior to Month A	(Start Point)	$\dfrac{\text{Total Pounds Used}}{\text{12 Months}}$	15,060
Month A	18,420	$\dfrac{15,060 + 18,420}{2}$	16,740
Month B	14,300	$\dfrac{16,740 + 14,300}{2}$	15,520
Month C	19,010	$\dfrac{15,520 + 19,010}{2}$	17,265

TABLE 14-2

Short-Range Forecast
Bulk Materials Vs. Monthly Usage

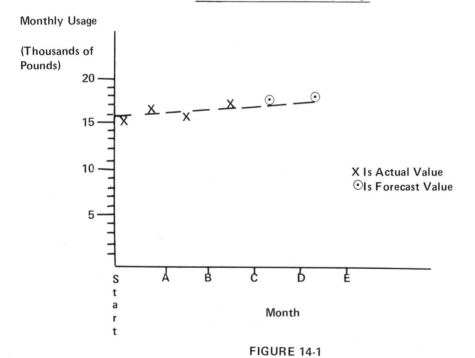

FIGURE 14-1

resulted in close control over the major investment in inventory. Restricting the use of the procedure to the important items keeps the cost of control to a minimum. Because the experience with the extrapolation procedure demonstrated the benefits that could be derived from its use, its use was extended further.

The production staff examined the history of products made and sold. It was found that for a few products, each item was sold every month even though the quantities sold for each varied considerably from month to month. After discussing these few items with the marketing staff, a decision was made to establish a finished stock inventory for some of these items resulting in:

— A corresponding decrease in the inventories of raw materials.
— An increase in the rate of response to customer demands for these items.
— The use of EOQ calculations to reduce operating costs and increase the plant capacity by decreasing downtime for changeovers.
— The elimination of the need for overtime.

The experiences at this plant bring to mind the adage that "half a loaf is better than none." There are important benefits to be gained from the use of a simple stopgap procedure in the absence of a sophisticated forecast. One of the additional benefits in the example is that the increased plant capacity relieves some scheduling restrictions and provides an opportunity for increased flexibility.

UTILIZE THE FLEXIBILITY OF ECONOMIC ORDER QUANTITIES

Not all opportunities for flexibility are readily visible. It is not commonly understood that the EOQ itself has a great deal of flexibility. As shown in Table 14-3, it is possible to vary the order quantity considerably, reducing it by 50% or increasing it by 33 ⅓% with little effect on total annual costs, only about 8%. The data in Table 14-3 can be used to state the flexibility in another way. The same small effect on total annual costs will be found even when the numbers of orders per year range from 7 to 15.

CASE IN POINT

In a midwestern millwork plant, when the use of EOQ's was introduced into the production and inventory control operations, funds available for finished goods inventory were limited. The decision was made to take advantage of the flexibility of the EOQ's by producing only 50% of the quantities resulting from the use of the formula. Because there was adequate production capacity to meet sales demands, the increase in downtime due to changeovers had no ill effects. The introduction of the new procedures yielded the results that had been expected from the use of the full EOQ's:

— Improvement in meeting promised delivery dates, going to a 98% performance of deliveries as promised from a 17½% performance.
— Elimination of overtime usually required during the peak summer months.
— Reduction of labor costs by about 10% throughout the year, including periods of high and low activity.

EFFECT OF

VARIATIONS IN ORDER QUANTITIES

ON

TOTAL ANNUAL COSTS

Order Quantity	Number of Orders Per Year	Annual Order Cost $	Average Number of Units in Inventory	Value of Average Inventory $	Cost of Carrying Average Inventory $	Total Annual Cost $	% Increase in Total Annual Cost	% Variation From EOQ
3,000	6.67	110.00	1,500	1,650	247.50	357.50	8.2	+ 50
2,800	7.15	118.00	1,400	1,540	231.00	349.00	5.6	+ 40
2,600	7.70	127.00	1,300	1,430	214.50	341.50	3.9	+ 30
2,400	8.33	137.50	1,200	1,320	198.00	335.50	1.8	+ 20
2,200	9.10	150.00	1,100	1.210	181.50	331.50	0.9	+ 10
2,000	10.00	165.00	1,000	1,100	165.00	330.00	[E	O Q]
1,800	11.11	183.50	900	990	148.50	332.00	1.1	- 10
1,600	12.50	206.50	800	880	132.00	338.50	2.5	- 20
1,400	14.30	236.00	700	770	115.50	351.50	6.9	- 30
1,200	16.67	275.00	600	660	99.00	374.00	13.2	- 40

Assumptions
for this
Table

1. Each order costs $16.50 for office and plant personnel.
2. The inventory carrying cost is 15% of the value of inventory.
3. Forecast requirement is for 20,000 units for the year.
4. The cost of each unit is $1.10.

TABLE 14-3

The use of order quantities that are 33⅓% greater than EOQ's can be used to increase plant capacity by reducing production time lost during changeovers.

CASE IN POINT

A midwestern hardware manufacturer had invested a great deal of time and effort in promoting a revised product line. The promotion effort was very fruitful, but the production facilities were unable to supply the sales demand. The slowing response to customers' orders resulted in the sales department asking for special treatment for important customers. If the plant was not producing the product that was ordered by an important customer, the sales department exerted pressure on the production department to stop its current production and to change over to produce the product asked for by the important customer. The extra changeovers resulted in increased downtime and the result was lost production capacity at a time when it was needed most.

Discussions were held with both sales and production and a decision was made to lengthen promised delivery lead times and to increase the production order quantities to EOQ's plus 33⅓%. The larger order quantities provided increased production capacity to the extent needed to meet the sales demands. The customers accepted the longer promised delivery lead times when they were assured that the lengthening meant that the promises would be kept. There is a variety of sources of flexibility. There is also a variety of occasions for being flexible.

STAY FLEXIBLE ON EOQ'S FOR PURCHASED MATERIALS

There are occasions for being flexible regarding when to use EOQ formulas. In the case of purchased materials for which vendors give price breaks the proper order quantity may be determined by comparing the results of using formula EOQ's with the results of capitalizing on the price break. The comparison is made by examining the total annual costs of the two alternatives.

CASE IN POINT

Vendors of packaging materials customarily offer quantity-price break schedules. In the case of cosmetics with low retail sales prices, the costs of packaging materials represent an important part of the total product cost. In one specific case, the conditions were:

Total annual usage: 70,000 units
Cost per purchase order: $25.00
Inventory carrying cost: 15% = .15
Cost for container:

Order Quantity Range	*Unit Cost*
Over 2,000 through 5,000	$1.44
Over 5,000 through 8,000	$1.39

$$\text{EOQ, @ \$1.44} = \sqrt{\frac{2 \times \$25.00}{\$1.44 \times .15}} \times 70,000 = 4025$$

$$\text{EOQ, @ \$1.39} = \sqrt{\frac{2 \times \$25.00}{\$1.39 \times .15}} \times 70,000 = 4098$$

The difference between $1.44 and $1.39 is small, $.05, but for 70,000 units it would represent an annual savings of $3,500. This potential benefit must be compared with the cost of carrying increased inventories resulting from increased order quantity. Examination shows:

— 17 orders per year for 70,000 total units calls for 4118 units per order. The 4118 is very close to the EOQ.
— 13 orders per year for 70,000 total units calls for 5385 units per order. The 5385 order is the least practical average order quantity that will qualify for the lower price.

Evaluation of the two alternatives can be easily made by comparing their total annual costs.

$$\begin{pmatrix}\text{Total Annual} \\ \text{Costs}\end{pmatrix} = \begin{pmatrix}\text{Annual Unit} \\ \text{Costs}\end{pmatrix} + \begin{pmatrix}\text{Annual} \\ \text{Order Costs}\end{pmatrix} + \begin{pmatrix}\text{Annual Inventory} \\ \text{Carrying Costs}\end{pmatrix}$$

At $1.44/Unit: $\begin{pmatrix}\text{Total} \\ \text{Annual Costs}\end{pmatrix}$ = ($1.44 × 70,000) + ($25.00 × 17) +

$$\left(.15 \times \frac{\$1.44 \times 4118}{2}\right) = \$101,269.74$$

At $1.39/Unit: (Total = ($1.39 X 70,000) + ($25.00 X 13) +
Annual Costs)

$$(.15 \text{ X } \frac{\$1.30 \text{ X } 5385}{2}) = \$ 98,186.39$$

The benefit of pay $1.39/Unit = $ 3,083.35

The increase in inventory carrying costs is unimportant when compared to the benefits of the lower unit cost and the reduction in ordering costs.

This example should demonstrate that the EOQ formula, although very useful, is only one of a number of concepts that can contribute to good control of inventories. The other concepts may operate wholly or partially with EOQ calculations, or their contributions may be entirely independent of the EOQ formula.

PUT BILLS OF MATERIALS TO WORK ON INVENTORY CONTROLS

Bills of materials can be useful to inventory control in at least two different ways. They can be used to support EOQ calculations, and they can be used with no relationship to EOQ considerations.

Bills of materials can be used to determine annual requirements for Class A materials. Application of forecast sales quantities to bills of materials provides information about quantities of Class A materials needed to meet the forecast. Those quantities are introduced directly into the EOQ formula. This procedure can cover both purchased and processed materials.

Bills of materials can be used to control disbursement of Class A materials. When production orders are issued, the quantities of product to be produced can be applied to the bills of materials to provide information about quantities of materials needed for the production orders.

The use of bills of materials for inventory control has been extended by converting them into production planning and scheduling tools, with no relationship to EOQ considerations. This technique has application in several classes of industries, and can provide excellent guidance toward minimum investment in inventory.

CASE IN POINT

To demonstrate the wide variety of industries for which this procedure is useful, the following relates to a manufacturer of industrial laboratory instruments and, also, to a manufacturer of pharmaceuticals and vitamins. Both companies followed almost identical steps.

The bills of materials were constructed to show different levels or steps in their processes. In their simplest form the bills of materials might show three steps for all products to be produced during a given period. The instrument manufacturer used a six-month period; the chemical manufacturer used a twelve-month period. The three steps are

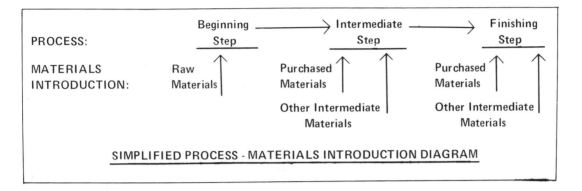

FIGURE 14-2

essentially those shown in greatly simplified form in Figure 14-2. That figure shows that raw materials are required for the first step, purchased materials and the products of other processes are required for the intermediate step and purchased materials and the products of other processes are required for the finishing step. Examination of Figure 14-2 shows that there are opportunities for keeping inventories at a minimum level by coordinating the production planning with the purchasing planning.

In both of these cases, the production supervisors coordinate their production planning so that, if the product from the process of one supervisor is needed for the process of a second supervisor, the first supervisor plans to complete his process before the time planned by the second supervisor for starting his process. Quantities of products to be produced are included in the plans. A simplified diagram for two processes is shown in Figure 14-3. The diagram shows that the beginning step for Product No. 1 is to completed before the beginning step for Product No. 2, so that material produced in the intermediate step of Product No. 1 will be available for use in the intermediate step of Product No. 2. The diagram also shows that material produced in the intermediate step of Product No. 2 is needed for the finishing step of Product No. 1. That information is used for planning the delivery of purchased materials required for the finishing step of Product No. 1.

The production plans of the production supervisors are given to individuals responsible for planning purchases. The production plans are applied to bills of materials that have been established for each production step. The result is a bill of materials explosion, showing quantities of purchased items needed, and the dates for which the use of the items are planned.

The laboratory instrument plant employs less than 100 direct labor employees. The planning of purchases is carried out by the purchasing agent. The chemical plant employs several thousand chemical operators. There, the planning of purchasing is performed by three people who provide the information to the purchasing agents. In both companies the production planning and the purchasing planning are carried out manually rather than by computer, although several attempts have been made to utilize a computer at the large chemical plant. The point to be emphasized is, even with manual planning, the cost of the planning is far less than the cost of carrying the large stocks of raw materials inventory that would have been otherwise needed.

No EOQ calculations are made for most purchased materials. For most items the quantities of materials ordered are the quantities to be used, plus a small safety factor, less

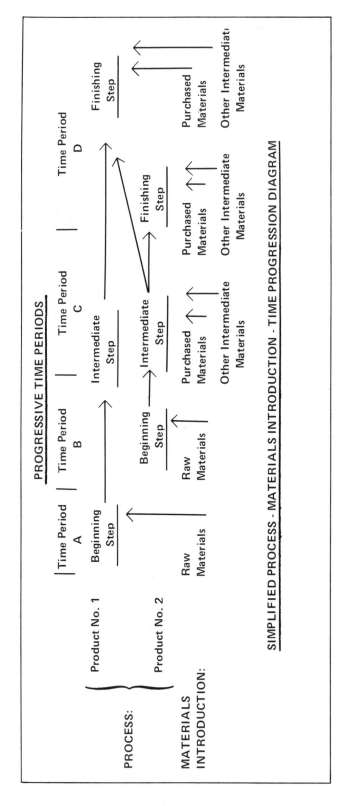

SIMPLIFIED PROCESS - MATERIALS INTRODUCTION - TIME PROGRESSION DIAGRAM

FIGURE 14-3

256

amounts on hand from previous orders. To some extent this procedure resembles that used in major automotive assembly plants. These cases demonstrate the use of detailed documentation. Some procedures operate in the other extreme, with very little documentation.

USE THE MATERIALS THEMSELVES AS INVENTORY RECORDS

For some Class C materials, good control can be exercised over their inventory levels without the expense of record-keeping. This applies particularly to materials that are staple items such as common hardware and common packaging supplies.

Such items can be purchased very readily and delivery is merely a matter of days. Generally, these materials are in supply in warehouses located near manufacturing plants. There is no need to maintain large inventories of these materials because, if a shortage develops, the shortage can be filled very quickly. The important consideration is for the shortage to become known in sufficient time for replacement. There must be enough material available to cover that lead time whether it's only one or two days. This outage is prevented by using a two-bin system.

In some production departments and in many maintenance departments the supply of the materials is divided into two bins. One bin furnishes the materials required on a day-to-day basis. The second bin is kept under lock and key. There is sufficient material in the second bin to cover the time required for replacement of the first bin. In the second bin there is a traveling requisition that can be directly processed by the purchasing department to replenish the supply.

The amount of material ordered generally does not have to be very large, probably enough to cover one month. In some cases, the total inventory for a very common item can be about five weeks' duration, enough to cover about one month's operation with the first bin, and in the second bin enough to cover the one week needed to bring in another month's supply. Part of the new supply then goes to replenish the second bin so that it is always kept at the proper level to cover the reorder time. This operation can be very successful. It can also be a disaster. Generally, when the operation is not successful, it is because the second bin is not maintained under good security.

The advantage of the two-bin system is that it can provide good control of inventory levels of some materials with the minimum of administrative costs and with a minimum of money invested in inventory. The materials can be treated this way because they have no extraordinary properties. Materials with extraordinary properties require somewhat different treatment.

CAREFULLY CONTROL CRITICAL MATERIALS WITH SMALL USAGE

A variation of the two-bin system can be applied to certain special, unique materials that are critical to production processes, but may not be required in large amounts. The purpose of the control is to ensure availability and so to prevent excessive costs that would arise if the materials were not available.

CASE IN POINT

In the pharmaceutical, food and confection industries, flavors and colorings have been found to fall under this classification. Often these materials have somewhat limited shelf lives; therefore, it is important to be certain that the materials on hand are suitable for use. They must be of proper strength or color, and if they change beyond the specified limits they must be replaced. There is no justification for buying large amounts of these materials because their rate of deterioration is faster than their rate of consumption. There is also no justification for maintaining detailed inventory records for these items; the amounts used are generally small and the costs are not a significant part of the product costs.

Control procedures for these items are designed to accomplish several objectives, depending on conditions specific to the materials. Two of the more common objectives are:

— Ensuring that a sufficient quantity is available in suitable condition to satisfy published production schedules.
— Ensuring that some quantity of the material is available in suitable condition to cover long procurement lead times.

Because of the suitable condition requirements, the control procedures always include provision for inspection or testing. In most cases the established control procedures call for examination of all items under this classification to be made within regular periods of time. It has been found that the cost of the examination and testing is much less when it is carried out regularly than if the materials are found to be unsuitable for use just at the time when they are needed for production. The control procedures generally contain provisions to take advantage of the fact that the materials are carefully tested at the time of actual use to determine the amounts required according to the condition at the time of use. The results of the tests that immediately precede actual use are noted in the inventory control logs, and are accepted in lieu of the periodic inventory control tests.

This procedure is designed to prevent stockouts of materials where the requirement for protection against this is critical and obvious. There are other materials for which the requirement for protection against stockouts is not so critical. There is another kind of requirement, however, which has been found to be not obvious, that is the requirement for knowing, before production orders are released, that the needed materials are available.

MAKE CERTAIN THAT MATERIALS ARE AVAILABLE BEFORE ISSUING PRODUCTION ORDERS

Experience in a wide variety of industries shows that production orders are frequently issued without verification that the materials needed for the orders are available for use. This occurs because one or more of the following assumptions are made:

— Inventory records that show materials on hand are accurate.
— Materials on hand are in usable condition.
— Vendors will make deliveries according to their promises.
— Materials delivered by vendors will meet specifications.
— Materials delivered by vendors will be available for use at the moment they are delivered to the plant.

— New items that meet published specifications are usable for production runs and do not need to be tried out.

All too often, these assumptions have been found to be false. In industries that employ packaging crews of considerable size, when those assumptions are false, the result is an accumulation of significant amounts of idle labor time. These industries include hardware, toys, confections, food, cosmetics, and pharmaceuticals. When a large crew is set up, ready to work, but is idle because of material problems, not much time has to elapse for the costs of the idleness to become excessive. This condition can be prevented by a very straightforward procedure.

The straightforward action consists simply of making sure that the needed materials are available for use before the production order is released. One step in this procedure occurs at the beginning of the inventory process. As a matter of principle, purchasing agents and buyers should be considered to have fulfilled their procurement responsibilities only after incoming materials have passed incoming inspection and are ready for use. As another matter of principle, those individuals who are responsible for warehousing and storage activities should be kept informed of the quantities that are recorded as being available. As another matter of principle, those individuals who are responsible for warehousing and storage should be alert to materials within their care that become unusable because of deterioration in physical condition.

Experience shows that the enforcement of these principles is practical. With these principles clearly stated, and their enforcement assured, the next step is to make certain beforehand that the materials required for a specific run are available, in proper quantity and in proper condition. There are various ways of accomplishing that, ranging from obtaining signatures on exploded bills of materials to simply using telephone contacts. If it is found that the materials are not available for a run, then that specific run is postponed and another run, for which materials are available, is planned.

It might seem that this planning activity will increase the number of people involved in inventory control activities. The opposite is true. Proper planning of material use eliminates the need for all of the expediting effort that is exerted in the absence of proper planning.

When planning is lacking, the expediters spend time searching for missing materials or trying to determine why the materials are unavailable, frequently while the packaging crew is sitting idle. It has been found that, in addition to reducing idle time, proper planning can yield as much as a 20% to 25% reduction in administrative staffs.

This procedure is designed for one specific purpose: maximizing the planned utilization of personnel and equipment. A separate procedure has been prepared to cover a related purpose: planning the utilization of personnel and equipment to replenish an inventory. As a matter of principle, a procedure should be designed to satisfy a single purpose. This principle helps ensure that each purpose is satisfied by the simplest possible procedure.

USE SIMPLIFIED MINIMUM-MAXIMUM DETERMINATIONS

Under some conditions there is justification for using procedures that are simpler than EOQ calculations for determining reorder quantities. Similarly, simple determinations of safety stocks are frequently in order. These conditions exist for most Class C materials as defined earlier and for some Class B materials for which substitute materials are regularly used.

CASE IN POINT

A typical, simple procedure is one that was installed for control of maintenance parts and supplies for a southern governmental agency. The procedures consist of these steps:

1. A purchase order and inventory record card is prepared for each item. The card shows complete identification of the item, the vendor, the most recent price, a historical record of purchases, additions to inventory, disbursements from inventory and the stock remaining on hand.

2. Periodically, annual usage of each item is determined from the record card. The results are entered into the form shown as Figure 14-4.

3. Information shown on the purchase order record card and inventory card will help determine how much time elapsed between the date the purchase order was prepared and the date the material was delivered by the vendor. For example, if the purchase order was dated January 2 and the record card shows the material was added to the inventory on January 29, the lead time can be accepted as being four weeks.

MIN-MAX CALCULATION FORM

Stock #	(A) Annual Usage	(B) Lead Time	(C) Annual Usage ÷ 50	(D) Column C × Column B Min.	(E) Annual Usage ÷ 2 Max.

FIGURE 14-4

4. The minimum inventory level is established by dividing the annual usage by 50 and then multiplying the result by the lead time. By using 50 instead of 52 a small safety factor is provided. Example: If annual usage is 2,000 units and if the lead time is five weeks:

$$\frac{2,000}{50} = 40 \times 5 = 200 \text{ units}$$

The minimum level is 200 units. When the inventory reaches that amount, the material is reordered. This information is also entered into the form shown in Figure 14-4.

5. The maximum level in this case is the same as the order quantity. It is set up as a six months' supply, calculated by dividing the annual usage by 2, with the result entered on the form in Figure 14-4.

The primary purpose of this procedure is to ensure availability of items needed for maintenance work. That objective is more important than minimizing the value of the inventory. The value of this procedure can be seen from the fact that it made an important contribution to the achievement of a reduction in maintenance labor costs amounting to about $120,000 per year. The use of a simple inventory control permits attention to be concentrated on the control of labor. The greatest control effort is being exercised toward the greatest potential benefits.

EXERCISE CONTROL OVER THE INVENTORY AT THE EARLIEST POSSIBLE POINT OF THE MANUFACTURING PROCESS

When the greatest potential benefit expected from a control effort has been identified as minimizing the investment in inventory, it should be recognized that there are two avenues of approach: quantity and unit value. The challenge to the control of inventory includes not only keeping the quantities at the lowest possible level, but also in keeping the materials at the lowest possible unit value. As the materials progress from the raw state to the finished form, costs are added. The value of the material increases merely because it is progressing through the production system and labor and other costs are being added. If the production cycle is short, inventories should be kept in the form of raw materials as much as possible. If the production process is long, efforts should be exerted to break up the process into several steps to allow materials to be kept in condition of the lowest possible value.

CASE IN POINT

An East Coast pharmaceutical manufacturer takes advantage of the fact that his product line includes different package configurations of individual bulk products. He places his inventory control emphasis on bulk products and raw packaging materials. His inventories of finished goods are kept low. Because of his supply of bulk product and packaging supplies he is able to respond to a stockout of finished product almost overnight. In this way he is able to keep his inventories relatively free of the packaging labor costs and those costs are an important part of the total costs of his finished products.

The ability to respond so rapidly to a finished goods stockout results in a slightly excessive labor force, but this was deemed to be justified by the fact that he is supporting sales at the rate per year of $10,000,000 worth of finished goods, at cost, by controlling an inventory worth less than $500,000, at cost. This represents a turnover of at least 20 to 1. He has found that his lowest cost protection against stockouts is something other than a safety stock of finished product.

BE CAUTIOUS IN THE USE OF SAFETY STOCKS

Safety stocks are intended to provide protection against stockouts resulting from irregularities in usage and variances against forecasts. The data shown in Table 14-4 show costs for various degrees of protection. The calculations for that data begin from the base of a safety stock valued at $100,000 that provides protection of one probable stockout per year. A stockout occurs when an item is out of stock for one week of the year. If a stockout is considered to occur when an item cannot be shipped the day the order is received, the cost of protection against that probability can be estimated to be about the same as for that shown in Table 14-4 for one stockout every five years. If protection is to be provided for one probable stockout per year, and if a stockout consists of being unable to ship the *day* the order is received, rather than the *week* the order is received the cost of the protection increases to roughly $126,000 from $100,000. Because protection against stockouts in the form of finished goods is costly, other methods of providing protection should be sought. Several alternatives have been discussed earlier in this chapter. They are:

— The first approach might be to install a forecasting activity in marketing, if there presently is none. If there is one, consideration should be given to possible ways of increasing its reliability.
— A strong effort should be made to accelerate final operations, so that safety stocks of unfinished materials, with lower costs, can be used in place of safety stocks of finished products, with higher associated costs.

Other practices have been used with success in a variety of industries.
In the absence of highly reliable forecasting, whatever the reason for the absence,

Keeping Probable Stockouts To An Average Of One Stockout	% Stockouts	Requires Protection Valued At
Every year	1.9%	100,000
Every two years	0.96%	114,000
Every five years	0.39%	126,000
Every ten years	0.19%	144,000
Never	0.00%	241,000

TABLE 14-4

arrangements have been made by some companies with some of their customers for a steady or regular delivery of some products. The customers retain the option to reduce or even cancel deliveries, with short notice. Despite the limited application and despite the short notice option these arrangements have proven to be useful. Regardless of the degree to which these arrangements can be utilized, they make a positive contribution to the reduction of safety stocks. Products for which such arrangements have been made include hardware, millwork, food and cosmetics. Customers covered by such arrangements vary from large store chains to small individual sales outlets.

Some manufacturers that operate by means of a chain of distribution points maintain safety stocks only at the beginning of the chain. Stockouts at the ends of the chain are corrected through the use of air shipments. The added expense of shipping by air has been found for them to be less than the expense of maintaining safety stocks at more than one location. This practice is particularly applicable to products that have a high ratio of value to weight. This includes jewelry and pharmaceuticals.

Because safety stocks cannot be avoided completely, they should be established with great care for items of high value, e.g. the Class A materials. The value of a specific material should be used as a guide for deciding how much accuracy in stocking should be sought.

ABOVE ALL: PLAN

Good inventory management practices are designed around the condition that plans are always subject to change. Nevertheless, planning of inventories is essential to the achievement of good control. An important element of the planning process is the identification and evaluation of alternatives. The various cases and examples presented in this chapter demonstrate how weak plans can be strengthened and how changes in plans can be easily accommodated. They also illustrate how inventory control procedures can be simplified and thereby rendered more flexible. The discussions have been directed toward providing help to make the planning of inventory control less abstract and more concrete.

Chapter 15

Slashing Costs Through the Work-In-Process Inventory System

Work-in-process inventory can be a substantial part of a company's assets. Where applicable, a reduction in work-in-process (WIP) inventories frees asset dollars that can be reinvested in new plants and equipment. A reduction in WIP also creates a one-time material requirement savings, a significant factor in a material scarcity situation. Another benefit is the reduction in inventory carrying costs.

It is necessary to keep WIP reduction efforts in line with overall production objectives. Optimal WIP is not necessarily zero WIP. In many cases too little WIP can cause downtime through inflexibility. Occasionally, benefits can be accrued from increasing rather than decreasing the WIP inventory.

WHAT IS WORK-IN-PROCESS?

Typically, a manufacturing company has three types of inventory accounts: raw materials, work-in-process, and finished goods. In theory, each of these three classifications is quite distinct. Raw materials inventory is the sum of the costs of those goods upon which no work has been accomplished, and, therefore, no value added while those goods have been in the plant. Finished goods inventory is the sum of the costs of products manufactured but not yet sold. All goods progressing through the manufacturing process, having been at the inception raw materials, and destined to be at the conclusion finished goods, are classified as work-in-process. The sum of the accumulated costs of all work-in-process items is the work-in-process inventory.

Raw materials are costed based on purchase price. Work-in-process gains additional value as it progresses through the manufacturing procedure. A casting purchased for fifty dollars is worth more than fifty dollars after the first manufacturing operation, for example, milling the referenced surface. How much more is normally determined by the cost of the milling operation. This cost is based on direct labor plus an overhead factor. If the milling required three dollars labor and the overhead factor was 120%, the value of the casting after the first operation would be:

Direct Material	$50.00
Direct Labor	3.00
Overhead ($3.00 × 120%)	3.60
Total Value	**$56.60**

Inventory value is based upon cost and not upon worth. The worth of a product is what someone else is willing to pay for it. *Worth is the basis of pricing, cost the basis of inventory.*

One cannot classify an item as raw material, work-in-process, or finished goods by merely looking at the item's physical characteristics. In practice, many judgment decisions are required in categorizing goods into the three types of inventory. Consider automobile radios. A finished radio awaiting shipment from a radio plant in Indiana is finished goods, but after it is shipped to a plant in Michigan it becomes raw material. It could be argued that the radio is not really raw material since it will not undergo any physical change during the manufacturing procedure. Likewise, it could be argued that the radio does not become work-in-process until it is incorporated into the dashboard subassembly, i.e., until the initial operation of the manufacturing procedure is performed.

The classification of inventory is often resolved by physical location. For instance, when parts are held in a storeroom awaiting assembly, they are usually called raw material. When they are issued to the assembly floor, they become work-in-process. But even this distinction can become blurred, as in a mobile home assembly plant where goods are received and stored "on-line" to be assembled in a home within just a few hours.

PRODUCTS AND PROCESSES

In some plants WIP control is of major concern, while in others it is insignificant. The importance of WIP is a function of two factors: products and processes.

In a chemical plant producing sulfuric acid via the contact process, the inventory concerns are limited to the (raw material) stockpile of sulfur and the (finished goods) tanks of acid. WIP is not considered as a separate entity, but rather as part of the process. On the other hand, in a brewery the aging process requires large quantities of WIP. To generalize, in the continuous process industries, managerial decision-making about WIP is superseded by process requirements as dictated by the laws of nature.

At the other end of the manufacturing spectrum is the machining job shop where WIP inventory value can easily be double that of raw materials and finished goods combined. Daily decisions about which products to manufacture and how they should be processed have impact not only on WIP but also on the entire profitability of the firm. Most companies are between the two extremes of continuous manufacture and job shop. WIP considerations for many companies are not usually a critical matter; nevertheless, they play an important role in the conduct of business and can be a source of cost reductions.

TRACKING WORK-IN-PROCESS INVENTORIES

Decision-making requires authentic information flows. The control and reduction of WIP inventories can only be attained by proper documentation and tracking of progress through the manufacturing process.

To illustrate the various documentation required, a simple product has been selected. It is a manually operated tire pump similar to those found in many large chain stores. Figures 15-1 and 15-2 are an explosion drawing and a bill of materials. The #1,000 tire pump is made of seventeen different parts: eleven are fabricated in-house and six are purchased.

The route sheet for the #5000 handle is shown in Figure 15-3. The route sheet calls out and describes each operation required to change the raw material into a piece part. It is required that direct labor employees submit a production report each day itemizing each employee's direct labor accomplishment. These reports are keyed to the operation numbers designated on the route sheet. If Jane Doe spent her full eight-hour shift working on operation 10 of the #5000 handle and she produces 11,260 parts, her production report would typically look like Figure 15-4. Using production reporting such as this as the source information, perpetual inventories of each shop item at each stage of manufacture are maintained.

Some companies have found that they can operate more effectively by delegating control of WIP to shop foremen and eliminating the paper work system necessary for perpetual inventory records. This is only successful when the time required by the foremen does not interfere with their supervisory duties. Large companies have automated this function with computerized on-line inventory control. A general rule that applies to all companies is "the value derived from the information should be greater than the cost of obtaining the information." The value of the information can be quantified in terms of increased cash flow from:

— Inventory carrying cost reductions.
— Increased customer service (previous lost sales that are recouped).
— Reduced unit cost of production by varying run size quantities.
— Reduced equipment downtime.

HOW MUCH WORK-IN-PROCESS?

The work-in-process value of materials increases as they progress from operation to subsequent operation. Understanding the value-added concept is important for daily decision-making. Graphically, value added looks like Figure 15-5, a typical value-added curve. Each operation adds value to the material. Total value added via the five operations is the finished goods value less the raw material value.

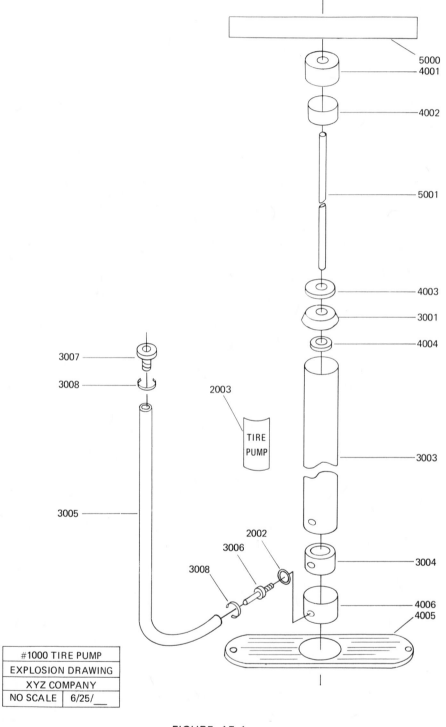

5000
4001

4002

5001

4003
3001
4004

3003

3004

4006
4005

3007
3008

2003

TIRE
PUMP

3005

2002
3006

3008

#1000 TIRE PUMP
EXPLOSION DRAWING
XYZ COMPANY
NO SCALE	6/25/___

FIGURE 15-1

BILL OF MATERIALS

1000	Tire	Pump			
	2000	Pump	Sub-Assembly		
		3000	Piston Weldment		
			4000	Handle Rod Weldment	
				5000	Handle
				5001	Rod
			4001	Top Cap	
			4002	Insert	
			4003	Backing	
			4004	Retainer	
		3001	Rubber Cup		P
		3002	Base Weldment		
			4005	Oval Base	
			4006	Base Cap	
		3003	Barrel		
		3004	Insert		
	2001	Hose Assembly			
		3005	Hose		
		3006	Check Valve		P
		3007	Screw-On Connection		P
		3008	Hose Bands (2 required)		P
	2002	Gasket			P
	2003	Label			P

(P indicates Purchased)

FIGURE 15-2

Route Sheet

Part No. ___5000___   Part Name ___Handle___

Material: 14 Ga. x 7″ Wide H.R.P.O. Coil

Operation Number	Machine Number	Set-Up Hours	Hours Per Pc.	Operation Description	Tooling
5	1492	2.3	.0005	Blank, Pierce	Die #5000-5
10	1383	1.8	.0020	1st Form	Die #5000-10
15	1438	1.8	.0020	2nd Form	Die #5000-15

FIGURE 15-3

Production Report

Clock Number 232		Name Jane Doe				Department 22
Part Number	Part Name	Operation	Start	Stop	Total Hours	Quantity Produced
5000	Handle	10	7:00	3:30	8.0	11,260

FIGURE 15-4

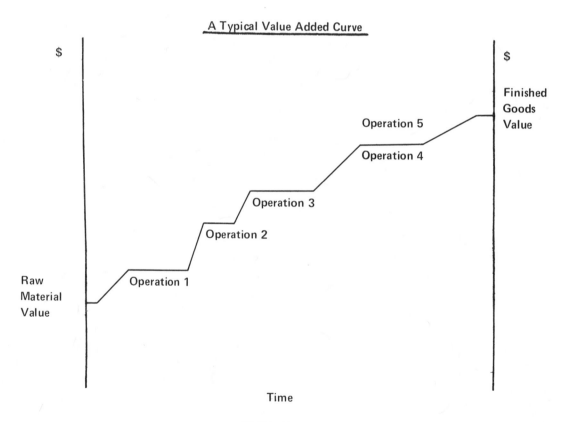

A Typical Value Added Curve

FIGURE 15-5

Some products are labor intensive and some are material intensive. The raw material value for the #5001 tire pump rod described earlier is $.08, with labor and overhead totaling $.03.

$$\text{(Value Added Percentage) rod} = \frac{\$.03}{\$.08 + \$.03} = 27\%$$

Compared with the 3003 tire pump barrel, the rod is more labor intensive.

$$\text{(Value Added Percentage) barrel} = \frac{\$.04}{\$.25 + \$.04} = 14\%$$

In both cases, the manufacturing procedure involves only a single operation. If a shop foreman "needed a job" to keep a man busy, which of these two parts should he run assuming: 1) ample material was available for both parts; 2) there was no immediate production requirement for either job but any parts run would be used in the not too distant future; and 3) the equipment necessary for running these parts was available? As a general rule, the more labor intensive parts should be run in such cases. The foreman should run rods. For every $1 of labor (including overhead) expended on barrels, $7.25 is put into WIP inventory; but for every $1 expended on rods, only $3.67 is put into WIP. Running rods keeps WIP inventory carrying costs as low as possible.

A similar analysis is often used in decision-making for production smoothing. Unfortunately, for most companies, output demand does not remain constant throughout the year; business is seasonal. Shipping demand for an East Coast cosmetics manufacturer is shown in Figure 15-6. The heaviest demand is for the Christmas season. The production rate was leveled by building finished goods inventory prior to demand. From the points of view of the availability of labor, product quality, and training requirements, smoothing was necessary. One third of the year, a partial second shift is employed to meet demand. The production planners in this cosmetics plant wisely produced labor intensive products in the summer months and material intensive

FIGURE 15-6

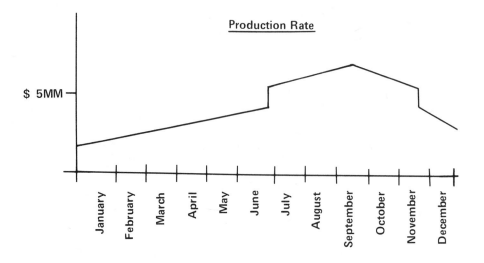

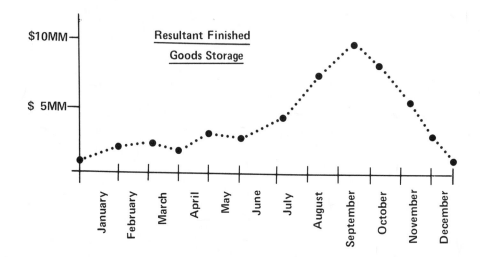

FIGURE 15-6 cont.

products during the "rush" season. Otherwise, inventory value in finished goods would have rocketed far beyond what was necessary.

REDUCING WORK-IN-PROCESS COSTS VIA ENGINEERING VALUE ANALYSIS: CHANGING DESIGN

In the 1960's, the concept of value analysis, sometimes called value engineering, came into vogue. The concept is to maintain without penalty the design function of a product while at the same time reducing the manufacturing cost to a minimum. This technique goes far beyond the traditional emphasis of cost reduction, work simplification and methods analysis. All of these traditional approaches take the product as given. Value analysis examines product design starting with the basic questions, "What is the purpose of this item? What else could do the same job?" Simplifying design and using less costly raw materials are most often the results of value analysis. Costs are routinely reduced by 30, 40, 50, and even 60 percent.

Value analysis indirectly reduces WIP inventory by reducing the number of component parts. From an operating point of view, simplified products decrease the number and complexity of manufacturing processes and operations. Scheduling is less complex. Lead time is shortened. Scrap loss is reduced. Material flow is enhanced.

MANUFACTURING ENGINEERING: CHANGING THE MANUFACTURING PROCEDURE

It is the function of manufacturing engineering or process engineering to review product drawings and other specifications and establish the manufacturing process. It is almost axiomatic that, throughout industry, most new product planning allows little time for the processing function. Processing usually gets caught in the time squeeze between completion of engineering design and the marketing demand for the new product. As a result, much initial processing is done that merely routes products through the operations to fabricate the parts, but not necessarily to fabricate them in the most efficient manner. Many times shop people have heard it said, "We'll do it this way just to get going. We can always come back later and do it right." The problem is that, many times, temporary, expedient methods become the permanent methods.

Less than optimal manufacturing engineering at new product introduction sets the stage for cost savings through later process improvements. Also, new developments in equipment and tooling compliment continual process improvements. Processing improvements can be defined into two categories: cycle time reduction and a recombination of work elements to reduce the number of operations required for part completion. Cycle time reduction involves improvements in speeds, feeds, tooling, fixturing, and equipment selection. Reducing the number of operations required has a direct bearing on the amount of WIP inventory needed to support the manufacturing procedure.

A prime example of good processing improvement is a revamp recently accomplished by the manufacturing engineers in the tire pump plant. They have retooled the #5000 handle (see Figure 15-3). Now instead of three operations, the handle is completely fabricated in a single operation. All work elements are completed in a progressive die. The die, and a new press of the required tonnage, were justified on the basis of direct labor savings. An added benefit was the elimination of 20 to 50 tote boxes of WIP material formerly stored between the three operations.

REDUCING WORK-IN-PROCESS COSTS VIA PLANNING LEAD TIME

In the aerospace industry long lead times are the rule, not the exception. Large transport planes, for instance, often take in excess of two years from the start of manufacture of the first part until the completed unit is "rolled out." Contrary to two years being considered a long time, it is amazingly short in view of the fact that over 300,000 parts and components are involved.

In general, the simpler the product, the shorter the lead time should be. The tire pump described earlier has a short lead time of only a few days. Lead times are not only determined by product complexity, but are also based on how well management plans and executes the manufacturing procedures.

Lead time determines how much WIP is required. Consider an "ideal plant" where the product output rate is constant throughout the year, and the value added curve is linear as shown in Figure 15-7. Time t is the lead time. If $t = 1$ year with an annual output of \$5MM and an annual raw material expenditure of \$1MM, then the average WIP value on hand throughout the year is $\frac{\$5MM - \$1MM}{2} = \$2MM$. If the lead time is shortened to $t = 9$ months, then $\frac{9/12 (\$5MM - \$1MM)}{2} = \$1.5 MM$. As can be seen, under these ideal conditions, the WIP inventory value is directly proportional to the lead time. A 25% reduction in lead time from one year to nine months resulted in a 25% reduction in WIP value.

THE "IDEAL PLANT" VALUE-ADDED CURVE

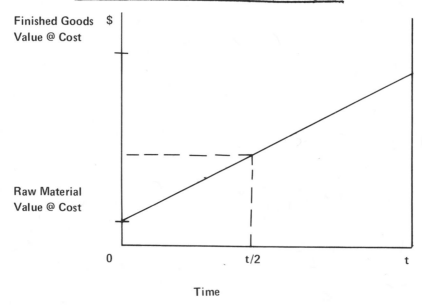

FIGURE 15-7

In the "ideal plant" just described, considerable cost savings accrue when the inventory carrying cost is considered. If the inventory carrying rate were 20%, savings would be (\$2MM − \$1.5MM) × 20% = \$100,000. This \$100,000 savings represents 2% of the annual sales at cost.

REDUCED LEAD TIME REDUCES WIP INVENTORY

In most companies, WIP inventory is larger than necessary. It's usually caused by long lead times. As an extreme, planned lead time in a machine shop with over 500 employees included 2 weeks delay *between each operation,* and at least one day for the performance of each operation. So for a skid of parts requiring 10 operations, the planned lead time would be at least 22 weeks. Yet in a confidential memo to the president, this company reported that "actual lead time as a percent of planned lead time fluctuated over the past year between 174% and 203%." No wonder the memo was confidential. Based on the memo, actual lead time for a 10 operation item was 38 to 45 weeks!

Most manufacturing men know from experience that excessive lead times with the corresponding high levels of WIP inventory cause problems on the shop floor:

— "Lost" parts
— Overflowing storage space
— Blocked aisles
— Confusion as to immediate production objectives

These are just a few of the resulting problems. Manufacturing management has a twofold incentive for reducing WIP: making their own jobs easier, and obtaining the savings of reduced inventory carrying costs.

1. Scheduling, Dispatching, Telescoping

Many production control systems in use today accomplish, as a bare minimum, the defining of shop requirements. For some this means taking a forecast, exploding the bill of materials based on the forecast, and generating the paperwork documents necessary for purchasing and shop production. For others, customer orders replace the forecast. Requirements planning is a basic production control function. Scheduling is another. However, in many plants, scheduling is given a lot of lip service but not much action. Many foremen have to do their own scheduling and dispatching. Quite often a production control department will place one of their people in each shop department or section. Sometimes this works out very well, but most often it has the net result merely of providing clerical service to the foremen who still have to bear the responsibility for "getting out the right production, and on time." Frankly, that is all right, except for one major flaw: the production control system thereby fails to regulate the production load to the plant capacity. When business is good, production requirements often outstrip capacity. Without production control regulations, large queues of work accumulate behind the overloaded equipment. WIP levels increase. Due dates are missed. Customers become disgruntled. Under such circumstances, production control is obligated to go one step farther than requirements planning and translate the production requirements into realistic shop loads. Scheduling should be a production control function. Actual machine run time is likely to be one of the smallest components of lead time. It is estimated that, on the average, the time jobs wait at each work center (queue time) can be at least 75% of the total manufacturing lead time.

The release of work orders has to be regulated so that materials do not build up excessively ahead of work stations. Whether done centrally by dispatchers or decentrally by foremen, dispatching has to take into account materials availability, tooling, minimizing set-up time, work load balance between work centers, and schedule dates. Working with all these factors toward the objective of reducing lead time requires considerable judgment, skill, and production knowledge. When properly done, effective dispatching smoothes material flow dramatically. Lead time shortens. WIP inventory investment declines.

One effective method of scheduling and dispatching is termed "telescoping." Briefly, telescoping is starting the second operation on some of the parts in a lot even before all of the parts have finished through operation one. Sometimes, even three or more operations may be in progress simultaneously. Figure 15-8 shows the Gantt chart illustration of how the tire pump handle #5000 was scheduled before and after telescoping. In this instance, lead time for the 10,000 piece lot of the tire pump handles was cut in half—from 7 days lead time back to 3.5. Admittedly, telescoping is not always possible. Small lot sizes, capacity bottlenecks, and other "disturbances" sometimes prevent its use. Telescoping, if applicable, can be an effective method of reducing WIP inventory levels.

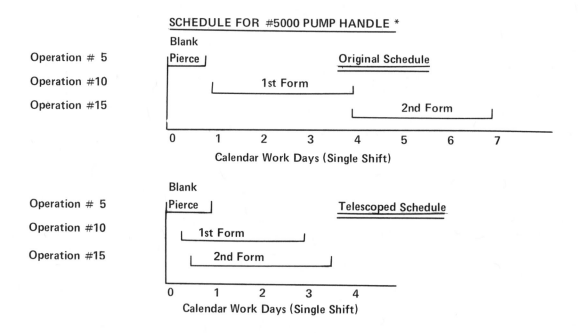

FIGURE 15-8

2. Group Technology

One of the ramifications of plant layout and material handling as pertains to reduced WIP levels is a concept first developed in Europe known as the Cell Concept, or most recently referred to as Group Technology. Group Technology is a compromise between the two basic philosophies of plant layout: process layout and product layout. Process layout groups together similar machines and processes. Plants under process layout might have a lathe department, a grinding department and a heat treat department. Layout by product is where the machines and processes are laid out one after the other with all necessary operations in their proper sequence. Product layout is normally associated with mass-production where specialized equipment and automated material handling are justified. Group Technology groups together processes necessary to produce similar products and/or components. For instance a "shaft group" would have all the equipment necessary to produce all the different sizes and types of shafts as required by the various product lines. Lathes, grinders, drill presses, keyway mills and heat treat facilities, would all be in the "shaft group."

Normally a shop organized under process layout can identify several categories of parts and components eligible for group technology. Typical groups include: shafts, gears, large castings, plastics, sheaves, cams, and linkages. In those shops where "group tech" has been tried, between 25% and 60% of the total output could be effectively covered. The balance of the output was of too low volume and/or high variability to be considered for "group tech."

Group Technology has many advantages:

   a. Drastically shortened lead times made possible by more expedient material handling, improved scheduling and telescoping, and singular responsibility for meeting schedule dates.

   b. Greater machine utilizations and lower setup times, because each machine performs a similar set of operations on similar parts.

   c. Elevated quality levels. Each machine operator specializes. Yet in the long run, operators can be rotated to give flexibility.

The most obvious disadvantage of "group tech" is that in every group there are one or more machines that are essential to the group but are not fully utilized. Sometimes this causes otherwise unnecessary duplication of some equipment. It is this factor that limits the application of "group tech" but wherever groups are feasible, the advantages of the concept are compelling.

Group technology also represents an effective way to manage people. The group is an independent entity that completes a production procedure from start to finish. Individuals can identify with such purpose, and work together in supportive and cooperative interpersonal relationships to meet the responsibilities of the group. Personal pride, involvement, and teamwork are key elements of group technology.

3. Other Factors

There are a number of other steps that are often taken in industry that have the effect of reducing WIP inventory. However, they are seldom justified solely on the basis of WIP related savings, although such savings are often a significant factor in cost-payback calculations. To illustrate the point, two examples follow:

a. *NC Machining Centers* (including automatic transfer machines).
Numerical controlled equipment is capable of producing very complicated parts with minimal tooling costs. NC machining centers routinely complete several dozen operations on a part within a single machine cycle. If these parts had to be tooled and scheduled on conventional machinery, the resulting lead times, along with the associated material handling and inventory carrying costs, would be much higher. These factors should not be overlooked when evaluating the possible procurement of NC equipment.

b. *Assembly Lines*
In the quest for labor efficiency, manufacturing engineers favor line production whenever possible. The production or assembly line is the best known way to produce large quantities of standardized products at low cost. The bonuses are that manufacturing lead time is short, material handling cost low, and WIP carrying costs are reduced.

WORK-IN-PROCESS STORAGE SPACE

Of all the criteria of successful layout planning, perhaps one of the most important is how well the layout fulfills the needs of WIP storage. A tendency for young, unseasoned layout engineers is to document all routings, flow chart the entire operation, anticipate that the manufacturing procedure should "click" smoothly as planned, and then sit down and design an "ideal layout." Chances are that such a layout does not provide sufficient WIP storage.

On the other hand, "old timers" on the shop floor often tend to be pessimistic and assume that no "ideal layout" can work. If a layout could be planned to cover all the contingencies they can mention, planned material flow and efficient material handling would suffer.

FIGURE 15-9

Typical Workplace Layout

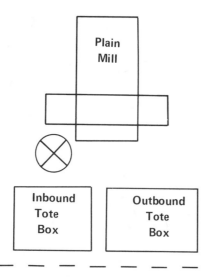

AISLE

The best layout solution lies somewhere between the two extremes. Careful analysis and creative engineering are required, and they need to include provision for normally expected contingencies. This is especially true in providing for WIP storage space. Space that is "theoretically enough" has to be supported by "overflow space."

A typical workplace layout is shown in Figure 15-9. In addition to the machine tool template, the operator and the inbound and outbound tote boxes are shown. Surprisingly, many layouts are attempted without showing the operator and handling containers.

As telescoping has become more prevalent in scheduling, many have found it expedient to provide additional WIP storage at each workplace as shown in Figure 15-10. In this way, material can flow directly from operation to operation without the necessity of maintaining a buffer WIP storage in a separate area. Additionally, in Figure 15-9, when the inbound box "runs dry" or the outbound box becomes full, the machine operator has to stop working and arrange for material handling. Often this causes considerable delay. Under Figure 15-10, such delays are avoided because the operator always has back-up tote boxes, and material handling can take place without significantly interrupting the operator's work pace.

FIGURE 15-10

Workplace Layout Providing Additional WIP Storage

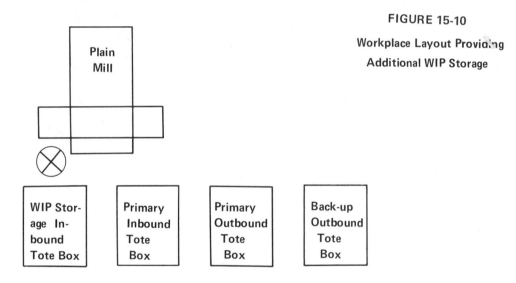

Providing sufficient WIP storage at workplaces does not eliminate the need for separate WIP storage areas. These are usually provided as an integral part of departmental inbound-outbound storage.

SUMMARY AND A WORD OF CAUTION

In this chapter we have seen the importance of controlling work-in-process inventory. WIP inventory is a substantial portion of a company's assets. Reducing WIP inventory frees asset-dollars which can be reinvested in new plants and equipment, and the expense of inventory carrying costs is reduced. As we have seen, all management levels, from first line supervision to the chief executive can have a meaningful impact on the level of WIP inventory. Reductions in WIP can produce significant profit contribution.

One last word of caution. Always keep WIP reduction efforts in line with overall production objectives. Optimal WIP is not zero WIP. Too little WIP causes downtime through inflexibility. In fact, it sometimes pays to increase WIP inventory.

It is not uncommon for a manufacturer to carry items in WIP rather than suffer excessive finished goods inventory. In Detroit, for instance, it is virtually impossible to forecast and build the right amounts of individual automobile models complete with the right mix of options and colors. The choices available to customers are far too numerous. On the other hand, it is not always possible to accurately forecast the requirements for major assemblies, produce to those forecasts, and hold the assemblies in WIP awaiting customer orders. The radios mentioned earlier are handled in this manner. So are engines, transmissions and air conditioning units.

Chapter 16

Determining the Aisle, Storage and
Order Picking Space Allocations

The basic purpose of the warehouse or storage facility is to act as a buffer between the supplier (producer) and the user of the stored goods. This also applies within the plant from department to department, and operation to operation as well as for distribution to outside customers. The ideal situation is not to need warehouse facilities at all, but few companies can manage to attain this unique position. Some factors that create the need for warehouses are:

— Variation in demand.
— The manufacturing process.
— Seasonal requirements.
— Fluctuations in economic conditions.
— Weather.
— Variety of goods produced.

Warehousing facilities fall into four major categories of storage:

— Raw material.
— Work-in-process storage.
— Finished goods storage.
— Process materials (not making up part of the end products).

Determining optimum needs for warehouse facilities is a difficult, complex task that varies from business to business. Companies in the same fields require different warehouse configurations and requirements. This is due to different determining parameters used in making warehouse policy. Some of the considerations for establishing warehouse policy are:

— Company policies.
— Customer requirements.
— Manufacturing processes.

— Inventory requirements.
— Volume of throughput.
— Variety of goods produced.
— Seasonal fluctuations in demand.
— Competition.
— Production lead time.
— Availability of manufacturing facilities.
— Geographic location of plant.
— Geographic location of customers.

To date, there is no known universal method for determining what optimum warehouse facilities are for all businesses. To determine optimum conditions each storage requirement must stand on its own merit. *Optimum* here is a misnomer, because this is an assumption that all the factors required to achieve such a goal are known and this is in reality an impossibility.

DETERMINING THE SIZE OF WAREHOUSE REQUIRED

The first phase is:

— Determining what must be made.
— How much is to be stored.
— What is to be stored.
— The inventory level that will be necessary to maintain an adequate supply.

The size will be dependent on what is being considered for storage:

1. Is storage for raw materials to supply production needs?
2. Is storage for component parts on subassemblies for interim and later production requirements?
3. Is storage for materials that are not part of the finished product but are necessary in the manufacturing process?
4. Is storage for the finished product for distribution to the company's customers?

Items one through three are usually storage facilities that are located at a plant site, while item four may be at a plant site but most likely will be in a distribution center.

Starting with the finished product, the warehouse determination can be made through two sources of data:

Method 1: Past sales data of the production products.
Method 2: Sales forecast of the company's potential share of the market for the next year and ensuing years. (This can be based on previous years' growth rates or trends.)

If it is a totally new product, method two will be the only available choice.

In method one, one year's data on shipped goods should be collected from shipping reports by product. If pallets are used to store materials in inventory, the dimensions of unit loads should be determined from pallet size. This dimension is also a determinate of rack and aisle parameters. If possible, a preferred pallet size is 48 × 40 inches; it is one of the most popular sizes in use today and is suitable for both truck and rail car usage giving good cube utilization in both. In addition, pallet pools can be formed.

When a unit size has been decided (this may be determined by the product, with no choice involved), the next step is to find out how many different categories of products are involved. This data should be available from the recap of past sales data or analysis of shipping reports. This figure will give the minimum number of access openings for obtaining the items stored. This is a relatively important figure because good warehouse policy should provide ready access to all materials stored with a minimum effort. The next step is to determine the multiple of access openings for material stored exceeding unit loads (greater than one pallet). The multiple access is also dependent upon the material handling equipment to be used in storage. For example, material can be stored on tier racks. This method permits multiple unit loads of the same material without access openings for each load. However, if pallet racks are used, each load must be placed in a unique access position. The access areas can be reduced using pallet racks if live conveyors and gravity feed are used so that when the first unit load is removed the rest move one position.

CASE IN POINT

A large food processor located in the Midwest was faced with the problem of inadequate storage space for its finished goods inventory. The initial judgment was to build additional warehousing space adjacent to the existing facility. However, the cost of constructing this new facility did not provide an attractive return on investment and alternatives had to be considered. An investigation of the existing warehouse facility revealed several interesting facts:

— Finished goods were stacked only two pallets high because of a lack of racking and carton strength. (The two tiers of the bottom pallet would buckle and damage the product inside if a third pallet load was placed on top.)

— There were many aisles because of the need to segregate by production date.

— There was a high incidence of inter-warehouse transfers due to quality control release procedures.

The conclusion reached by the task force was that a new facility would not be needed if the cube of the existing warehouse were used more effectively. The final decision was to install flow through gravity feed racking three tiers high serviced on both ends by stacker cranes. This solution increased storage capacity to the required amount at a considerably reduced cost. An added benefit was a reduction in fork lift travel time and a better controlled system of stock rotation and shipment by production date.

Stored material or items can follow the ABC inventory theory. That is, 10 to 20 percent of the material may represent 80 to 90 percent of the volume. If this is so, multiple factors can be developed for the different items stored when the desired inventory levels are determined for each product.

CASE IN POINT

A fiber manufacturer wanted to improve his sheet fiber storage which was an ineffective operation. Customers were complaining about delays, receiving wrong material and the company was experiencing increased costs in its warehouse operations. There were 256 varieties of the material. In analyzing the shipping reports, it was found that over a one-year period 25 percent of the items represented 80 percent of the volume. The current sales were approximately four million pounds per year. The fiber was made in four-foot by seven-foot sheets. It was stored on pallets with a maximum of 6,000 pounds per pallet. Because it was decided to store the material in racks, the minimum number of access positions would have to be 256. However, because 64 items represented 800,000 pounds or 80% of the volume, this meant that the average volume of these items would require an average of two pallets per item. The inventory requirement was set at 1,000,000 pounds with possible expansion to 1,500,000 in the future. Since the business growth was averaging 4 percent a year, the new facility should be adequate for ten years under the plan.

Storage is not the only facility requirement when considering space needs. Some others are:
1. Areas required other than storage
   — Aisles
   — Receiving
     • Receiving stage or loading areas
   — Shipping
     • Shipping staging area
     • Packaging
     • Staging area packaging
   — Office area
   — Inspection area
   — Pallet storage (empty)
   — Material handling equipment maintenance
   — Packaging material storage

2. Considerations in planning warehouse
   — Allow for additional ground area for future expansion
   — Taxes
   — Transportation
     • Truck
     • Rail
     • Air
   — Customer location
   — Source of production (supply)
   — Material handling equipment
   — Design facility for ten-year growth

3. Material Handling
   — Hand carts

— Narrow aisle fork truck
— Conveyors
— Counter balanced fork truck
— Stacker crane
  • Manually operated
  • Semi-automated
  • Fully automated
— Pallets
— Tier racks
— Tote boxes
— Portable line
— Steel pallet boxes
— Straddle trucks
— Elevators
— Hydraulic lifts
— Pallet racks
— Wire containers
— Dock facilities
— Portable ramps
— Adjustable dock board

CASE IN POINT

A sheet fiber warehouse was planned to initially operate with one 6,000 pound capacity counter-balanced lift truck. The equipment dimension and pallet size (4 X 7 feet) were the major determinants in the minimum aisle size. For a 90 degree rack entrance from the aisle, it was necessary to have a minimum aisle of 11.25 feet. Two feet were added to increase ease of handling and safety to those operating in the area. The final aisle size was 13.25 feet.

In addition, the warehouse facility had a 12-foot center aisle for access to the storage aisle and the aisle configuration required 63 percent of the warehouse floor space. This was not an efficient use of the space and was due to the selection of the type of truck. The lift truck was also to be used for other purposes besides warehouse operations. The other purposes were chiefly responsible for the lift truck's configuration. There was only one truck to be purchased, so the facility was really designed around the handling equipment in this instance.

At some future point the capacity of the sheet fiber warehouse could almost be doubled by:

1. Going to a narrow aisle truck.
2. Eliminating the center aisle.
3. Installing more racks.
4. Placing entry doors at the end of each aisle.

This would require the existing racks to be turned 90 degrees from their present position and nested closer together. This change would result in a ratio of 39.6 percent aisle space and would increase the number of access spaces to 480. The maximum capacity would then be 2.88 million pounds, almost three times the original requirement.

AISLE REQUIREMENTS

Two of the most important factors determining aisle requirements were mentioned earlier:

1. The type of handling equipment.
2. The dimensions of the largest stored item or load.

The minimum aisle requirements are determined from the basic dimensions of equipment and loads of hand trucks, conveyors, lift trucks and stacker cranes.

The next factor to consider is the volume of movement by asking:

1. Is two-way traffic needed?
2. Can some aisles be two-way and others one-way?
3. Should there be one-way traffic only?

Where conveyors are used, consider:

1. Can one conveyor supply in both directions?
2. Are two conveyors required (one in and one out)?

If conveyors are planned, be sure to provide means for ease of maintenance. This implies ease of access with the proper equipment to make repairs or to pull and/or replace equipment.

Where stacker cranes are the handling equipment, the load size usually controls the aisle dimensions, and the equipment is customized for this dimension.

ORDER PICKING AND PLACING IN STORAGE

One area that is a major concern in warehouse operations is the provision for staging areas. These staging areas provide for preparation, temporary storage, empty containers, pallets, packaging facilities, order put-up and many other miscellaneous warehouse activities. Adequate consideration in providing staging areas can greatly enhance the effectiveness of the warehouse activity. The situation in most warehouse units is one of variable demand in input and output. There are times when the facility is nearly empty and times when it is full. It is important at these peaks and valleys of activity that the proper continuity of the staging areas be maintained.

Location of staging areas can significantly improve order picking. High volume items should be located nearest the picking assignment areas and also be closest to the floor. In most instances high volume items represent 10 to 30 percent of the stored items. In the example cited earlier on the sheet fiber facility, 25 percent of the stocked items were 80 percent of the activity. These items were located closest to the floor and nearest to the order assembly and picking assignment areas.

Other considerations to examine in warehouse operations are: Can order picking and warehouse storage be combined? Can a picker, after assembling an order, then warehouse incoming material? Some stacker crane installations are set up in this manner; each time the crane picks an item, it stores another item on the return trip. This setup minimizes empty traveling.

Taking another approach would be to bring all materials to the picker from the warehouse by automated means and input new materials from the same area. Approximately 90 percent of warehouse activities involve: travel, search, locate, place and retrieve. Automating these activities could reduce the manpower requirements by 90 percent. Therefore, in a ten-man operation, a dollar figure of approximately $468,000 could be spent on an automated project for an ROI of 20 percent figuring a $5.00 hourly rate including fringes.

One area of assistance that should be explored by more companies is the utilization of the computer. In too many instances, this giant tool is dormant or not being used as effectively as possible.

CASE IN POINT

One instance involved a client who was printing orders directly at warehouse locations through his computer system. The only thing that improved was the speed of getting the order to the warehouse by one hour or so. The orders were made up the same way as under the old system except for printing.

The computer already had in its files the location and inventory of all items warehoused. With a little more programming effort, each item listed on an order could have been listed in the picking sequence designed for the minimum distance traveled. If out-of-stock conditions existed, these could have been indicted on the order.

In reviewing the current system, it was estimated that 35 percent of the order picking time could have been saved if the computer order system was revised as stated. There were approximately 84 people at three of the warehouse locations. About one-third were involved in order picking. By incorporating the sequence and out-of-stock system on the computer, a potential reduction of nine warehousemen, or approximately $100,000 per year, could have been realized.

In the design of warehouses, each situation should be considered unique and not approached with predetermined answers. This includes situations where the same products are involved. New methods and handling equipment are being developed and improved every day. What was true last year may have been surpassed by developments this year. Improvement in handling equipment has a direct effect on aisle size, storage height and manning requirements. Each new or revised facility should stand on its own merits and be planned based on the current state of the art in warehousing operations.

Chapter 17

Minimizing Distribution Costs by Defining and Selecting Off-Site Warehousing Needs

AVOIDING THE "BOOBY TRAPS" IN OFF-SITE WAREHOUSING

Effects on Total Inventory

Off-site warehouse locations, and additional locations in general, always add to the total inventory required. Off-site space can serve a number of purposes and has advantages. The objective is to select and locate this space so that cost savings more than offset any additional inventory costs.

Chances Are

The chances are high that your decisions on utilizing off-site space will be wrong and will add major excess cost to your inventory control program. Many well-managed companies and professional managers "trip" in this area and the penalties can destroy an otherwise good control program for on-site operations. The booby traps are many and come in both large and small sizes. This chapter outlines how to avoid many of the pitfalls in considering off-site warehouse operations.

The economics are basically simple. Properly used, off-site space can add elasticity and flexibility to your production planning program. It can provide long-range space expansion, reduce freight costs and generate its own cost savings. But only sometimes and only when properly and totally analyzed; if not it can become a nightmare of added handling costs and/or fixed costs.

The Approach Sequence

To approach the problem, and this perhaps unfamiliar area, the following sequence is recommended:

1. Determine the prime purpose.
2. Determine the types of space suited to that purpose.
3. Size the requirements.
4. Select several locations.
5. Within service limitations, correctly compare the costs of alternatives and make the final selection.

PURPOSES OF OFF-SITE WAREHOUSING

Off-site warehousing space can beneficially serve a number of purposes. The major categories are listed and discussed below. The prime purpose of the off-site operation is a key factor in determining the type of outside space that would be best. The best geographical location will also vary depending on the purpose or prime mission of the space.

Raw Materials

Main raw materials are usually not candidates for outside warehousing because of their volume and activity and because your vendors may do some warehousing for you. Minor raw materials may be candidates if a large price differential can be obtained or if a single annual purchasing time is involved. A number of companies hold a small inventory of some raw materials in a commercial warehouse as an emergency back-up.

Packaging Supplies

Packaging supplies are ideal candidates for outside storage and often are overlooked by the manager. Especially suited are the denser items such as chipboard carton blanks and plastic bags. Bulkier items such as those that are corrugated, may not adapt to outside storage as well, nor offer the same economies.

Larger Production Runs

Outside space can be used to obtain longer production runs on certain items. Whether this is practical depends on the trade-off of reduced manufacturing costs versus increased space and carrying costs and the additional handling costs. High volume items generally are better held on-site. Mid-volume or low volume items, where the run size might be increased from a two-month to a four-month inventory, are sometimes candidates—but an individual item cost analysis should be made.

Seasonal Inventory Variations

Items with seasonal variations are preferred candidates for outside storage. Because of the elasticity of commercial space, it can be cheaper to handle seasonal surges off-site. Use of outside space for seasonal demand is well-recognized. Antifreeze is a classic example that is not only seasonal but has a few short weeks of peak sales demand. The extent that such items are warehoused off-site depends on whether they will return to the plant for shipment and whether they are predispersed geographically. Keeping the on-site inventory at the annual mean inventory level can reduce total costs.

Improved Delivery and Customer Service

A common purpose for off-site space is to reduce delivery time and improve customer service. Sometimes it is used to serve a coastal region or to serve one or several major accounts. In-transit times vary considerably, depending on the mode of transportation (truck, rail, water, air) and whether the shipment is a full or partial load. Management usually sets total delivery time parameters. These should be clarified with respect to full or partial loads and the percentage of the time such as "90% of the time the product should be delivered within 5 days of order receipt." These limits are to be met. Total delivery time restraints may dictate certain space requirements and freight costs. Be sure to clarify the service and activity parameters that the location is to provide.

Temporary/Special Needs

Any experienced inventory control manager knows that there is frequently some temporary or special program that throws inventory out of control for months and plays havoc with storage space. Examples include:

- Product line additions or eliminations
- Work stoppages, actual or potential
- Facilities expansions or contractions
- Quality or engineering "holds"

It is to your advantage to get these temporary/special needs into off-site warehousing. The integrity, organization and sanity of the on-site warehouse is maintained. Off-site operations have better cost isolation that can aid in evaluating the costs of a new venture. Surprising as it may seem, some managers defeat their own programs by retaining special inventories on-site and forcing standard, high turnover inventory into an off-site location.

Long-Range Expansion

A warehouse operation may be a preliminary step to expanding into a region with a manufacturing facility. This purpose is not often recognized by managers but can materially affect the type of space that is required.

One company wanted to penetrate the southwestern United States but knew from its long-range planning that three to six years would be required to support a facility in this area. A short-term leased warehouse, utilizing co-packing and relabeling provided the least cost approach for obtaining space and penetrating that region.

TYPES OF SPACE AND ADVANTAGES

Five types of off-site space are discussed, including their advantages and limitations. Two broad categories of space also exist: public and captive (or company controlled).

Type	Category
Commercial	Public
Pooling point	
Carrier owned	Semi-public
Company leased	Captive
Company owned	

Common Advantages and Limitations

Public space has certain common advantages. The two key advantages are that it is elastic and, within limits, can be expanded or contracted. It also has low administrative costs that are included in other charges. Its main limitation is that handling charges are high and can accumulate to become excessive on high turnover items, especially when compared to captive or company operated space.

Captive space tends to be inelastic in its space charges but usually offers lower handling charges. Administrative services such as management, supervision, security, maintenance, secretarial, and communications must be provided at a company owned or leased location. In some cases these costs can add 35% or more to the operating cost. For example, an operation involving eight to ten warehousemen may require three to four support or administrative personnel.

Commercial Space

Commercial space is elastic and charges include low administrative costs. Handling charges are high. Picking accuracy is usually good, if the items per order are limited.

Pooling Point

Pooling point space is generally public space but is located at certain key transfer points. For example, pooling point cities exist for grocery products in both Utah and Nevada. It has the same advantages and limitations as commercial space with an added advantage of lower long distance freight rates. Its special limitations are that these rates are usually only in one direction. Another limitation is that delivery times are subject to more variability due to pooling.

Carrier Owned

Certain carriers, particularly smaller, independent ones, own or lease warehouse space. It usually is semi-elastic and could be expanded or contracted with some notice or planning. Pick-up and shuttle service is usually good. Use of this type of space presumes maintaining a level of business with the carrier and sometimes restricts route selection. It is also vulnerable to the carrier's financial viability.

Company Leased

The advantages of this type of space are low handling costs and good control. Disadvantages include inflexibility and high administrative costs. A further advantage is that no capital investment is involved in land and buildings. For this reason, this type of space is ideal to penetrate a new region. Warehouse buildings are often built for speculation and may be available for immediate lease without construction delays. Legal, insurance and tax matters usually require clarification and attention. Leased warehouses are often "late to develop" or "early to develop" sites and special attention must be paid to site drainage, site foundations and floor load capacities of the space. An "early to develop" site is usually built on a land fill project. Caution should be exercised relative to floor weight loading since these buildings have not totally settled.

Company Owned

This type of space is truly captive and has the accompanying captive advantages and limitations. It has good control along with low handling costs, but may have high administrative costs and inflexible space and fixed costs. It requires capital investment and may require lead time to be constructed. Long-range space needs and potential facility plans in the area should be fully explored before proceeding with this type of space.

Commercial Space Turnover

As mentioned several times in the chapter a frequent mistake is to place high turnover items in commercial space and consequently handling charges go out of control. It is the inventory control manager's responsibility to prevent an "out-of-control" situation and to minimize these charges, but not beyond the point of no return. The commercial warehouse, pooling point, or carrier must make some profit and consider your account a sound business arrangement.

DETERMINING THE AMOUNT OF SPACE NEEDED

To determine the space need, requirements will have to be expressed in several units including:

Square feet
Pallets
Weight or hundred weight

To do the best planning job you also should know the minimum and maximum limits of each of the above units for the first year. The first year limits should also be forecasted by month especially if seasonal items will be handled. You should provide a rough estimate of off-site space needed for at least a three to five-year period.

Square Footage

Current square footage is usually known but must be converted to equivalent cubic capacity at other locations. As simple as this sounds, many companies fail to compare equivalent square footages. For example, 100,000 square feet of current storage that is stacked two pallets high, and concrete pillar impeded, may require only 30,000 to 40,000 square feet of four high, clear span storage space. The converse situation can also exist.

Pallets

Pallets are the unit basis used to invoice from many commercial or public warehouses. Typically, there is a charge for each pallet in or out, in addition to a charge per square foot assigned and/or a charge per month on the total pallets in inventory.

To compare the costs on alternative types of space, and to compare public versus captive alternatives, you should know the number of pallets in and out per month and have a monthly projection of total pallets in inventory throughout the year.

Weight

If the off-site location is to be a shipping point you will also need to know weight in and out. This will be required for distribution studies and a convenient unit is hundred weight (since most freight rates are in these units).

The Nature of the Beast

A realistic philosophy on the percent utilization of space is vital. Understanding the beast is half the problem. Empty warehouse space behaves like a vacuum; it quickly fills up with something, and often to the detriment of warehouse utilization and space efficiency. Two important considerations in determining space requirements are:

- Recognize the true efficiency of the current on-site space and fairly assess how much it might be improved.
- Provide some, but not all, of your growth requirements in improved utilization of space at both on-site and off-site locations.

Sampling techniques can be used to develop space utilization and efficiency figures on existing space. For example, sample fifteen random rows to determine the percent of space currently occupied. Resample fifteen *full* rows and determine the percentage of pallet capacity achieved or current efficiency. The product of these two ratios is your current true space utilization.* The amount of space devoted to aisles, if excessive, would also be a factor but can otherwise be ignored.

The axiom that warehousing will expand to fill almost any space *applies to your current on-site space.* A realistic assessment of your current space utilization is a must. It may show a quite low utilization and avoid the need for off-site space or it may show some improvement is possible—which could be used to partially cover anticipated growth.

SELECTING THE LOCATIONS

Locating the off-site space is usually the fourth step in the decision process. Location will be a function of the purpose, types that meet the purpose, and size requirements.

The approach in analyzing locations usually falls into one of the following three groups of purposes.

Supporting an Existing Facility

A number of the purposes for an off-site space is essentially to support or amplify an existing facility. In these cases, the off-site space is usually within the same metropolitan area as the facility. A number of sites or companies are explored and compared. If your company will operate its own trucks and provide its own drayage or shuttle service, it is desirable to be within a few miles of the facility; otherwise the location can be anywhere in the metropolitan area.

Expansion into a Region

When the purpose is to expand into a region, an analysis of several states is usually made. Warehouse costs, service and delivery times are gathered for several cities in the

---

*Space utilization is commonly the ratio of storage row area to total area. True space utilization, as used here, is the ratio of the actual pallets held to the total pallet capacity.

region. Delivery times from the location and in-bound freight to the region are frequently key considerations.

Improved Customer Service

When the objective is to improve delivery and customer service, either on a national or special account basis, a distribution location study should be made. Using linear programming, a minimum cost solution is determined by computer for the service constraints specified.

This distribution analysis assumes either plants or warehouses can be shipping points and the problem can be complex. It can be simplified in several ways. Some shortcuts include using a "canned" program that assumes a finite number of destinations or customer cities, restricts the candidate cities, and repeats the minimum cost solution if necessary with replacement candidate cities.

Some general observations can be made on distribution location studies. With six manufacturing points or less, these studies tend to select one or several of the manufacturing locations. This is because of the impact of rehandling expenses. Over ten manufacturing locations tend to favor a true *general* distribution center or warehouse. In-between 6 and 10, the solutions are unique to the special facets of the problem.

Special Considerations

Relationship to other divisions of the company must also be considered. Many companies are making major savings by combining warehousing for all divisions. One firm dropped from 42 locations to 18 on a national basis.

Opportunities for pooling points on finished goods and in-transit privileges on both raw and finished goods should also be thoroughly explored.

Certain states such as California have inventory taxes, and this added cost must be considered and included in alternative comparisons.

COMPARING COSTS CORRECTLY

Final decisions and selections are made by comparing the costs of alternatives. As stated before, this is with given service limits and within the purposes of the location. However, costs must be compared *correctly* and many an error is made at this point.

Figure 17-1 shows the development of five different *Delivered Costs* for five different routes of shipment and handling. The exhibit shows a simple case involving two plants and one warehouse location.

COMPARING DELIVERED COSTS

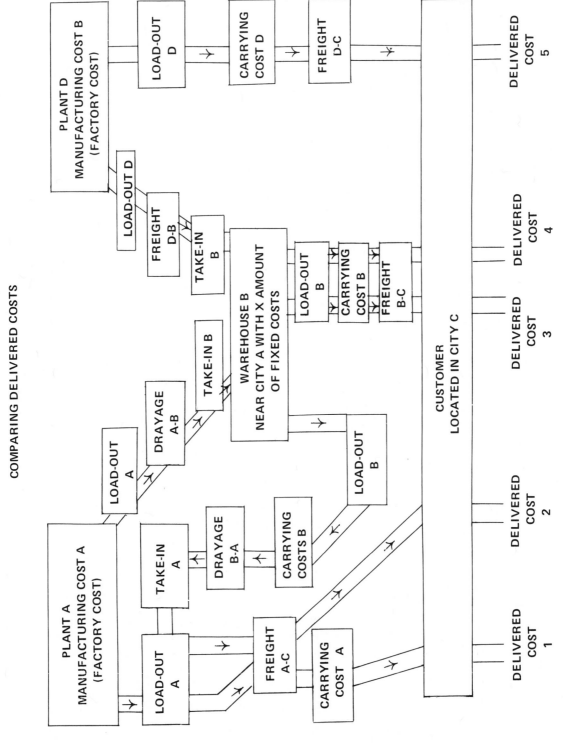

FIGURE 17-1

Note that handling costs are isolated and the number of loading and unloading operations carefully documented. The same is done for drayage. Note that Delivered Cost 2 has two drayage charges and five handling charges while Delivered Cost 3 has one drayage charge and three handling charges. Frequently the proper number of handling operations are not charged to the proper alternative.

Note also that factory cost, freight, and carrying charges will vary with the alternative and the material flow.

Carrying Costs

Carrying costs are composed of three major elements:

Direct space costs
Inventory investment costs
Obsolescence or deterioration costs

Direct space costs are the cost per square feet of the space including heat, light and building taxes.

Fixed Charges

In some warehouse solution problems the administrative costs (management, security, communications, etc.) are treated as a total fixed cost. Administrative costs can be treated as either a total fixed cost or as a fourth part of carrying costs, so long as the treatment is consistent. There is a tendency to ignore the administrative costs for existing facilities or space. Though they are smaller, they should not be ignored.

Major Costs Assumed

Though some may disagree, experience has shown up to 70% of carrying costs may lie in inventory investment and in obsolescence or deterioration. Direct space costs themselves may be only 30% of carrying costs. This will vary somewhat depending on the type of items stored. The point is space costs themselves are not the major costs assumed by off-site warehousing. In magnitude order they usually are:

Inventory investment
Obsolescence
Handling costs or administrative costs

The above are frequently higher than direct space costs.

An Example of Cost Savings

A large food company through general growth had saturated its original manufacturing facility with additional production equipment until there was no space remaining for finished goods. Over the years it had also expanded into private labeling, which required further finished goods space and an extensive packaging materials inventory. In desperation, its high volume standard business was moved to commercial storage and shipments were made both from commercial warehouse and by backtracking to the plant. Outside warehouse charges zoomed to a half a million dollars per year.

The solution to these problems was dramatic. Warehouse space across the street was put under long-term lease and company tractors were used to shuttle all finished goods across the street to the new location. A cost saving of $400,000 resulted even though material was being rehandled.

The above saving was just in warehousing expense. Needless to say, the savings in production control and inventory management were also large and dramatic.

Chapter 18

Pinpointing the Timing for Converting Manual Systems to EDP Applications

THE USE OF ELECTRONIC DATA PROCESSING IN INVENTORY AND PRODUCTION MANAGEMENT

High speed, large volume electronic data processing equipment, once possible only for larger firms that could justify the cost of an in-house installation, now is available to companies of all sizes. The combination of a time-sharing service bureau, an on-site terminal, and high-quality data transmission lines gives the smallest company the option of using the most powerful computers and most sophisticated software.

This availability of computing capacity on a "utility company" basis means that managers who once were called upon to evaluate and decide between using various manually applied systems and techniques now must determine *if and when to utilize* the computer. Additionally, once the decision to use the computer is made, such concerns as batch processing, on-line processing, and point-of-action inputs must also be considered.

Many new smaller suppliers of hardware are entering the field of computers. More recently a third option has become available, the "mini" or desk top computer. Originally developed for scientific applications as a high technology programmable calculator and later used for process control applications, the capabilities of mini-computers have been expanded to the point that they can be used for many general purpose business applications. The minis have been developed, for the most part, by newer manufacturers with more flexible pricing and selling practices than the older, more established suppliers of hardware. Examples have been seen where the entire computer needs of medium-sized companies have been filled with a purchased dedicated mini-computer at costs that are half to two-thirds of those using either time-sharing or large centralized installations.

The language and terminology of the computer programmer and systems analyst, the rapid change in types of equipment available, and decision-making on the selection of off-the-shelf programs all contribute to the confusion and difficulties of the company manager in decision-making regarding use of the computers.

Five system choices are available:

1. **Manual,** using paper and pencil, slide rule, adding machine and calculator computations, graphic solutions and displays.
2. **Mini-Computer,** with one "dedicated" installation serving a department or office.
3. **Large Volume In-House**
4. **Time-Sharing** through a service bureau.
5. **Combinations** of the first four.

Fundamental considerations to the decision of when to use EDP equipment and what type to use for PIC applications include: direct costs of operating the system; speed of processing data and preparing reports to allow more timely decisions to be made; accuracy in processing; reliability of systems; control over system integrity; ease of expansion and potential; capability for making more sophisticated analysis leading to improved operations.

DIRECT COSTS OF OPERATING THE SYSTEM

Manual systems' direct operating costs that are potentially reducible by using EDP equipment are primarily in clerical labor for data collection, recording, analysis, and summarization for reports. When these transactions are repetitive they are good candidates for substantial cost reduction. Others concerned with exceptions and irregularities will require the same and perhaps more manual processing under an EDP system than with a manual system.

Projected savings in direct and indirect clerical costs used to justify an EDP program often fail to materialize in many installations or are realized much more slowly than projected. The failure to achieve projected clerical savings most frequently results from the inevitable expansion of services provided using the computer, services that were not requested under the manual system and not foreseen when the cost projections were made.

The timetable slippage in achieving savings invariably results from the more stringent requirements for precision and accuracy on the input data imposed by the computer.

Components of costs related to an EDP system include:

— High one-time system analysis, development and programming costs
— One-time equipment installation costs
— One-time systems installation costs
— On-going equipment ownership costs or equipment leasing costs
— On-going systems operating labor costs
— On-going operating supply costs
— On-going shared-time charges

— On-going transmission line costs
— On-going space costs
— System and programming revision costs when change occurs

It has been observed that, with equal attention to system analysis, design and installation, a manual system involving ten or less capable people, properly supervised, can frequently be operated more economically than many EDP systems provided a satisfactory level of service is attainable.

The cost justification from smaller systems therefore must be made on the basis of the potential from increased services that are not practical to perform manually. The large computer in a centralized installation promises economies through high-speed processing that makes effective use of powerful equipment and shared cost of software.

Changes are occurring in the hardware-software cost relationship as smaller, more versatile, economical computers are developed and software complexity and personnel costs increase. Software development and maintenance costs are replacing hardware as the major cost area in an installation.

Cost projections of alternate systems must be based upon projections of the life-cycle of each of the options considered.

THE MANAGEMENT INFORMATION SYSTEM

The appealing idea that all management decision-making could be made by a super system (the "total management information system") leaving managers to devote their energies to policy making has faded into history. The practical approach of independent complementary systems interfaced with managers' intervention at key points has replaced the super system approach.

Many observations indicate that the potential for economies in the direct costs of operating a system vary greatly by functional activity, and the Production-Inventory Control system design should be organized to recognize these observations. Typical PIC activities are tabulated and indicate the relative potential for economies using EDP.

Activity	Potential for Economies thru Data Processing Application	Related Functional Areas to Share EDP Services with PIC
Forecasting Requirements	High	Marketing, Budgeting, Purchasing
Maintain Perpetual Inventory	Medium	Finance, Purchasing
Calculating Economical Lot Sizes	High	Purchasing
Replenishment Order Point Calculation	Medium	Purchasing
Maintaining Bills of Material	High	Financial Purchasing Costing
Material Requirements Planning	High	Purchasing
Developing Capacity Plan	Medium	Financial, Personnel, Marketing, Purchasing

Customer Order Entry and Invoicing	Medium	Sales, Sales Services
Maintaining Shop Routings	Low	Manufacturing Engineering, Cost Accounting, Budgeting
Machine Loading	Medium	----------
Project Planning and Control	Medium	----------
Shop Order Selection	Low	----------
Detail Daily Shop Planning and Scheduling	Low	----------
Dispatch Control	Medium	----------
Priority Determination	Medium	Marketing, Customer Services
Floor Progress Reports	Medium	Payroll, Bonus Calculations

Speed is Where It's At in Management Information Systems

The speed of processing data and preparing reports with EDP systems allows more timely decisions to be made. Here the potential of the computer can exceed the best manual systems. The possibilities of cost benefits through timeliness are both elusive and difficult to quantify. They depend upon two important considerations:

- The willingness and capability of managers who receive timely reports to take timely action.
- A priority in system use that assures that processing is carried out when PIC needs it.

The indecisive, timid, procrastinating manager (or worse yet, committee of managers) who will not react nullifies all the potential for benefits gained by rapid processing of information.

Managers who have, of necessity, become accustomed to making decisions using intuition and judgments based upon skeletal information when faced with fast, factual processed information requiring objective decision-making, occasionally fail to react. The availability of more details than they are accustomed to often triggers requests for still more facts for further analysis thereby delaying the decision-making process so that it is slower than it would have been with less information. Another reaction is to seize on real or imagined omissions or errors in the processed information that have no impact on the conclusion that should be made and use the error or omission as a basis for not making a decision.

When it is Proposed that a Computer Be Shared with Financial Groups, the Wise PIC Manager Will Reject the Entire Proposal

After the nearly inevitable top management directive that follows this rejection, the wise PIC manager will then insist upon standing arrangements for optional and alternate provisions for all essential service requirements.

When a computer is shared with other users PIC's priority will always end up lower than accounting and financial users. Accounts receivable, payroll, and month-end financial statements will always, and perhaps should, take priority over PIC needs.

Workable, time-capacity-priority arrangements can nearly always be made to share a computer with engineering, marketing, purchasing, and personnel, but never with accounting.

Accuracy in Processing

Calculation errors caused by equipment malfunction are almost nonexistent with present day equipment. Errors that do occur are inevitably caused by human error made while inputting information or by failure to maintain management discipline over the system. Simple input audit programs for both the stored data base and for one-time use variable data should always be developed and applied.

In one example, a data file of shop routing information was maintained in a random accessible tape storage system. The data was used for calculating operating performance indices, man-load projection, machine-loan projections, calculating cost standards, projecting processing times, calculating economical order quantities, and maintaining control over work-in-process inventories.

An audit of the accuracy of summary reports indicated that over thirty percent of the data used in these reports was in error. Errors were a combination of clerical errors in original input compounded by the failure to fully enter and process all changes as they occurred over a period of years. Since recreating the entire data base was impractical, an audit program that verified *logic* was developed and applied. The logic audit was programmed to verify that recorded machine numbers were actually in the stated departments and departments were in sections. In addition, upper and lower limit values were established for the labor time standards for both setups and running by machine number.

This audit program screened out all routings that failed any of the five checks made on each line item for manual editing as the part numbers came up for scheduling. Routings screened out had all data validated. Later audits indicated active routings to be over 98% accurate.

The application of this corrective program was immediately effective as the audit routines were applied to parts as they came up for release to production.

Reliability of Systems

Machine downtime with electronic equipment is such a low percentage of the total time as to be of little consequence. If an auxiliary power supply is provided and an exchange agreement developed with another user of similar equipment in the immediate area, the PIC needs can be adequately provided for in case of system failures.

Do not overlook the local hospitals or banking institutions as a possible source for backup computing service in cases of failure.

Control over System Integrity

Human intervention with its subsequent errors is minimized in a computerized application. The system will repeat each of its steps exactly as programmed each time it cycles. However, absolute discipline must be maintained over the input to the system for both the variable data and the data base. The data base of any system should be subjected to periodic audit to ensure that all needed changes and revisions are incorporated.

The maintenance of an on-going system will require programming changes as the methods, processes and other service needs change. Revision and reprogramming at times is as involved as the initial installation. A prime requirement for system maintenance is documentation of the original programs as well as all subsequent revisions. This step-documentation is all too often left undone causing much unnecessary expense and error in the future.

CASE HISTORIES THAT INVOLVE COMMON PITFALLS; THE CORRECTIVE ACTION TAKEN; AND THE RESULTING PAYOFF

CASE IN POINT

The subject of this case history is a manufacturer of a standardized line of proprietary products assembled from a combination of both purchased and locally fabricated parts. There were 12 basic models, each with from 2 to 10 options. Lead times were such that sufficient stocks of parts and components had to be maintained to permit assembly from inventory.

The final bill of material for each model had from 300-350 piece parts, subassemblies, and purchased components. Many parts and subassemblies were common to all models. Stocks were maintained both as individual parts and at various levels of subassembly. Materials made up 75% to 80% of the total manufacturing cost.

Month-end financial statements showed widely fluctuating profits as indicated material inventory values varied dramatically. Parts outages with line shutdowns were frequent.

An inventory management system had been installed by the systems people who were a part of the financial organization. The system involved computerized perpetual inventory both in units and dollar value of every part and every subassembly at each stage in the process. Some subassemblies went through five tiers before they were ready for final assembly and the cost of labor and manufacturing overheads was applied to the perpetual inventory at each level. Options were handled on an add/delete basis. Summary reports were run weekly, priced and used to value closing inventories of materials and work-in-process inventory for financial statements. After more than a year of application of this theoretically sound system, the monthly statements still showed wide potential savings in inventory levels, outages continued at the same level and the task of correction was assigned to another group made up of people with manufacturing, purchasing and PIC viewpoints.

The first step in the corrective program was to redefine the real needs that the system had to fill. The needs ultimately were only three:

— Provide stock status reports, so that purchasing knew when a new order should be placed.
— Provide plant scheduling with a stock status report so that they would know when to issue new shop work orders.
— Provide accounting with an accurate inventory value at the end of each month.

There was no real need to know the inventory level of subassemblies or the inclusion of the labor cost of subassembling in the inventory valuation.

An examination of the usage rates, ordering quantities, and achievable rate of turnovers revealed that there was no real need to have an on-going, up-to-date perpetual inventory record for a handful of very expensive components.

The second step was to audit all bills of materials and create a single level engineering type bill of material for each model/option combination that could occur.

Step three was to identify those commodities and components that had continually been troublesome in the initial system. Metal bar stock, paint, coatings, fasteners, and cartons were all found to have been heavily involved in the faults and errors of the original system. Alternate approaches to the computerized perpetual inventory system were considered for each. Bar stock, paints, coatings, and fasteners were removed from the system. A weekly physical inventory was instituted to determine their stock levels which was punched into the records. A two-bin system was organized to control fasteners and they were expensed as received. After developing a distinct part numbering system for each carton and carton insert they were retained in the perpetual inventory.

A twice weekly physical inventory of a few selected very high cost items was instituted.

Step four was to establish an independent control system for subassemblies based on a simple replenishment order point and lot size for each subassembly that was to be built up for stock.

Step five was the establishment of reorder points for all items included in the revised perpetual system.

Working of the Simplified System

At the start-up of the revised system the plants were shut down and a full physical inventory was made of all stores and work-in-process by individual piece part numbers. The count of subassemblies that were built up were exploded back to their individual piece parts as a beginning inventory record in units was established.

Thereafter receiving reports were keypunched daily as was the final assembly tally by model/option identity.

At midmonth, an updated inventory record was produced in units by adding all the receipts, exploding the final assembly tally using the single level bills of materials and deducting it from the inventory, and inputting the count of those items that were physically inventoried. The final printout showed the unit basis and, in units, the starting inventory, additions to inventory, deductions, theoretical ending inventory, and the reorder point for each line item.

An adjustment column was incorporated to cover shipments of individual parts as spares, scrap losses, and error corrections.

At month end another printout was run which included all the derived information plus the standard unit cost and its extension by the calculated ending inventory level to arrive at the total value of the ending inventory.

Within sixty days the occurrence of unanticipated parts outages was completely eliminated, irrational fluctuations of inventory value were eliminated and an inventory reduction program was underway. Computer time charges were reduced to 20% of the original level.

It should be recognized that this oversimplified system was successful whereas the "complete" system failed because of a number of unique characteristics:

— Lead times for fabricated parts were short, typically two to four weeks.
— Economical order quantities for most purchased parts tended to be large compared to usage rates.
— Safety stocks had to be relatively high to meet the sales policy criteria that all models and options could be assembled from stocks on hand.
— The few high cost, high usage parts that required more precise control were interwoven with all parts.

CASE IN POINT

The subject of this case is a plant that fabricated individual piece parts that fed other assembly plants. There were about 20,000 active part numbers requiring from 3 to as many as 15 operations. Less than 50 had to be run continuously, all others were produced in lots determined by 12 to 18 month forecasts of usage rates. Total volume was subject to large swings predictable 2 to 4 months in advance but the part number mix stayed nearly constant. Approximately 5% of the part numbers were obsoleted each year with an equivalent number of new ones being added.

Lot sizes had been established intuitively under a manual production control system. As computer capacity became available for production control use the original lot sizes were incorporated into the new system.

It was quickly recognized that economical order sizes could be calculated to replace the intuitively established number so a program was written using the classic straight-line usage rate:

$$\text{formula EOQ} = \sqrt{\frac{2AS}{IC}}$$

Standard accounting costs were used and an interest or holding cost was assumed. The program, recognizing that total volume was subject to wide swings, was written to express the EOQ lot size in terms of weeks of usage.

When reviewed, the total volume was almost twice that of the period when the program was installed, the shop was clogged with excessive work-in-process inventory with most shop work orders being split in half at early operations, and often split again at later operations on an expedited basis in an attempt to supply needed parts.

A typical part with an original forecast annual usage rate of 2,500 units annually had an economical order size of 700 which was expressed as 14 weeks using 50 parts per week. When the usage rate was doubled to 5,000 per year or 100 per week, the lot size was calculated to be 1,400 parts. A correct recalculation of the EOQ using a forecasted annual usage of 5,000, assuming all cost factors remained fixed, would result in an EOQ of 1,000 or 10 weeks of usage.

The obvious corrective measure was a one-time recalculation of the EOQ for those parts that should have been properly controlled with an order point system and the installation of a material requirements planning system for those parts that did not fit an order point usage pattern.

Achievable savings were projected at $1,200,000 through modifying the overly simplified application of the essentially correct assumption that this was a proper application of EOQ and order point inventory management.

CASE IN POINT

One theory with great appeal is that economies can be made and large computers justified by means of many different functions using the same data base.

The subject of this case history is a large job shop operation employing 500 people. A job cost accounting system was used for control and a number of different old direct labor incentive systems were employed in different operations. All direct labor standards were expressed in man-hours per unit counted. The general accounts, payroll, incentive bonus payment calculations and job lot cost accounting reports were all calculated and prepared using an old, limited capacity, early generation computer.

Plant scheduling, machine loading and capacity planning were all done manually and were neither accurate nor timely. Promises were made to customers when machine capacity was in fact not available and work forces were frequently out of balance with the true needs.

It was proposed that a larger new generation computer be installed on the basis that it would be used for scheduling and machine loading in addition to taking over the services already being provided. Systems were designed and programs written to input orders, calculate flow times, generate promise dates and calculate man and machine backlog reports all making use of the existing data base of time standards that were being used for the incentive bonus calculation. Near term previous average efficiencies were used to factor standard hours and project actual hours for scheduling man and machine loading systems.

The result was near failure. Schedules and machine loads were nearly irrational and deliveries deteriorated. The fault? Not the system, not the new computer, but the data base. The incentive time standards as the result of poor maintenance, years of loosely negotiated times, standards juggled to compensate for inconsistent bonus pay lines rarely reflected the actual times that operations should or did take.

The solution was a second data base of "scheduling time standards" selected from historical records of good running days to be used only for the production control portion of the system.

CASE IN POINT

A hydraulics manufacturer had a diverse sales line consisting of many models of pumps, valves and cylinders. The production control system was based on two time-sharing programs, one for production planning and the other for material planning. The production planning program was based on infinite capacity and therefore all customer orders were processable. The material requirements were driven by customer delivery dates and were not filtered for capacity constraints. The end result was a delivery delinquency of 35%.

The solution to the problem was to create CPM charts and load work centers on a weekly basis based on man and machine constraints. The time-sharing programs were abandoned when the company purchased an in-house computer. The production planning and material requirements were processed in-house resulting in more timely information and exception reports for problem parts.

Each of these case histories demonstrates a fault in analysis that was independent of the computer application itself illustrating the need for analysis and full understanding of the level of needs, the underlying principles of the technique applied, and a comprehension of the data used. Each had within it the potential for success which was eventually achieved once the pitfall was recognized and eliminated.

The production control department of every company of 100 employees can both improve its effectiveness and perhaps effect economies through the judicious use of the computer on selected applications. Whatever difficulties are encountered, converting to computerization is likely to result in decreased costs, increased productivity, and greater profits provided the PIC manager remains aware of certain factors such as

— Analysts and programmers frequently lack a business perspective.
— The "total system" approach will result in high costs.
— Your friendly computer salesman is not a good source of objective information on the effectiveness of alternate systems. You, the user, have to make those decisions!
— Don't try to "do it all" on the computer.
— Dedicated mini-computers have the highest probability of successful cost effective applications of the various systems available.
— Use the pilot approach to prove out new installations.
— The users of the system must be able to understand it.
— Costs are declining as a result of the move towards smaller computers. Avoid long-term irrevocable commitments.

Index